Y0-ENR-971

WITHDRAWN

SALES ANTICIPATIONS AND INVENTORY BEHAVIOR

28407

SALES ANTICIPATIONS AND INVENTORY BEHAVIOR

Albert A. Hirsch

U.S. Department of Commerce

Michael C. Lovell

Carnegie-Mellon University

HF
5415
H527

JOHN WILEY & SONS, INC.

New York · London · Sydney · Toronto

OHIO UNIVERSITY
LIBRARY

Copyright © 1969, by John Wiley & Sons, Inc.

All rights reserved. No part of this book may be reproduced by any means, nor transmitted, nor translated into a machine language without the written permission of the publisher.

10 9 8 7 6 5 4 3 2 1

Library of Congress Catalogue Card Number: 73-88313

SBN 471 40070 x

Printed in the United States of America

Preface

This study analyzes a new body of data provided by the Manufacturers' Inventory and Sales Expectations Survey of the Office of Business Economics, U.S. Department of Commerce. Our interest centers on the way in which businessmen form their expectations, the precision of their predictions, and the impact of forecasting errors on inventories and production. The new data enable us to study these problems at the firm as well as the aggregate level.

Although these topics are of obvious concern to business economists and cycle theorists, our investigation may also interest economists concerned with other problems involving *ex ante* concepts. For example, our analysis of alternative structural hypotheses explaining the generation of sales expectations may be applicable to the problem of explaining the term structure of interest rates. Furthermore, our study touches on a number of points pertinent to the field of industrial organization. In particular, our analysis in Chapter 6 of the relative flexibility of large and small firms is relevant to the question of what determines the optimal size of the firm, for we find empirical evidence supporting the proposition that an advantage of smallness is a greater degree of flexibility in responding to fluctuating demand conditions. For the most part, we shall rely on standard econometric procedures, but we do develop an alternative to the "realization function" procedure frequently employed in studies of *ex ante* data. It is conceivable that our procedure will be of use to econometricians interested in the determinants of such phenomena as plant and equipment expenditure as well as inventory behavior.

Our greatest debt is to the thousands of anonymous respondents to the Manufacturers' Inventory and Sales Expectations Survey; we have also accumulated a host of obligations to an innumerable list of friends and colleagues during the five years devoted to this research project. We especially thank Lawrence Bridge, Murray Foss, Maurice Liebenberg, and Irving Rottenberg of the Office of Business Economics. David H. Nickerson, Michael Gold, and Roy Weil of the Carnegie-Mellon Computation Center cooperated in working out procedures enabling us to process individual firm data on the computer without compromising the integrity of confidentiality restrictions. We are particularly indebted to John A. Carlson, W. W. Cooper,

Franklin M. Fisher, Edward Greenberg, William T. Newell, Edward Prescott, Mitchell Rothman, and Thomas J. Sargent for constructive comments on preliminary drafts of the manuscript. Also, many helpful suggestions were received when we presented preliminary reports on our project at the 1965 Universities-National Bureau Conference on Determinants of Investment Behavior* and at the December, 1966, meetings of the Econometric Society. William H. Friesell, Theodore Ikola, Pamela Meyers, James Matthews, Howard Pifer, Charles Upton, and Warren Weber labored as programmers at various stages of our project. Elaine de Martino prepared the individual firm data for processing. Financial support and released time for this project were provided in part by a Ford Foundation Faculty Fellowship, by National Science Foundation Grant GS 1293, and the Graduate School of Industrial Administration. We also thank Mrs. Eleanor Balocik and Mrs. Norma Ziker for their patience in preparing the manuscript for publication.

Albert Hirsch
Michael Lovell

August, 1968
U.S. Department of Commerce and
Carnegie-Mellon University

* See Lovell [1967] and the comments by Millard Hastay and Robert Eisner.

Contents

Chapter 1 **INTRODUCTION** 1

1.1 The Cost of Forecast Errors 1
1.2 The Inventory Cycle 3
1.3 A Guide for the Reader 11

Chapter 2 **MEASURING EXPECTATIONS** 13

2.1 The Manufacturers' Inventory and Sales Expectations Survey 13
2.2 Measuring *Ex Ante* Concepts 16
2.2.1 Preliminary Data Adjustments: Benchmark Alignment, Seasonal Adjustment, Price Adjustments, Systematic Bias Correction 17
2.2.2 Omitted Variables—Price, Advertising, and Orders 20
2.2.3 Alternative Data Sources Used in Earlier Studies 23
2.3 Statistical Procedures 25
2.3.1 Security Restrictions 26
2.3.2 Sample Design 26
2.3.3 Choosing Among Alternative Hypotheses 27
2.3.4 Aggregation, Data Pooling, Homogeneity, and Homoscedasticity 29
Appendix: Format for Presenting Regression Results 33

Chapter 3 **ON THE ACCURACY OF EXPECTATIONS** 35

3.1 Introduction 35
3.2 Measures of Forecast Accuracy 35
3.3 Forecast Accuracy—Industry Data 42
3.3.1 Turning-point Errors 42
3.3.2 The Magnitude of Forecast Errors 46
3.3.3 Comparison with Alternative Estimates of Forecast Accuracy 49

3.4 Firm Data and Aggregation Effects 51
3.4.1 Firm Turning-point Errors 53
3.4.2 The Magnitude of Firm Errors 53
3.5 Conclusions 58

Chapter 4 **THE COMPOSITION OF FORECAST ERRORS** 62

4.1 Introduction 62
4.2 Systematic Errors in Forecasting 62
4.2.1 Perennial Optimism 66
4.2.2 The Variance of Anticipated Change, Three Types of Forecasts 73
4.3 Underestimation of Change 79
4.3.1 The Probability of Underestimating Change 79
4.3.2 Regression Analysis of Change Underestimation 91
4.4 Market Share Decomposition 95
4.5 Waves of Optimism and Pessimism 100
4.5.1 Correlation Matrices 101
4.5.2 Principal Components 104
4.6 Summary and Conclusions 107
Statistical Appendix 110

Chapter 5 **THE STRUCTURE OF EXPECTATIONS** 112

5.1 Introduction 112
5.2 Ferber's Law of Expectations Formation 115
5.2.1 Short Anticipations 116
5.2.2 Long Anticipations 121
5.2.3 Regressivity of Expectations 129
5.3 Adaptive Expectations 141
5.3.1 Short Anticipations 144
5.3.2 Long Anticipations 153
5.3.3 Expectation Revision 161
5.4 "Rational" or "Implicit" Expectations 169
5.4.1 On the "Sufficiency" of Anticipations 171
5.4.2 Actual Realizations as a Proxy for Anticipations 177
5.5 Summary and Conclusions 189

Chapter 6 **INVENTORIES AND PRODUCTION** 193

6.1 Introduction 193
6.2 Planned Production and Finished Goods Inventory Behavior 194
6.2.1 The Model 194
6.2.2 Empirical Evidence 201

6.3 Finished Goods Inventory Behavior 204
6.3.1 The Structural Equation 208
6.3.2 Reduced Form Estimates 212
6.3.3 Sales Proxies in Predicting Inventory Behavior 217
6.4 Stocks of Purchased Materials and Goods in Process 220
6.5 Aggregate Inventory Behavior 225
6.6 Summary and Conclusions 229

Appendix on Estimation Procedures 234
A. Inventories Versus Production, and the Choice of Dependent Variables 234
B. Nonlinear Estimation of the Reduced Form Equation 235
C. Simultaneous Estimation of Planned and Realized Inventory Investment 236

Epilogue 239

Bibliography 245

Index 253

List of Tables

Chapter 1

Table	1.2.1	Hypothetical Inventory Cycle Data	10

Chapter 2

Table	2.1.1	Variables of the Manufacturers' Inventory and Sales Expectations Survey	14
	2.1.2	Industry Identification Codes	15

Chapter 3

Table	3.3.1	Turning-Point Errors, Aggregate Sales Data	43
	3.3.2	Accuracy Analysis, Aggregate Data	46
	3.3.3	Accuracy of Sales Anticipations Relative to Ferber's Naive Test, Aggregate Data	50
	3.3.4	Railroad Shippers' Forecasts, 1957–1964	51
	3.4.1	Turning-Point Errors, Firm Sales Data	52
	3.4.2	Sales Accuracy Analysis, Firm Data Averages	53
	3.4.3	Sales Accuracy Analysis, Aggregate Figures from Sampled Firms	57

Chapter 4

Table	4.2.1	Structure of Anticipation Errors, Aggregate Data	67
	4.2.2	Forecast Decomposition, Firm Data	72
	4.2.3	Forecast Accuracy versus BIASP, VARP, and DISP	78
	4.3.1	Over- and Underestimation of Change Probabilities—Industry Data	82
	4.3.2	Over- and Underestimation of Change—Individual Firm Sales Probabilities	90
	4.3.3	Underestimation of Change—Regression Results	94

4.4.1 Share and Industry Decomposition—Pooled Regressions, Short Sales 99
4.4.2 Share and Industry Decomposition—Pooled Regressions, Long Sales 99
4.5.1 Mean and Frequency Distribution of Correlation Coefficients—Benchmark Adjusted Industry Aggregates 102
4.5.2 Average Value of Correlation Coefficients—Individual Firm Data 103
4.5.3 Principal Component Analysis—Benchmark Adjusted Industry Aggregate 106

Chapter 5

Table 5.2.1 Ferber Extrapolations—Short Sales 118
5.2.2 Ferber Extrapolations—Short Ratio 122
5.2.3 Ferber Extrapolations—Long Sales 126
5.2.4 Ferber Extrapolations—Long Ratio 130
5.2.5 Regressivity of Expectations 133
5.2.6 Ferber Extrapolations—Actual Short 134
5.2.7 Ferber Extrapolations—Actual Long 138
5.3.1 Adaptive Expectations—Short 146
5.3.2 Adaptive Expectations—Short Ratio 150
5.3.3 Adaptive Expectations—Short Ratio Seasonal Dummies 154
5.3.4 Adaptive Expectations—Long Ratio 158
5.3.5 Adaptive Expectations—Long Ratio Seasonal Dummies 162
5.3.6 Expectation Revision 166
5.4.1 Rational Expectations—Short 174
5.4.2 Rational Expectations—Short Ratio 178
5.4.3 Rational Expectations—Long 182
5.4.4 Rational Expectations—Long Ratio 186

Chapter 6

Table 6.2.1 Planned Finished Goods Inventory Investment 201
6.3.1 Finished Goods Inventory Realizations 209
6.3.2 Reduced Form Finished Goods Inventory Investment 213

6.3.3 Sales Proxies in Predicting Inventory Behavior with Seasonal Dummies 218
6.4.1 Planned Purchased Material and Goods in Process Investment with Seasonal Dummy Variables 221
6.4.2 Purchased Material and Goods in Process Investment with Seasonal Dummy Variables 223
6.5.1 Maximum Likelihood Parameter Estimates 228

List of Figures

Figure 1.1	Components of private domestic investment spending, 1929–1967.	3
Figure 1.2	The role of inventory investment in business cycles.	5
Figure 1.3	The Lundberg-Metzler inventory cycle.	6
Figure 1.4	Planned and realized inventory investment.	8
Figure 2.1	Price versus quantity response.	22
Figure 4.1	Predicted and realized three-month sales changes.	63
Figure 4.2	Illustrative prediction-realization scatters.	64

SALES ANTICIPATIONS AND INVENTORY BEHAVIOR

CHAPTER 1

Introduction

1.1 THE COST OF FORECAST ERRORS

Members of the business community frequently lament the limited degree of accuracy that economists achieve when they attempt to forecast future business developments. More precise sales forecasts would permit a closer meshing of production schedules with demand and an economizing on inventories. If sales developments could be predicted with greater precision, it might be possible to avoid much of the overtime and other costs occasioned when forecast errors force an abrupt readjustment of production schedules.

This volume is not a manual prescribing how firms *should* forecast. Rather, we shall examine a new body of data revealing the degree of precision actually achieved by the typical manufacturing firm in forecasting short-run sales and inventory developments. The evidence is provided by the Manufacturers' Inventory and Sales Expectations Survey of the Office of Business Economics, Department of Commerce. When we examine the magnitude of prediction errors displayed by the data, we shall use a variety of yardsticks for measuring forecast accuracy; these same measures could be used by a firm to monitor the predictive achievements of its marketing department.

In addition to looking at the forecasting records of representative manufacturing firms, we shall examine time series derived by summing the predictions of individual firms to both the two digit industry and the durable and nondurable levels of aggregation. Such aggregates are often used by business analysts. The effects of aggregation upon forecast accuracy are of some interest, for it certainly is conceivable that the sum of inaccurate firm forecasts might yield quite accurate predictions of aggregate economic activity.

The composition of forecast errors is the concern of Chapter 4, where we look at certain types of systematic bias that tend to crop up in business forecasts. We shall discover that while some firms are perennially optimistic when it comes to forecasting future sales, others persist in making unduly pessimistic predictions. The data reveal that firms quite generally tend to underestimate future inventory accumulation. We shall consider the possibility of improving the accuracy of raw forecasts by eliminating systematic bias.

The immediate costs experienced by the firm as a result of its prediction errors do not necessarily reflect the full cost to the economy of inaccurate forecasting. Remember, the advocates of socialism traditionally assert that a fundamental defect of capitalism is that the difficulties experienced by firms in predicting sales lead to inconsistent behavior and social waste. Furthermore, professional economists have long argued that prediction errors may contribute to the generation of the business cycle. Professor Pigou [1922, p. 84] explained:

> If the passengers of a ship always walk about independently, there is little danger of their causing much disturbance to its equilibrium, but if they rush in combined panic from side to side, there is very great danger. It is, therefore, important for us to inquire how far, in the matter of expectations concerning the future, those persons whose action controls business do, in fact, tend to act in droves.

John Maynard Keynes followed Pigou in stressing the psychological factor, arguing in *The General Theory* [1936, Ch. 22] that the trade cycle, if not the trend level of unemployment, is largely the consequence of expectational shifts in the marginal efficiency of capital and the liquidity preference schedule. The error theory of the business cycle may have a history that is exceeded in length only by the "sunspot" and "harvest" theories.

How important a role the psychological factor actually plays in the generation of business cycles is a question that has caused disagreement among generations of economists. Pigou [1929, p. 220] was inclined to argue that monetary and expectational factors play equally important roles:

> . . . the importance of the error factor is of the same order as that of the monetary factor: that, if all errors were eliminated, the normal range of industrial fluctuations would be reduced substantially, perhaps to the extent of one-half; but that considerable industrial fluctuations would still remain.

But he also conceded:

> Here again our estimate of quantities must rest on judgment and guesswork.

One essential ingredient for obtaining answers to such questions is provided by our evidence on the degree of precision actually achieved by business firms in predicting the future. Our new evidence reveals that firms are able to forecast developments with considerable precision; predictions of future sales volume are much more precise than prior empirical studies have suggested. Of course, since the timing as well as the magnitude of forecast errors may be critical, we must also examine in Chapter 4 the interrelationships among prediction errors made by different firms in different industries to see whether there really are Pigouvian waves of optimistic and pessimistic error. In later chapters, we shall employ the more formal framework provided by the theory of the inventory cycle.

1.2 THE INVENTORY CYCLE

Members of both the psychological and the monetary schools of business cycle theorists indict inventory investment as a particularly critical factor in the generation of the business cycle. While Hawtrey [1928, 1937] argued that monetary variables had their primary effect on the economy via their influence on inventory investment, the models of Lundberg [1937] and

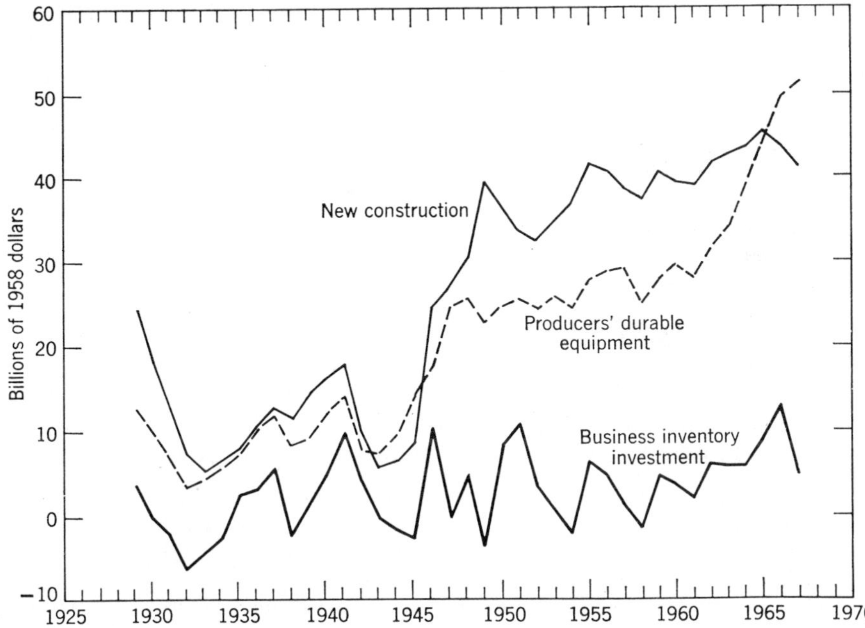

Figure 1.1 Components of gross private domestic investment. (Annual data, 1929–1967, in billions of 1958 dollars. *Source:* 1968 *Economic Report of the President*, U.S. Government Printing Office, p. 211.)

Metzler [1941] stressed the role of expectational errors in the generation of the inventory cycle.

Empirical confirmation of the critical nature of inventory investment has been provided by the important contributions of Moses Abramovitz [1950] and Thomas M. Stanback [1962]. As indicated on Figure 1.1, inventory investment is subject to more violent fluctuations than other components of investment spending. A closer inspection of the historical record will reveal that during recessions, when high inventory investment would have generated income and added to effective demand, stocks have moved in the wrong direction. In periods of boom, when excess demand prevails, inventory investment has been large in magnitude, contributing to inflationary pressure.

An estimate of the extent to which the recessions of recent decades have been the consequence of changes in the level of inventory investment is provided by Figure 1.2, where fluctuations in actual gross national product are contrasted with a hypothetical GNP series corresponding to the path that effective demand would have followed if there had been no fluctuations in inventory stocks. The hypothetical series is obtained by subtracting from actual GNP both inventory investment and an estimate of the consumption it generates.[1] If there had been no inventory liquidation in the thirties, an inspection of the hypothetical series suggests, the trough of the great depression would not have been so severe. The 1937 and 1949 recessions can both be explained, as a first approximation, by the liquidation of inventory, for without fluctuations in stocks these two years would have been characterized by only slight interruptions in the rate of growth rather than definite declines in GNP. The sizable replenishment of stocks in 1946 did smooth the task of reconversion following World War II. During the Korean mobilization, the contribution of record-breaking levels of inventory accumulation to effective demand constituted a serious source of inflationary pressure. At the close of the Korean emergency, a reduction in inventory investment served to deepen the recession. The 1958 recession is only partially explained by inventory liquidation. In contrast recessions remain in the second hypothetical series, which shows GNP less producers' durables and consequent consumption. It is clear that this category of investment spending has made a major contribution to the growth in effective demand but not to cyclical reversals in

[1] The curve suggesting the way in which effective demand would have behaved if there had been no inventory investment or disinvestment was derived by subtracting the effects of inventory investment upon GNP, as estimated with the Klein-Goldberger econometric model of the United States, from actual GNP. A brief description of the procedure used is provided in Lovell [1962a, p. 261]. For more sophisticated simulations of the 1953–1954 and 1957–1958 recessions, see Klein and Popkin [1961] and Gary Fromm [1962]. Note that the simpler procedure of utilizing "final sales" (GNP less inventory investment) to measure the impact of fluctuations in inventory investment upon GNP is only a rough approximation, for it neglects the impact of changes in income upon consumption spending.

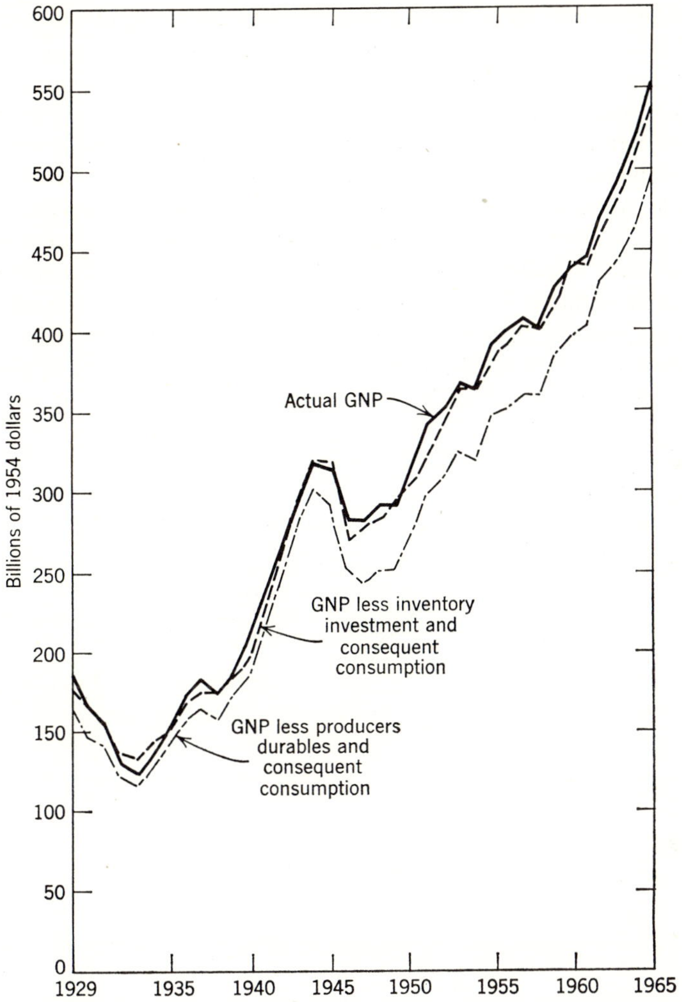

Figure 1.2 The role of inventory investment in business cycles.

economic activity.[2] Thus, investment in inventories has been perverse in timing and magnitude, contributing to fluctuations in economic activity, to booms, and to unemployment.

Although this historical review reveals that fluctuations in stocks are a critical link in the causal chain leading to the generation of cycles in economic activity, it tells us nothing concerning the complex of factors that lead, via

[2] The effect of zero investment in plant and equipment upon capacity is suppressed in analyzing the contribution of this category of investment spending to effective demand.

their effect upon inventory investment, to cyclical reversals in economic activity. The Lundberg [1937] and Metzler [1941] aggregate inventory cycle models provide a simplified explanation of this phenomenon. This theory is of particular interest to us, for the assumption that inventories are drawn down below planned levels when sales volume is underestimated constitutes the cornerstone of their analysis. Figure 1.3 illustrates one of the hypothetical cycles described by Metzler. Observe the marked fluctuations in inventories and output that are generated when this model is excited by a single disturbance in autonomous government spending. For Lundberg and Metzler, it is the induced fluctuations in inventory investment and consequent consumption spending that prevent output from adjusting promptly to the new equilibrium. Cyclical movements persist, but the system gradually converges to the new equilibrium.

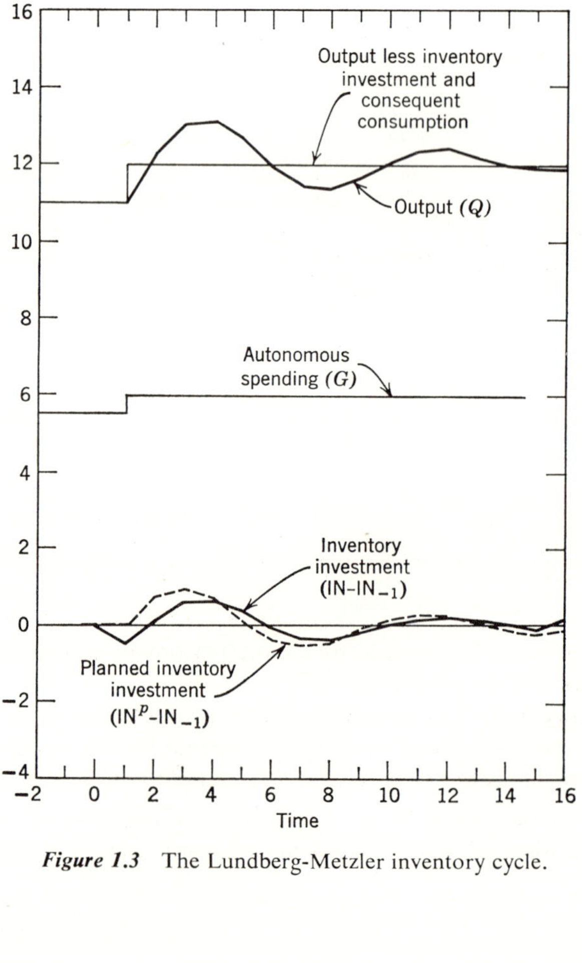

Figure 1.3 The Lundberg-Metzler inventory cycle.

A few brief paragraphs summarizing Metzler's assumptions will serve to explain how these cycles are generated by his model. We must review his behavioral assumptions before we can outline the research strategy employed in later chapters when the time comes to subject the basic building blocks of inventory cycle theory to empirical test. Although empirical studies of inventories have been handicapped by inadequate data that forced earlier investigators to rely upon grossly imprecise measures of sales anticipations or to resort to surrogative procedures, our new data will permit us to test, in considerable detail, many of the behavioral assumptions underlying the Lundberg-Metzler theory of the inventory cycle.

A quite elementary theory explaining the generation of prediction errors and consequent departures of inventories from their planned level is customarily utilized in models of the inventory cycles. Suppose that equilibrium inventory, IN_t^e, is a linear function of actual sales volume, A_t; in other words, suppose that if sales volume remained constant, the representative firm would eventually adjust its inventory to achieve:

$$\mathrm{IN}_t^e = \beta_0 + \beta A_t \tag{2.1}$$

This line is plotted on the upper panel of Figure 1.4. Note that IN_t^e is a long-run objective, and at the time when production decisions must be made, actual sales may not be known precisely. Rather, if the firm predicts sales of P_t, its anticipated equilibrium inventory level will be

$$\widehat{\mathrm{IN}}_t^e = \beta_0 + \beta P_t \tag{2.2}$$

The firm may not attempt to adjust its stock promptly to this level. Instead, costs involved in rapidly changing output may cause the firm to attempt only a partial adjustment of inventories toward this anticipated long-run level. Specifically, planned inventory may be simply

$$\mathrm{IN}_t^p = \delta(\widehat{\mathrm{IN}}_t^e - \mathrm{IN}_{t-1}) = \delta\beta_0 + \delta\beta P_t + (1 - \delta)\mathrm{IN}_{t-1},\ 0 < \delta \leq 1 \tag{2.3}$$

where IN_{t-1} is the actual inventory stock inherited from the preceding period; these points are indicated on the upper graph.

That errors in anticipating sales will, in practice, cause actual inventories to depart from the planned level is revealed by the lower panel of the graph; thus, if actual sales exceed P_t, inventories may be drawn down below IN_t^p by the full amount of the forecast error, leaving actual end-of-period inventories of

$$\mathrm{IN}_t = \mathrm{IN}_t^p - (A_t - P_t) \tag{2.4}$$

as indicated on the lower panel of the graph. The line with slope -1 on the graph indicates actual inventory as a function of realized sales, given sales anticipations of P_t. Furthermore, if we substitute equation 2.3 into 2.4, we

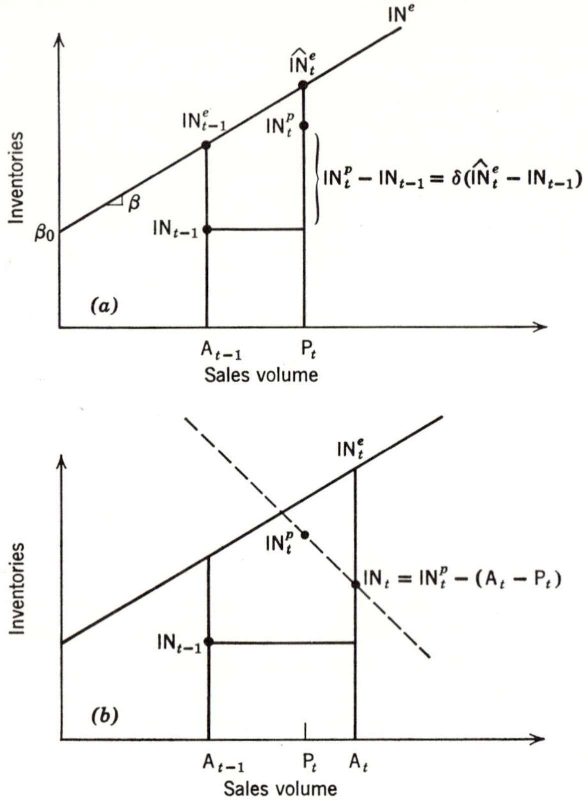

Figure 1.4 Planned and realized inventory investment. (*a*) Planned inventory investment. (*b*) Realized inventory investment.

obtain as the "reduced form" equation for inventory investment:

$$IN_t = \delta\beta_0 + (1 + \delta\beta)P_t - A_t + (1 - \delta)IN_{t-1} \tag{2.5}$$

Thanks to the new data on sales anticipations and planned inventory investment it will be possible for us to subject these last three equations to empirical scrutiny. Thus, in Chapter 6 we shall explore, by stage of fabrication, the determinants of planned inventory investment. In addition, we shall consider equation 2.4 and a somewhat more general hypothesis concerning the way in which errors in predicting sales volume cause inventories to depart from the planned level. We shall also estimate reduced form equations similar to 2.5.

Of course, a study of how changes in such variables as expected sales influence inventory investment will not suffice to explain the inventory cycle.

There are other fundamental building blocks that must be mentioned in providing an explanation of the structure of the model generating the hypothetical data displayed in Figure 1.2. First, it is necessary to have an equation explaining the generation of sales expectations. The simplest hypothesis is to suppose that firms expect no change:

$$P_t = A_{t-1} \tag{2.6}$$

With the aid of this hypothesis, equation 2.5 reduces to

$$\mathrm{IN}_t = \beta_0 + (1 + \beta)P_t - A_t = \beta_0 + (1 + \beta)A_{t-1} - A_t \tag{2.7}$$

provided we simplify by supposing that firms attempt a prompt adjustment of stocks to equilibrium ($\delta = 1$). Inventory investment is simply

$$\mathrm{IN}_t - \mathrm{IN}_{t-1} = -A_t + (2 + \beta)A_{t-1} - (1 + \beta)A_{t-2} \tag{2.8}$$

Since all output must be sold or else added to inventory, we also have as an identity for output:

$$Q_t \equiv A_t + (\mathrm{IN}_t - \mathrm{IN}_{t-1}) \tag{2.9}$$

and substituting from 2.7 reveals

$$Q_t = (2 + \beta)A_{t-1} - (1 + \beta)A_{t-2} \tag{2.10}$$

If aggregate sales are the sum of an endogeneous consumption component and an exogeneous term G_t representing the sum of government spending and fixed investment, so that

$$C_t = cQ_t \tag{2.11}$$

and we have

$$\begin{aligned} A_t &= C_t + G_t \\ &= cQ_t + G_t \end{aligned} \tag{2.12}$$

We then obtain by substituting this last sales expression into 2.10 the following equation for output:

$$Q_t = (2 + \beta)cQ_{t-1} - (1 + \beta)cQ_{t-2} + G_{t-1} + (1 + \beta)(G_{t-1} - G_{t-2}) \tag{2.13}$$

This second order linear difference equation has as its equilibrium solution $Q^e = 1/(1 - c)G$, which is the product of the multiplier times autonomous spending. The cyclical movements in income illustrated in Figure 1.3 were generated by Metzler with the above equation, for hypothetical parameter values of $c = \beta = 0.5$, by having an initial equilibrium with $G = 550$ and $Q = 1000$ disturbed by an increase in autonomous spending to $G = 600$; the data are recorded on Table 1.2.1. As is well known, this inventory cycle

TABLE 1.2.1. HYPOTHETICAL INVENTORY CYCLE DATA

Time Period t (1)	Autonomous Spending G_t (2)	Predicted Sales $P_t = A_{t-1}$ (3)	Desired Inventory $IN_t^p = 0.5P_t$ (4)	Planned Inventory Investment $IN_t^p - IN_{t-1}$ (5)	Production Q_t = cols 3 + 5 (6)	Consumption $C_t = 0.5Q_t$ (7)	Realized Sales A_t = cols 2 + 7 (8)	Inventory Investment $\Delta IN_t = IN_t - IN_{t-1} = Q_t - A_t$ (9)	Inventory Stock $IN_t = \Delta IN_t + IN_{t-1}$ (10)
0	550	1100	550	0	1100	550	1100	0	550
1	600	1100	550	0	1100	550	1150	−50	500
2	600	1150	575	75	1225	612	1212	13	513
3	600	1212	606	93	1305	652	1252	53	566
4	600	1252	626	60	1312	656	1256	56	622
5	600	1256	628	6	1262	631	1231	31	653
6	600	1231	615	−38	1193	596	1196	−3	650
7	600	1196	598	−52	1144	572	1172	−28	622
8	600	1172	586	−36	1136	568	1168	−32	590
9	600	1168	584	−6	1162	581	1181	−19	571
10	600	1181	590	19	1200	600	1200	0	571
11	600	1200	600	29	1229	614	1214	15	586
12	600	1214	607	21	1235	617	1217	18	604
13	600	1217	608	4	1221	610	1210	11	615
14	600	1210	605	−10	1200	600	1200	0	615
15	600	1200	600	−15	1185	592	1192	−7	608
16	600	1192	596	−12	1180	590	1190	10	598
.									
.									
.									
∞	600	1200	600	0	1200	600	1200	0	600

will be damped rather than explosive only for certain values of the model's parameters.[3]

Among these many ingredients of the inventory cycle, the problem of obtaining an equation providing an adequate explanation of how expectations are generated will warrant our close attention. Equation 2.6, the assumption that expectations are static, is recommended only by its simplicity. Chapter 5 will be devoted to testing alternative hypotheses concerning the generation of expectations that have received attention in the literature. In Chapter 6, we shall also examine inventory investment equations that are similar to 2.8 in that the expectations variable has been eliminated by substitution, but are based on more complicated hypotheses concerning the structure of expectations.

1.3 A GUIDE FOR THE READER

A reading of this book must begin with a perusal of Chapter 2, where problems of measuring expectations are reviewed and the details of the data provided by the Office of Business Economics survey of inventory and sales expectations are described. In particular, the reader will find it useful to refer repeatedly to two tables in that chapter that present symbols for the basic variables and list the code numbers used throughout the study to identify specific industries. Chapter 2 also discusses certain strengths and limitations of the data and reviews problems involved in adjusting for such complications as seasonal movements and price changes. It concludes with a discussion of certain recurrent statistical problems and an appendix explaining the format of standardized statistical tables used for summarizing regression output in subsequent chapters.

Since the empirical chapters that follow are more or less self-contained, they can be read in any order once the basic material in Chapter 2 has been examined. Each of the empirical chapters contains a detailed introduction providing motivation for the analysis that follows. In the concluding section of each empirical chapter, the results of the analysis are summarized in detail. The implications of the analysis for empirical research and business cycle theory are briefly discussed in the Epilogue.

The reader will note that the chapters in this book are divided into sections, and that the sections, in turn, are often subdivided. We have found it convenient to adopt a decimal convention for reference purposes. Thus, "Chapter 3.2.1" denotes the first subsection of Section 2 of Chapter 3. It has proved most convenient to delete the chapter number when referring to

[3] See Metzler [1941] for an analysis of the stability conditions for this and a variety of related models.

equations; further, we disregard distinctions between subsections in the serial numbering of equations. Thus, when we mention "equation 2.2" without specifying the chapter we mean the second equation of section two of this present chapter; to refer to the second equation of the second section of Chapter 4 we write "equation 2.2 of Chapter 4." With tables, we retain the chapter numbers and delete subsections; thus, Table 5.2.1 is the first table in Section 2 of Chapter 5. All books and articles cited in the text are listed in the bibliography; reference is made by the author's name followed by the year of publication in brackets; where appropriate, the year is followed by a specific page or chapter number. Additional references will be found in the extensive bibliography of Eisner and Strotz [1963].

CHAPTER 2

Measuring Expectations

2.1 THE MANUFACTURERS' INVENTORY AND SALES EXPECTATIONS SURVEY

Certain characteristics of the firm and industry data provided by the Office of Business Economics (OBE) quarterly survey will be discussed in this chapter. Problems involved in adjusting for such complications as seasonal movements deserve careful evaluation. In addition, it is necessary for us to consider the effects of certain omitted variables and to compare the time series available for our study with alternative data sources. Furthermore, we must describe the strategy we followed in analyzing our data, discuss certain recurrent statistical problems, and explain the format employed in tables reporting our regression output.

Initiated on a semiannual basis by the OBE in the spring of 1957, the inventory and sales expectations survey has been conducted quarterly since the beginning of 1959. Respondents are asked to report both the expected level of inventories at the end of the current quarter and the level anticipated for the end of the next quarter; in addition, they report on actual inventory at the beginning of both the current and previous quarters. The survey also inquires as to expected sales volume for both the current and the succeeding quarter. In addition, information concerning the discrepancy between desired and actual inventory stocks is provided in terms of the percentage of firms reporting inventories as high, about right, or low, relative to total sales and the unfilled orders backlog. The scope of the survey is suggested by Table 2.1.1, where the different variables are listed together with the symbols that will be utilized to identify them throughout our study.

TABLE 2.1.1. VARIABLES OF THE MANUFACTURERS' INVENTORY AND SALES EXPECTATIONS SURVEY[a]

Variable Code	Definition
IN_t	Actual total inventories at end of quarter t
$INAS_t$	Short inventory anticipation (plans as of the beginning of the quarter concerning end of quarter inventories, IN_t)
$INAL_t$	Long inventory anticipation (plans as of the beginning of quarter $t - 1$ concerning end of quarter t inventories)
SALE	Actual sales of quarter t
ASSALE	Short sales anticipation (anticipations held at the beginning of quarter t concerning that quarter's sales volume)
ALSALE	Long sales anticipation (anticipations held at the beginning of quarter $t - 1$ concerning quarter t's sales volume)
FIN_t	Actual finished goods inventory at end of quarter[b]
$FINAS_t$	Short finished inventory anticipation (plans as of the beginning of the quarter concerning end of quarter finished goods inventory)
$FINAL_t$	Long finished inventory anticipation (plans as of the beginning of quarter $t - 1$ concerning end of quarter t inventories)
COND	Condition of inventory (proportion of firms in industry reporting their total inventories as high in relation to total sales and unfilled orders less percentage reporting inventories low)
PT_t	Inventory position dummy variable, all inventories[c]
PF_t	Inventory position dummy variable, finished goods inventory[c]
PO_t	Inventory position dummy variable, purchased materials and goods in process[c]
$PM \equiv IN - FIN$	Stocks of purchased materials and goods in process
$PMAS \equiv INAS - FINAS$	Short anticipated purchased materials and goods in process stocks
$PMAL \equiv INAL - FINAL$	Long anticipated purchased materials and goods in process stocks

[a] The subscript "t" is usually suppressed in the text.

[b] Data on finished goods inventories were not added to the survey questionnaire until the third quarter of 1959. Observations on FINAS begin with the first quarter of 1960 and on FINAL with the second quarter of 1960. The data utilized in the aggregate regressions were not partitioned by stage of fabrication.

[c] For firms, the condition data is analyzed with a dummy variable that assumes the value of -1, 0, or $+1$, depending on whether inventories are regarded as low, about right, or high, relative to current sales volume and unfilled orders.

The length of the horizon involved for the various forecasts depends, in part, upon the freshness of the forecast that the respondent reports; a minimum estimate of the length of the horizon is provided by the timing of the receipt of returned questionnaires by the OBE. Approximately half the questionnaires are returned to the OBE by the end of the first month of the quarter. Since small companies generally respond sooner than large, an average response date weighted by company size is around the tenth day of the second month of the quarter. Thus, the average forecasting horizon for the inventory figures involves, as a minimum, about fifty days for the short forecast; for the long forecast, the average forecast horizon is at least four

TABLE 2.1.2. INDUSTRY IDENTIFICATION CODES

Aggregate Study (fall of 1957 through second quarter of 1963)

	Code	Industry
Durables:		
	1.	Primary iron and steel
	2.	Primary nonferrous metals
	3.	Electrical machinery
	4.	Machinery except electrical
	5.	Motor vehicles and equipment
	6.	Transportation equipment (excluding motor vehicles and equipment)
	7.	Other durables
Nondurables:		
	1.	Food and beverages
	2.	Textiles
	3.	Paper and allied products
	4.	Chemicals and allied products
	5.	Petroleum and coal products
	6.	Rubber
	7.	Other nondurables

Firm Analysis

	Number of Firms				Date of
Industry	Small	Large	Total	SIC Number	Last Survey
1. Nonferrous metals	5	5	10	33	64-4
2. Electrical machinery	9	8	17	35	64-4
3. Nonelectrical machinery	9	7	16	36	64-4
4. Chemicals	10	10	20	28	64-4
5. Petroleum	10	10	20	29	65-2
Total	43	40	83		

and one-half months. The short sales forecast may have been made after somewhat more than one third of the period being forecast has actually expired, while the long sales forecast is made at least one month in advance of the beginning of the quarter for which the forecast is being made. The variables are measured in millions of dollars for the analysis of the industry aggregates and in thousands of dollars for individual firms.

The sample used by the Office of Business Economics consists of about 1200 manufacturing firms; the firms in this sample hold about 70 percent of the book value of U.S. manufacturers' inventories.[1] Obviously, this is too much data to be conveniently analyzed *in toto.*

Our strategy was to divide the investigation into two phases. The first phase involved an analysis of aggregate industry time series adjusted to benchmarks by the Department of Commerce.[2] The seven durable and seven nondurable industries used in this phase of the study are identified on Table 2.1.2. The second phase of our investigation focused upon time series data for 83 individual firms in five industries: nonferrous metals, electrical machinery, nonelectrical machinery, chemicals, and petroleum. Because we were interested in such questions as whether large firms can predict more accurately than small, we selected approximately equal numbers of "large" firms, with assets in excess of $10 million, and "small" firms, with assets below that cutoff point. Table 2.1.2 lists the number of large and small firms in each of the five industries for this microphase of our study.

2.2 MEASURING *EX ANTE* CONCEPTS

Do the figures reported to the Department of Commerce adequately represent the anticipations used by the firm in making operating decisions? Since point estimates rather than confidence interval predictions are provided by the respondents to the OBE survey, we do not have a subjective measure of forecasting precision.[3] The questionnaire for the OBE survey is generally

[1] Murray Foss [1961] provides a detailed discussion of the sampling procedure utilized by the OBE.

[2] Section 2.1 will briefly describe the benchmark adjustment procedure by which the quarterly survey figures are adjusted to conform to the estimates provided by the Manufacturers' Shipments, Inventories and Orders Survey, which is based on a larger sample.

[3] We may hope that the point estimate constitutes an expected value in the statistical sense, but it is easy to think of circumstances in which it may be particularly hard for a respondent to reply with a single number. For example, if a firm is certain that it will ship 10 units if there is a steel strike and 100 units if there is no strike, and if it subjectively evaluates the probability of a strike as 1 in 3, should it report a prediction of $70 = \frac{1}{3} \cdot 10 + \frac{2}{3} \cdot 100$, an event that is practically impossible, or 100? In principle the answer hinges upon the way in which the respondent is penalized for incorrect predictions; thus, he should forecast 100 if an error, whatever its magnitude, costs $1.00.

returned by the company's controller, treasurer, or one of their assistants. Thus, there exists the distinct possibility that the figures do not correspond to a simple aggregate expectation of production and purchasing departments. But Murray Foss does report that seven out of every eight respondents stated that the sales anticipations figures "played an important part in the company's production and purchasing policies" when this question was raised as a supplemental question on one of the earlier surveys. The proportion was somewhat higher in durables than in nondurables; in the food and beverage industry more than one in three firms answered in the negative. Foss also reports that five out of every six firms reported that they utilized the inventory forecast in production and purchasing policies. Field interviews conducted by the OBE confirmed that the sales forecast lies at the heart of most companies' future plans.[4]

2.2.1 *Preliminary Data Adjustments*

The information provided by respondents to the OBE survey has been subjected to certain adjustments in advance of data processing. Thus, the aggregate industry data have been aligned to industry benchmarks. On the other hand, we adjusted the data for seasonal movements only for certain explicitly noted applications. Neither the sales nor the inventory figures have been deflated for price movements. Furthermore, this set of *ex ante* data has not been subjected to prior adjustment in an attempt to improve predictive accuracy through the elimination of systematic forecasting errors. All of these adjustments deserve detailed discussion.

BENCHMARK ALIGNMENT. The aggregate industry data have been adjusted to benchmarks provided by the larger sample figures of the monthly sales and inventory survey conducted jointly by Census and the OBE.[5] One advantage of employing benchmark adjusted figures is that they are not so sensitive to irregular response records. Without adjustment there is a danger that the observed forecasting error might be distorted as a result of fluctuations in response rates between the survey in which the *ex ante* figures are collected and the subsequent survey in which the *ex post* realizations are reported. Individual firm data cannot, of course, be adjusted to benchmarks, and

[4] See Foss [1961, p. 237] for additional information concerning the relevance of the forecasts for company planning.

[5] Foss [1961, p. 234] explains that for each industry the firms in the sample are partitioned into two cells on the basis of size. For each size cell of each industry, the anticipated inventory figure is multiplied by a blowup factor. The blowup factor for inventories is simply the ratio of the actual inventory book value figure from the regular larger monthly survey to the inventory figure reported by firms in the anticipations survey. A similar procedure is employed for sales.

allowance for nonresponse was made by programming the computer to delete all observations for which relevant data had not been supplied by the respondent.

Seasonal Adjustment. Throughout most of our analysis the data are analyzed without prior seasonal adjustment. This is the appropriate approach for regression analysis when the seasonal fluctuations in the dependent variable are thought to be generated by the seasonal in the explanatory variables. For example, in Chapter 5 we utilize unadjusted data in analyzing Ferber's Law of expectations formation because his model explicitly incorporates the way in which seasonal movements in sales influence expectations. Occasionally, however, it was appropriate for us to subject the data to prior seasonal adjustment. Thus, in analyzing the accuracy of forecasts we were interested in whether a naive forecaster knowing only the seasonal pattern of sales could achieve as accurate a prediction record as that of the firms responding to the OBE survey. Furthermore, we used seasonal dummy variables in analyzing the adaptive expectations model. On the other hand, in certain stages of the analysis, it proved more convenient to run regressions on data subject to prior seasonal adjustments. The technique of seasonal adjustment employed is equivalent to utilizing dummy variables; appropriate adjustments were made for loss of degrees of freedom occasioned by seasonal adjustment in accordance with the argument of Lovell [1963].

We must also note the possibility that responding firms might report their anticipations on a seasonally adjusted basis. Two factors suggested to Foss [1961] that this is not a serious source of ambiguity. First, on a supplemental questionnaire about half the firms checked "normal seasonal change" as a factor influencing their forecast. Second, when Foss compared the anticipations figures without seasonal adjustment with the seasonally adjusted realizations he did not find any decisive improvement in forecast accuracy.

Price Adjustments. The data have *not* been deflated for price movements, primarily because of the difficulties involved in accurately observing changes in the prices used by firms in measuring their sales volume and inventory levels. The sophisticated price deflation procedure employed by the National Income Division in adjusting inventories for the GNP accounts requires knowledge of the extent to which LIFO and various alternative accounting procedures are employed, the average length of the inventory turnover period, and the composition of raw material inventory. Such information is not available at the firm level, and in any case the computations would have been quite involved. Potentially, the neglect of price movements can be quite serious. For example, during a period of inflation the book value of inventories may increase, suggesting positive inventory investment when, in fact, the actual magnitude of stocks has declined. The effort involved did not seem worthwhile, given that the data period is one of fairly stable prices.

Furthermore, any distortions appear in practice not to create serious difficulty for the econometrician, judging by the interesting comparative analysis of Paul Kuznets [1964].[6]

A second problem involving price movements concerns the question of whether the forecasts are being made in terms of current prices rather than in terms of prices expected to prevail three or six months hence. Foss [1961, p. 236] reported that the absence of a marked inflationary trend meant that the movements of the series were subject to only minor change when adjusted under the assumption that respondents were making the forecasts in terms of current rather than expected prices.

Systematic Bias Correction. Compilers of *ex ante* data customarily attempt to eliminate systematic biases from their forecasts. This seems to be the case with at least part of the data collected for the railroad shippers' forecasts to be discussed in Section 2.2.3.[7] Similar adjustments for systematic biases are made by the OBE-SEC in publishing the results of the businessmen plant and equipment expenditure survey. Econometric studies of expectational behavior may be distorted when compiling agents have adjusted *ex ante* data in an attempt to improve its forecasting ability. Corrections are also made by the OBE in preparing their inventory anticipation data for publication in the *Survey of Current Business*. Specifically, it has been found that the magnitude of the COND variable can be used to improve the predictive ability of the raw inventory forecasts.[8] Obviously, when the objective is the prediction of future business conditions, it is advantageous to examine *ex ante* data from which systematic biases have been eliminated. But we were fortunate to be able to work with the data in *un*corrected form, for our concern is with the structure determining inventory movements, and systematic forecast biases are in themselves a phenomenon of interest. Indeed, if we had worked with data from which systematic biases had been eliminated we would have underestimated, in Chapter 3, the magnitude of the errors that firms typically make in forecasting inventory developments.[9]

[6] In the course of analyzing the effects of interest rate movements on inventory investment, Kuznets compared the regression coefficients obtained from undeflated data with estimates from data adjusted in several alternative ways for price movements. He found that his parameter estimates were quite insensitive to the choice of deflator, and were essentially the same as with undeflated data.

[7] A personal interview conducted by Lovell several years ago indicated that at certain Regional Boards of the American Railway Association individual replies are edited in order to eliminate predictions that appear unreasonable. This may tend to eliminate large changes.

[8] The correction procedure is described by Foss [1961].

[9] Conversely, it is necessary for the reader to remember that the anticipated inventory figures published quarterly in the *Survey of Current Business* have a much more precise forecasting record than the inventory data analyzed in Chapter 3 precisely because of the success of the OBE in eliminating systematic bias.

2.2.2 *Omitted Variables—Price, Advertising, and Orders*

More often than not the econometrician is frustrated by being unable to observe certain variables that would be useful for his investigation. Our study is no exception. In analyzing the determinants of sales expectations and production and inventory behavior, it would be particularly useful to have observations on the flow of new orders and the unfilled orders backlog. Information on the firm's cost of capital would enable us to evaluate the sensitivity of inventory holdings to changes in carrying costs. Accurate observations on price movements might be used to deflate our data, although prices were fairly stable over most of the period of our study. Price anticipations data would assist in testing whether price hedging considerations influence the magnitude of raw material stocks.[10] Furthermore, it would have been helpful in studying the way in which firms respond to errors in forecasting to have data on planned and actual selling price and advertising expenditure. Our inability to observe such variables raises problems in measuring forecast errors and studying the structure by which sales anticipations and inventory movements are generated.

Only indirect evidence concerning unfilled orders is provided by the OBE sales and inventory anticipation survey. Although firms are asked to consider the backlog of orders as well as sales volume in evaluating the condition of their inventories as high, low, or about right (the COND variable), they do not report the dollar magnitude of the order backlog. It proved practical to obtain data on the orders variable from the OBE-Census monthly manufacturing survey only at the durable and nondurable aggregate level.[11] Studies by Stanback [1958], Darling [1959], and Lovell [1961] have stressed the importance of unfilled orders as a determinant of the desired level of purchased materials and goods in process inventory. Presumably, information on the magnitude of new orders might be useful in explaining the generation of anticipated sales volume.

The distinction between production to order and production to stock, emphasized by Moses Abramovitz [1950] in his study of inventories in the interwar period, is also critical in the analysis of the structure of sales expectations and the production decision.[12] In many industries, production is largely to order. In durable manufacturing, the backlog of unfilled orders

[10] Lovell [1961] assumed that anticipated price changes were proportional to actual changes in attempting to measure the importance of the speculative motive for holding inventories. The evidence suggested that firms do *not* successfully speculate in raw material inventories.

[11] Classification procedures differed at the industry level between the monthly and quarterly surveys.

[12] The distinction between production to order and production to stock has received considerable attention in recent empirical studies of the production decision by Gerald Childs [1967], T. J. Courchene [1967], and David A. Belsley [1965].

is about six times the magnitude of finished goods inventory, while the situation is reversed for nondurables. The Commerce Department classifies production as being entirely to stock in the food and kindred products, tobacco, apparel, petroleum and coal, motor vehicle, chemicals, and rubber industries. On the other hand, the value of unfilled orders exceeds the dollar value of inventories for fabricated metal products, both electrical and non-electrical machinery, and transportation equipment.

Even without observations on orders, we can still anticipate that certain inter-industry differences in behavior may be explicable in terms of the relative importance of production to order. Thus, one might suppose that firms producing to stock would be less accurate in predicting sales volume. For the firm producing items to specific order, the sales anticipation may in large measure be a reflection of production plans. After all, a firm with a nine-month backlog of unfilled orders knows the short-run demand for its product. Any error made by such a firm in predicting sales volume must be the consequence of the firm's inability to forecast the precise time at which it can effect delivery. Thus, actual sales may fall short of the anticipated volume if machinery breakdowns or difficulties in procuring raw materials make it impossible to achieve planned production levels. The finished goods inventories held by firms producing primarily to stock cushion the impact on sales when production schedules are interrupted by technical difficulties.

For firms producing to stock, the analysis of sales anticipations and inventory behavior is simplified to the extent that it is reasonable to assume that firms do not respond to short-run surprises by adjusting price or advertising expenditures. Relaxation of these simplifications, which were invoked by Lloyd Metzler [1941] in his buffer-stock analysis of the inventory cycle, compels us to recognize that sales anticipations may be conditional statements concerning how much a firm expects to sell at a planned future price and a planned level of advertising expenditure; or to put it another way, anticipated sales volume is a point on the *ex ante* demand function evaluated at planned magnitudes of certain control variables. A firm may respond to surprise by adjusting price or advertising expenditure rather than by letting quantity assume the entire burden. How accurately the discrepancy between anticipated and actual sales volume measures forecast error depends on the extent to which the firm is willing to adjust price and advertising expenditure; it also hinges upon the sensitivity of demand to these control variables.

The nature of the problem is elucidated by Figure 2.1. Suppose that the firm's marketing department believes that curve $\hat{d}$-$\hat{d}'$ constitutes the short-run demand curve that it will face in the coming period. And suppose that in the light of this forecast and other relevant information the firm determines that profits will be maximized by price $\hat{p}$ and quantity $\hat{q}$. If the firm finds, *ex post*, after production decisions and other commitments have been finalized, that

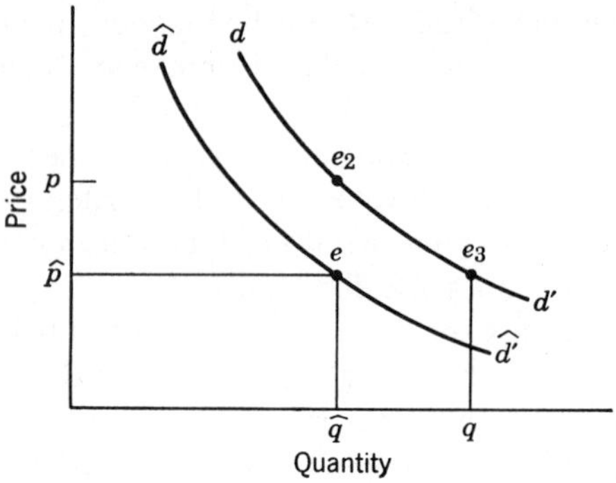

Figure 2.1 Price versus quantity response.

demand is actually *d-d'*, it might respond by raising price to p and selling the planned quantity $\hat{q}$. In terms of predicting *quantity* sold, such a firm would have a perfect forecasting record although its sales revenue forecast would be overfulfilled. Alternatively, the firm might maintain the planned price and sell q units by revising production schedules or drawing down inventories of finished goods—which is what Metzler assumed. Or the firm might respond by selecting some point intermediate between e_2 and e_3 on the *ex post* demand curve. It might even sell quantity $\hat{q}$ at price $\hat{p}$, leave a fringe of unsatisfied demand for tomorrow, but achieve a perfect record in terms of predicting both quantity sold and sales revenue.

The optimal response to forecast error hinges upon such dynamic factors as the expense of abruptly changing production levels, the likelihood that customers will postpone their purchases for a period rather than turn to an alternate supplier, and the possible costs in terms of a loss of customer goodwill involved in short-run price adjustments. The possibility that the firm may respond to an unexpected shift in demand by adjusting its advertising expenditure constitutes a further complication.

In order to investigate the extent to which firms in practice respond to forecast errors by adjusting price, it would be necessary to have accurate data on realized (rather than list) price at the firm level. Unfortunately, such data are not available; it is clear that the price indices compiled by the Bureau of Labor Statistics are inadequate for this task. There is at least some evidence, however, that in practice firms find it inadvisable to meet short-run shifts in demand with price adjustments. For example, George Katona [1951, p. 223] has argued:

> Price increases are often considered to be risky. Prices are frequently a matter of public knowledge, whereas output . . . is not . . . Retracting a decision after it has been put into effect is easier with respect to changes in output. . . . Reducing prices to the previous level may be considered as a public acknowledgment of a mistake . . . .

Furthermore, the management science literature prescribing optimal techniques of production scheduling and inventory control presumes, for the most part, that prices will not be revised as a result of short-run errors in predicting demand conditions.

It is most convenient if our reader will allow us to proceed under the assumption that firms absorb unexpected shifts in demand by adjusting their inventory of finished goods and revising their production schedules. Under this assumption, no serious problem is created by the fact that our variables are measured in current dollars rather than physical units. It can be shown, however, that the fact that our sales data are measured in current dollars does not mean that the assumption of price rigidity is critical. Indeed, the problem of measuring the magnitude of forecast errors would be more serious if sales were measured in quantity units. Thus, the error in forecasting the demand curve's position on Figure 2.1 would be correctly measured in physical units only if the firm avoids price adjustments and sells q units. In terms of sales evaluated at market price, on the other hand, the accuracy with which unanticipated shifts in demand are measured hinges upon the elasticity of the short-run demand curve; in particular, if the short-run demand curve d-d' in Figure 2.1 is of unit elasticity, the difference between realized and anticipated dollar revenue would accurately measure the error (q-$\hat{q}$) in forecasting the quantity that can be sold at planned price. Unless the elasticity of demand is less than one half, sales revenue will provide a more precise measure than actual shipments of the error made in estimating the position of the demand curve.[13]

2.2.3 *Alternative Data Sources Used in Earlier Studies*

Admittedly, quarterly time series covering only a short span of years do not provide as broad a range of observations as we would like to have, although the period analyzed does encompass one recession; but the difficulty is mitigated by the detailed industry breakdown of the aggregate data and the availability of observations at the individual firm level. Certainly, the

[13] To see this, suppose that anticipated demand is $\hat{q} = \hat{\alpha}\hat{p}^{-\eta}$ while realized demand is $q = \alpha p^{-\eta}$; that is, the error involved in incorrectly predicting the position of the demand curve (α instead of $\hat{\alpha}$) has led the firm to charge price p rather than planned price $\hat{p}$. Realized sales revenue is then $qp = \alpha p^{1-\eta}$ instead of $\hat{q}\hat{p} = \hat{\alpha}\hat{p}^{1-\eta}$. It is easily verified that the gap between realized and anticipated sales revenue is the more precise measure of the error in predicting α unless η, the elasticity of demand, is less than one half. If price only affects current demand, of course, a profit maximizing firm would always sell at a point where its elasticity of demand is greater than unity. In fact, however, firms recognize that today's price may affect the availability of customers tomorrow and not fully exploit the instantaneous inelasticity of their demand schedule; but an elasticity of less than one half seems very unlikely.

anticipations data provided by the OBE survey constitute a much more fruitful source of information on short-term anticipations than has been available from other sources.

The railroad shippers' forecasts, conducted since 1927 by the Regional Shippers Advisory Boards under the auspices of the Association of American Railroads, provided the data base for pioneering investigations by Ferber [1953] of the structure of sales expectations and by Modigliani and Sauerlander [1955] of production and inventory behavior. This extensive body of data is derived from a survey of traffic managers concerning the number of railroad carloadings that they anticipate their firm will be using for the shipment of their finished product. Serious questions concerning the validity of this body of data as a measure of actual anticipations have been raised by a number of authors who have objected that actual forecasts could not contain the gross errors and regressivity property revealed by the railroad shippers' forecasts. Albert Hart [1960] has suggested that the figures must be "reconstituted" before they can provide a valid measure of actual anticipations, and Edwin S. Mills [1962, Ch. 11] argued that his "implicit" procedure for obtaining a surrogative measure of expectations might constitute a more accurate index of actual anticipations than is provided by the railroad shippers' forecasts. Lovell [1964, Appendix] argued that since the questionnaire utilized for the shippers' forecasts asked about actual carloads shipped in the corresponding quarter of the preceding year (C_{t-4}) as well as anticipated shipments ($\hat{C}_t$), the respondent may be tempted to obtain his forecast by simply blowing up the corresponding same-quarter-of-last-year carloading figure by the ratio of the company's sales forecast ($\hat{C}_t$) to actual year-ago sales (S_{t-4}); i.e., $\hat{C}_t = C_{t-4}(\hat{S}_t/S_{t-4})$. In support of this hypothesis, Lovell found that estimates of sales anticipations ($\hat{S}_t$) derived with this equation for the cement industry are much more accurate predictors of future developments than the original carloading anticipations ($\hat{C}_t$) data published by the American Railway Association.[14] We shall see in Chapter 3 that the magnitude of forecast errors does appear to have been grossly exaggerated by the railroad shippers' forecast data. Nonetheless, the analysis of Chapter 5 will reveal that Ferber's results concerning the structure of sales anticipations survive replication on the new data provided by the OBE survey.

A second source of *ex ante* firm data is provided by the Commerce-SEC

[14] The S_t series was measured in terms of barrels. Even though the carload anticipation may provide the same forecast of the relative increase expected over the corresponding quarter of the preceding year, this does not imply that the barrel and carloading forecasts will be equally accurate. Lovell found that anticipated and actual sales, measured in barrels, were much more closely correlated than forecast and actual carloadings. Although a large proportion of cement output is shipped by rail, barrel shipments and carloadings are *not* highly correlated in all quarters, and the carloading anticipations are particularly inaccurate in quarters in which the correlation is low.

annual survey of business anticipations of capital and sales expenditures. B. Peter Pashigian [1964] analyzed the accuracy of these forecasts over the period 1948–1955; these same data had been utilized by Modigliani and Weingartner [1958] in predicting capital expenditures and by Pashigian [1965] in his study of inventory investment. Although these studies are of great interest, the time series utilized by these authors is shorter than that now provided by the OBE sales and inventory survey, and their data have not been analyzed on a firm-by-firm basis.

Direction of change surveys provide a third source of *ex ante* data. Beginning in 1950, the IFO-Institut fur Wirtschaftsforschung sent monthly questionnaires to approximately 5000 firms in Western Germany. Inquiry was made concerning the anticipated and actual direction of change for a wide variety of operating variables on a monthly basis. These data have been analyzed by H. Theil [1958, 1966], T. Thomstad and D. B. Jochems [1961], and several other investigators. Similar data for United States firms provided by Dun and Bradstreet have been studied by Modigliani and Sauerlander [1955] and Millard Hastay [1960]. Usually, the procedure is to use diffusion indices based on the excess of firms predicting an increase over those anticipating a decrease. Obviously, considerable precision is sacrificed when the only information available concerns the direction rather than the magnitude of change.

Several other sources of *ex ante* data have been employed in studies of inventory behavior. In particular, Murray Brown [1961] used aggregate data for the period 1956–1959 from *Fortune's* Business Roundup survey, which involves a sample of about 200 firms. Furthermore, Gilbert R. Whitaker, Jr. [1966] analyzed monthly data from four firms in his investigation of the production and inventory decision. Most other sources of *ex ante* data, such as the McGraw-Hill survey, involve a longer forecasting horizon, and are most fruitfully employed in studies of fixed investment rather than inventory and production behavior. While our catalog of the various sources of *ex ante* data relevant to the short-run decision-making problems of the firm may be incomplete, it does suffice to illustrate that the body of data provided by the OBE survey constitutes a most useful source of information.

2.3 STATISTICAL PROCEDURES

Since the empirical chapters that follow are devoted to an analysis of a number of related topics on the same body of data, it is obvious that many of the practical problems of data processing and statistical analysis must also be very similar. We shall now discuss these common problems.

2.3.1 *Security Restrictions*

In order to insure that the confidential nature of the individual firm's response would be preserved, only Albert Hirsch, the coauthor associated with the OBE, was authorized to see data pertaining to individual firms. Programs were written that were capable of processing the data "blind." That is, the computer performed such tasks as editing the data cards at appropriate stages of the analysis in order to delete a firm's observations for dates when it neglected to provide relevant information. Furthermore, Hirsch personally supervised the processing of the individual firm data and observed the degaussing of the data tapes after they had been used on the computer. As an additional precaution, the firms were identified by code number rather than by name.

Because of these security restrictions, we planned our project in a way that would permit us, at least in principle, to process all the firm data in a single day. This restriction limited the flexibility of our approach, and for the most part we had to content ourselves with the use of standardized linear regression procedures. In effect, turn around time was almost infinite, but this restriction did insure that we did not engage in sequential statistical "experimentation" on our body of data.[15] A wide variety of competing models that have been advanced in the literature on inventories and expectational behavior warranted consideration, and approximately 10,000 regressions were run on individual firm data alone. This is an outrageous number, but the reader of the chapters that follow will be frustrated from time to time by the fact that our output was too small! We lost a small portion of planned output as a result of programming problems. And as always, it is apparent in retrospect that a number of hypotheses warrent further consideration.

2.3.2 *Sample Design*

The sample of firms utilized for the microphase of our study was selected on a systematic rather than a random basis. The nature of ongoing clerical

[15] In practice, three separate passes on the firm data were made, necessitating three trips by Albert Hirsch to Pittsburgh. The first pass was unsuccessful because of a programming error that distorted the sequence of firm observations; another "bug" occurred when incomplete questionnaires caused zero observations to be available for a particular firm's regression. Most of the second pass was successful, although the firm data on waves of optimism and pessimism, presented in Chapter 4.5.1 was lost. The third pass corrected this error, and in addition, we attempted some minor elaborations on the basis of our output from the second pass. Specifically, we obtained on the third pass the results on the sign of turning point errors of Chapter 3 and on purchased material and goods in process inventory of Chapter 6; also, a minor change was made in the treatment of the COND dummy variable and some alternative procedures for handling seasonal complications were introduced.

operations at the OBE would have made it extremely difficult to transcribe data for certain firms in the OBE sample for our study. Since time and funds available for coding the data were limited, we would not have been able to obtain nearly as large a sample if we had tried to select a purely random subsample of firms from the 1400 included in the OBE survey. Furthermore, it seemed advisable, since data for only a limited number of firms were to be analyzed, to attempt to focus upon firms that responded regularly to the survey and consistently answered most of the items on the questionnaire. So, we decided to select firms that had a good response record from among those with records that could be accessed easily. Firms that merged or had major acquisitions during the sample period were excluded.

If our objective were to estimate the magnitudes of such variables as anticipated sales, the systematic nature of our procedure for selecting the sample of firms might introduce serious bias. Although we shall have to consider the possible effects of sample bias in Chapter 3, where we shall be concerned with estimating the magnitude of forecast errors made by the average manufacturing firm, it is clear that the sampling issue is not so serious when our objective is to obtain regression estimates of the parameters of behavioral equations. In particular, for models that are sufficiently rich to explain differences in the behavioral patterns among individual firms, so that there are no interfirm differences in parameter values among firms in the same industry, it does not matter which particular firms happen to fall into our sample.[16] Under these circumstances, our systematic sampling procedure is obviously preferred to a much smaller randomly selected sample. On the other hand, it is obvious that quite serious biases might be introduced if the firms with good response records prepare their forecasts and adjust their inventories in fundamentally different ways from firms that do not respond regularly to the survey.

2.3.3 *Choosing Among Alternative Hypotheses*

A recurrent problem will involve the task of choosing the valid regression model from among a number of alternatives explaining the same variable. For example, in Chapter 5 we will be interested in comparing the validity of the adaptive expectations model with an alternative hypothesis of Ferber. The problem is not trivial, for neither model constitutes a special case of the other; more precisely, neither model can be obtained from the other by the imposition of linear restrictions on the parameters; as a consequence, standard t-test or F-test procedures are not directly applicable.

Several alternative approaches to this problem are employed by practicing

[16] That is, the expected values of the parameter estimates are insensitive, although the efficiency of the estimating procedure is obviously sensitive to sample design.

econometricians. One approach is to fit the competing models and then compare them on the basis of goodness of fit as measured by the correlation coefficient. An alternative procedure, frequently utilized in selecting which econometric model is preferable, concerns a different measure of their relative predictive abilities. That is, one may fit the models to one part of the data and use the parameter estimates obtained from this process in testing the predictive ability of the rival models on the remaining observations. The model yielding the smallest mean-square predictive error over the testing period is selected as valid. A third procedure, with which we became acquainted only near the end of our study, involves the application of Bayesian analysis.

Theil [1961, pp. 212–214] has provided justification for the first approach. Specifically, he considers the procedure of simply accepting as true that model which has the smallest standard error of estimate, corrected for degrees of freedom. He shows that this decision procedure leads "on the average" to the correct choice.[17] Precisely the same choice will be made if one selects the model with the highest $\bar{R}^2$ (adjusted for degrees of freedom) provided that missing data or other complications do not prevent both models from being applied to precisely the same time period. Theil also emphasizes that his proof rests on the assumption that the dependent variables are identical; for example, he has not shown that the criterion is appropriate in choosing between y and log y as the dependent variables. In his demonstration, Theil assumes that the disturbance for the correct model is independently distributed with constant variance and zero mean and that the explanatory variables are nonstochastic. This last proviso is honored only in the breach when lagged dependent variables appear in the equation. A further difficulty arises because we do not know by how much the probability of making a correct decision exceeds one half, but this problem can be at least partially surmounted in our study. Since we have data for a sizable number of firms, it will be possible for us to use the binomial theorem. Specifically, we shall determine the probability of the observed majority of k out of n firms yielding a tighter fit with a particular model if, for each firm, the probability of accepting the model is 0.5. This is not a powerful approach, but it is one luxury permitted by having data on a number of individual firms.

Although we have followed the procedure analyzed by Theil in our study, the possibility of dividing the data into estimation and testing sets does

[17] Hodson Thornber [1966, Section 2.4] has shown that the $\bar{R}^2$ criterion serves to minimize expected loss in choosing between alternative models if the loss function is symmetric, the prior judgement is that each model is equally likely to be correct, and both models have the same dependent variables and the same number of explanatory variables. Unfortunately, the standard adjustment of $\bar{R}^2$ for degrees of freedom is not the appropriate correction for minimizing expected loss when the models do not have the same number of explanatory variables.

deserve some discussion. Indeed, one critic has argued that we should have estimated the parameters of a variety of models on the data for half our firms and then ranked the models on the basis of how well they did when these parameter estimates were utilized on the data for the firms reserved for prediction purposes. Whatever its merits, programming and data processing constraints precluded this approach; but these same constraints prevented us from "mining" our data by generating hypotheses through a prolonged sequence of "experimental" runs on the computer. Nonetheless, we do have a vested interest in looking with jaundiced eye upon certain implications of the data partitioning procedure.

We shall compare the large sample implications of the two approaches. To do this, it is necessary for us to worry about how many observations should be used for fitting and how many reserved for predictive testing. If too few are used for fitting, the procedure will be subject to considerable risk because of imprecise parameter estimates. On the other hand, if too many observations are used for estimation, the results obtained in the prediction period will be quite noisy because of the effect of the stochastic disturbance. Let us suppose that the decision has been made to reserve some definite fraction, say one half, for fitting and the remainder for predictive testing. It is clear that, for each model, as the sample size increases the parameter estimates obtained on the fitting portion of the data will approach those that would be generated with the full body of data; furthermore, the mean square error in the prediction period will have as its probability limit the same standard error of estimate provided when all available observations are used for estimation.[18] Consequently, with sufficiently large samples, the ranking of models in terms of predictive ability will be the same regardless of whether the standard error of estimate or the data partitioning procedure is employed. For small samples, we should obviously use the method that is most likely to yield the same ranking that would be generated by either procedure for large samples. This means that with a finite sample the best way to rank the models is on the basis of the observed variance of the residuals obtained when *all* the data are used in the regression.

2.3.4 *Aggregation, Data Pooling, Homogeneity, and Homoscedasticity*

Data are available for 83 firms and 14 industries, but the temptation to construct various aggregates and to pool our data in a variety of ways has

[18] To define these concepts for the incorrect specification, we can follow the procedure of Theil, who defined the parameters of the wrong model as the expected value of the estimates obtained by the application of least squares. Certain obvious regularity conditions must be imposed when this approach is employed in analyzing the effects of variations in sample size.

been too much for us to resist. As a result, we shall see, there is a potential set of 148 regression results to examine for each model considered.

Our data are aggregated in at least two senses. First, we have the 14 sets of time series derived at the OBE by adjusting the full sample estimates to industry benchmarks. But we also have summed these benchmark industry time series into durable and nondurable aggregates. Furthermore, it has proved useful in certain instances to examine aggregates derived for the subsample of firms in each of the five industries for which we have firm data; and we did this for all firms, for all the large firms and for all the small. Thus, in addition to calculating the durable and the nondurable aggregates from the industry benchmark data, we also have three other aggregates for each of the five industries for which we have firm data.

The aggregates have been computed in all instances before data transformation. For example, certain models involve the ratio of the short sales anticipation to actual sales of the previous quarter, denoted ASSALE/ $SALE_{-1}$. This is *not* an aggregate of the ratios, but the ratio of two aggregates, $\sum_i ASSALE_{t,i}/\sum_i SALE_{t-1,i}$, where the second subscript denotes the industry or firm.

The durable and nondurable aggregate regressions are of interest primarily because they yield direct information about the behavior of the more readily observable macrovariables used in econometric model construction. Of course, perfect aggregation is achievable when a model linear in the variables is sufficiently rich to explain interindustry differences, so that there is no variation among industries in the magnitude of the parameters.[19] This does not mean, however, that it will be immaterial whether we fit the model to the aggregates or to the industry benchmarked data. Quite the contrary, the appropriate procedure under this homogeneity postulate is to pool all of the data in a single long string of observations to be processed as a single regression. In this way we have, for example, seven times as many observations to estimate the durable manufacturing sector's parameters as we would if we fitted the data to the durable manufacturing aggregate data. It is also of interest to see the effect of hypothesizing that all parameters are the same except the intercepts, for perfect aggregation is still possible with a linear model even if the intercepts are not all the same. For most models we calculated pooled regressions and pooled regressions with separate intercepts for both durables and nondurables.

[19] By perfect aggregation we mean that the model can be applied to aggregate data without having to worry about distributional complications; e.g., in the simple consumption function model $C_i = \alpha_i + \beta_i Y_i$, where the subscript i denotes the ith individual, information on the distribution of income will be of no help in predicting aggregate consumption if β_i, the marginal propensity to consume, is the same for all individuals.

The homogeneity assumption is convenient, because it facilitates aggregation and provides a substantial gain in degrees of freedom by data pooling. It can also be subjected to empirical test. Whenever we pooled data we calculated two F statistics providing approximate tests of the hypothesis that there are no interindustry differences in the parameters of the model. More precisely, the first F statistic is pertinent for the null hypothesis that all industries have the same parameter values, while the second is pertinent for the null hypothesis that only the intercepts vary from one industry to the next. The full sequence of F tests involved in the covariance analysis of the homogeneity assumption that there are no interindustry differences in the various parameters of the model has not been applied;[20] this approach involves certain conceptual difficulties[21] and would have required considerable additional computer time.

The assumption of homoscedasticity, it must be emphasized, is particularly open to question with the pooled regression. Although it is possible that all industries have the same slope parameters for a particular model, the variance of the disturbances may well be greater for large than for small firms or industries. Of course, violation of the homoscedasticity assumption does not in itself serve to introduce bias. But it does mean that more efficient parameter estimates might have been obtained by a two-pass procedure in which the observations are transformed in a second "weighted regression" pass on the basis of estimates of industry standard errors of estimate obtained in the first pass. Furthermore, two problems of statistical inference are created when the homoscedasticity condition is violated. First, the standard errors of the regression coefficients for the pooled regressions are distorted. Second, the F tests of the homogeneity hypotheses are not valid. For these two additional reasons, also, it is unfortunate that we did not have the computer time and flexibility to undertake the additional computations involved in the two-pass procedure. However, in certain instances, we did work with models in ratio form; this approach reduces the disparities in industry size, and in certain circumstances achieves homoscedasticity.

Grounds for suspicion with regard to both the standard errors of the regression coefficients and the F tests for homogeneity arise because of the

[20] For a discussion of covariance analysis, see Mood [1950] and Kuh [1963].

[21] The two F statistics we report are based on the standard procedure described in such textbooks as Johnston [1963]. They are concerned with the question of how much is gained in terms of a tighter overall fit when the homogeneity restriction is relaxed. The covariance analysis discussed by Mood involves a sequence of F tests casting further information on such questions as whether the hypothesis of identical intercepts should be accepted as opposed to all parameters being identical except the intercepts. But because it involves the computation of a sequence of F tests, which are nonindependent, it is impossible to determine the precise probability of erroneously rejecting the null hypothesis if it is, in fact, correct.

possibility that the stochastic disturbances are autocorrelated. We present the Durbin-Watson statistic for the aggregate regressions. The reader is reminded, however, that this test is not valid when a lagged dependent variable appears in the model as an explanatory variable; this same complication introduces Hurwicz [1950] bias in the absence of autocorrelation and generates inconsistent parameter estimates when the disturbances are, in fact, autocorrelated.

In analyzing data for individual firms, we proceeded in much the same way as with the benchmark adjusted industry data. For each model, we ran a regression on each firm. In addition, we pooled the data for all the observed firms in each industry, both with and without separate intercepts. Furthermore, we ran a regression on data aggregated over each industry subsample. But this is not all. We were also interested in observing whether there were noticeable differences in the behavior of large as opposed to small firms. Therefore, we ran pooled regressions, with and without separate intercepts, and the aggregate regression on all the large firms with assets in excess of $10 million and again on all the small firms. For each model this involves a large number of regressions; specifically, there are potentially 83 individual firm regressions; and for each of five industries there are three aggregate regressions, three pooled regressions, and three pooled regressions with separate intercepts. This adds up to some 128 regressions run on the firm data for each model, although the full potential was often not realized because of incomplete firm response.

Appendix: Format for Presenting Regression Results

Obviously, space limitations, if not our readers' patience, preclude the presentation of 148 sets of parameter estimates reported in our computer printout for each model. Instead, we present on the first page of each table the pooled regressions obtained for each of the five industries for which we have firm data. Furthermore, we report on two facing pages the durable and nondurable results obtained with the benchmark adjusted industry data. We deviate occasionally from this pattern. Thus, in Chapter 6, we cannot always present the industry benchmark results because industry finished goods inventory data were not available. Furthermore, we include in Chapter 6 an additional page reporting pooled regressions for small and for large firms separately by industry, for these results proved of somewhat special interest.

We shall first explain the format for presenting the benchmark industry regression output. Each column summarizes a regression. The first seven are individual industries, and they are identified by number in accordance with the code translated on Table 2.1.2. The AGGREGATE column obviously reports the regression obtained by aggregating the data over all industries while the POOLED and POOLED WITH SEPARATE INTERCEPT columns report results for the pooled regressions with and without the intercepts being constrained to be the same in all industries. In the first few rows we report the number of degrees of freedom,[22] the value of $\bar{R}^2$, the standard error of estimate, and the Durbin-Watson statistic.[23] Both $\bar{R}^2$ and the standard error of estimate are

[22] Note that six fewer degrees of freedom are available for the POOLED WITH SEPARATE INTERCEPT than for POOLED because of the additional intercepts.

[23] The Durbin-Watson statistics for the pooled regressions are only approximations. When the data is pooled by literally forming a string of observations and then processing with the standard regression package the program will yield a statistic distorted by the jump in the residuals between industries, and the computed figure will depend on the arbitrary order in which the industries are arranged. We also used a more sophisticated program that operated by summing individual moment matrices and that did not yield even a pseudo-pooled Durbin-Watson statistic.

adjusted for degrees of freedom. The pairs of numbers in the following rows are the regression coefficients with standard errors immediately below. Below the matrix of regression coefficients and standard errors, we present the two alternative F statistics. Finally, we report a pooled standard error of estimate obtained from the regressions for individual firms.

The pooled individual firm results are reported on tables in five separate columns, one for each of the industries for which we have data. We indicate in the title whether or not the reported regression and F statistic have constrained intercept.[24] No attempt was made to compute a pooled Durbin-Watson statistic with the firm data, but $\bar{d}$ denotes the average Durbin-Watson statistic obtained with the individual firm regressions. The "Partial $\bar{R}^2$" reported for each separate intercept pooled regression is actually a partial-multiple coefficient of determinations in the following sense: it is computed by subtracting from unity the ratio of the standard error of estimate to the variance of the dependent variable, where the latter is computed around individual firm means rather than the grand mean. Since this variance is smaller than the second moment about the grand mean, the ratio is larger, and the resulting coefficient of multiple determination is reduced in magnitude. Of course, appropriate adjustments are made for lost degrees of freedom. It must be remembered that the same problems with regard to both the homogeneity assumption and the independence assumption may also be involved with firm data.

In any statistical study, it is important to consider the possibility that the data are sufficiently ill-conditioned to generate inaccurate results through the excessive accumulation of roundoff error. That the problem can be of serious proportions even when processing data on the electronic computer has been demonstrated recently by James W. Longley [1967], who obtained grossly different answers when he processed highly colinear data on IBM and GE equipment with standard packaged computer programs. Of course, the matter is of particular concern when, as in this study, the data must be processed "blind." Our matrix inversion operations were performed in double precision on a Control Data G20 computer. That roundoff error is not serious for our study is suggested by the fact that we were able to achieve extremely accurate results in a special test with our programs on Longley's highly collinear data.

[24] If f denotes the number of firms pooled, k the number of parameters in the regression and n the number of degrees of freedom reported on the table for the regression, then F is distributed with n_1 and n_2 degrees of freedom; here $n_1 = k(f - 1)$ for the pooled or $(k - 1)(f - 1)$ for the separate intercept regressions while $n_2 = n - n_1$.

CHAPTER 3

On the Accuracy of Expectations

3.1 INTRODUCTION

How accurately does the representative firm forecast its future sales developments? In which industries are firms most successful at predicting demand conditions? Are firms more precise at predicting inventory developments or at forecasting the demand for their product? Should the theory of inventory cycles rely on the presumption that errors made by firms in predicting short-run sales movements are of critical importance in generating economic fluctuations? Studies of the railroad shippers' forecast data have suggested that firms are grossly inaccurate forecasters. New evidence on the degree of forecasting precision achieved by respondents to the OBE quarterly inventory and sales anticipations survey will be appraised in this chapter. Various measures of forecasting precision must be discussed before we turn to the empirical evidence. Then, in Section 3.2, we shall examine the data at the industry level and compare our results with alternative estimates that have been derived from other data sources. Firm data and the effects of aggregation are discussed in Section 3.4. Finally, the argument will be summarized in Section 3.5.

3.2 MEASURES OF FORECAST ACCURACY

What is the appropriate yardstick for measuring the degree of accuracy achieved by a forecaster? Although predictive ability is often advocated by economists as an appropriate criterion for selecting the best model from a variety of candidates, the question of how one measures forecast accuracy has not been entirely resolved. Rather, we find that in prior investigations of *ex ante* data, a variety of alternative statistics have been utilized for this task. Here we shall briefly discuss certain merits and deficiencies of the more popular candidates and define those that merit application to the anticipations data available for our study.

Several criteria may be used in appraising alternative yardsticks. First, it is obviously advantageous to work with a measure that may be regarded as an index of the cost to the firm of erroneous forecasts. This suggests that a simple tabulation of the proportion of errors made in predicting the direction of change will not suffice, for this approach neglects the magnitude of the error. Although we shall report information on the frequency of turning point errors, it should be noted that a small turning point error may be less costly to the firm than a large overestimate, but with correct sign, of the actual realized change. Second, it is useful to have a measure of forecast accuracy that is independent of units of measurement so that the relative accuracy of forecasts by large and small firms will be comparable. Third, it is helpful, at least for certain purposes, if the yardstick of precision rates the forecaster relative to the difficulty inherent in the type of series he is trying to forecast. Thus, if two forecasters make prediction errors of equal magnitude on the average, we might still wish to assign a higher score to the first forecaster if he is charged with predicting a time series characterized by erratic fluctuations while the second forecaster is attempting to predict a series dominated by stable trend and seasonal components. This is the type of comparison we will have to make, for we wish to evaluate the relative performance of forecasters who are attempting to predict different time series relevant only to their own firm; our task would be easier if the forecasters were all concentrating on the same variable.[1] Finally, it is useful to judge the forecasts both with and without adjustment for simple systematic biases. Obviously, no single yardstick of forecast accuracy can be ideal in terms of all such criteria, and a number of alternative statistics will need to be considered.

It is customary in analyzing the accuracy of forecasts to work in terms of predicted and actual relative changes. Otherwise, there is a danger that the presence of a marked trend in the series will give an inflated picture of the accuracy of the forecast. This convention will be followed here. Thus, if A_t denotes the actual realization of the variable to be predicted, while P_t is the value forecast for time t, we consider the actual relative change

$$a_t = \frac{A_t - A_{t-1}}{A_{t-1}}$$

[1] In econometric work, a variety of models may be compared in terms of their ability to forecast a particular time series; in these circumstances, the task of comparing relative predictive ability is simplified considerably.

and the anticipated relative change

$$p_t = \frac{P_t - A_{t-1}}{A_{t-1}}$$

Thus, if the forecaster consistently makes the naive prediction of *no change*, p_t will have a mean and variance of zero.[2]

The first measure is the mean-square-error, which is defined as:

$$\text{MSE} = \frac{\sum (p - a)^2}{n} = \frac{1}{n} \sum \left(\frac{P - A}{A_{-1}} \right)^2 \tag{2.1}$$

where n is the number of observations.[3] The forecast error is squared, which is consistent with a quadratic loss function imposing a penalty in proportion to the square of the forecast error. In many studies the square root of the MSE, the root mean square error (RMSE), is reported. Although the actual costs to the firm of forecast errors obviously can not be measured without detailed knowledge of the decision-making problem confronting the firm, the theory of production smoothing and inventory control, as developed by Holt, Modigliani, Muth, and Simon [1960] and by Theil [1961], suggests that, at least for simple examples, these costs will be *proportional* to the MSE.[4] It should be noted that this statistic is independent of the units of measurement when relative changes are employed.

[2] Theil [1966, pp. 47–49] has pointed out that there is a certain asymmetry in working with relative changes. Thus, if a series first increases and then decreases by, say, 25%, it will not have returned to its original level. So, in contrast to his earlier work [1961], Theil now uses the log change, defined as log (A_t/A_{t-1}). For series that are not subject to large fluctuations, however, the difference between the relative and the log change approach will not be pronounced. In retrospect, we are willing to concede that something is to be said for using the difference $P_t - A_{t-1}$ rather than the relative change. For one thing, the problem of aggregation is simplified, for the industry anticipated change is simply the sum of the anticipations of individual firms. But throughout we have followed convention on this issue.

[3] It is conceivable that the $p - a$ may constitute drawings from a distribution for which the first and second moments do not exist. Then the population value of MSE would be nonexistent, and the sample statistic might increase without limit for larger and larger sample sizes. Throughout, let us assume that such pathological problems do not confront us.

[4] The actual cost of forecast errors, of course, depends upon the parameters of the loss function. The MSE will be proportional to these costs only for simple applications. In more realistic applications, several predictions (e.g., sales in several future periods) may be involved in making a single decision; then the loss becomes a more complicated expression involving such factors as the correlation of the various prediction errors as well as their MSE. But in these circumstances no single measure of the cost of forecast errors can be constructed without knowing the parameters of the loss function. Further, it must be conceded that the loss function rationale for using the MSE is strictly applicable only when working with the actual rather than the relative change.

A second measure is the coefficient of correlation between predicted and actual changes. Although this yardstick has been used in many empirical studies of forecast accuracy, a disadvantage is that it does not penalize the forecaster for systematic linear bias. Thus, a forecaster who always underestimates actual changes by fifty percent receives a perfect score of unity. Nonetheless, the correlation coefficient is not without merit, as may be seen by considering the following formula for r^2:

$$r^2 = 1 - \frac{S_e^2}{S_a^2} \tag{2.2}$$

Here S_a^2 denotes the variance of a and S_e^2 the variance of the discrepancies about the regression line of predicted on actual change. Now S_a^2 is the MSE that would be obtained by a naive forecaster whose prediction is always $p_t = \bar{a}$, where $\bar{a}$ denotes the average value of a_t over the sample period. On the other hand, S_e^2 denotes the MSE that would have been obtained with the forecaster's predictions after optimal linear correction for systematic bias. So the correlation coefficient compares the MSE that would result from using the forecast corrected for linear bias relative to the MSE that would be obtained from a naive forecast of $\bar{a}$.

A third measure of the accuracy of forecasts is provided by Theil's inequality coefficient. In *Economic Forecasts and Policy*, Thiel [1961] advocated the use of the statistic:

$$U = \frac{\sqrt{\text{MSE}}}{\sqrt{\sum a^2/n} + \sqrt{\sum p^2/n}} \tag{2.3}$$

An advantage of this statistic is that it is bound between the range of zero for perfect forecasts and unity. Furthermore, it penalizes for systematic linear bias, which r^2 does not. This statistic has been used by econometricians to appraise the relative forecasting abilities of econometric models. Thus, John Meyer and Glauber [1964, p. 218] employ U, $\bar{R}^2$, and the standard error of estimate as alternative criteria in comparing several single equation models of investment behavior. Nonetheless, this inequality coefficient does not always provide a reasonable ranking of alternative forecasting procedures. The anomaly with regard to U may be clarified with a simple example. Suppose that our forecaster knows that $\bar{a} = 0$ and the magnitude of S_a, and nothing more. He might simply forecast no change, in which case he would have a mean-square-error of S_a^2. Alternatively, he might draw his forecast randomly from a distribution with mean zero and a variance of S_a^2. Although the second strategy is manifestly worse than the first (it yields a mean-square-error of $2S_a^2$), it receives a better rating in terms of Theil's U statistic; specifically $U = \sqrt{\frac{1}{2}}$ rather than unity when the noise is added.

In more recent work, Theil [1966] has reverted to the following alternative inequality measure:

$$U_1 = \sqrt{\frac{\text{MSE}}{\sum a^2/n}} \tag{2.4}$$

This measure is again zero in the case of perfect forecasts. A value of unity means that the forecaster could have obtained the same MSE as he actually achieves by always reporting a naive forecast of no change ($p_t = 0$). A value larger than unity implies that a naive forecast of no change would be more precise than the actual achievement of the forecaster.[5]

It proves more convenient, in discussing the accuracy of forecasts, to apply a simple transformation to Theil's second inequality coefficient. Consider the following coefficient:

$$r_1^2 = 1 - \frac{\text{MSE}}{\sum a^2/n} = 1 - U_1^2 \tag{2.5}$$

As with r^2, a value of r_1^2 of unity implies perfect forecasting. On the other hand, a value of zero implies that the forecaster is achieving a MSE that is as bad as would have been obtained by simply forecasting no change. A negative value implies that the forecaster's record is *worse* than that which might have been obtained by always forecasting no change.

While this "pseudo" coefficient of determination constitutes a convenient measure of forecast accuracy, it is useful also to consider slightly more difficult naive-forecaster benchmarks in the denominator. Specifically, the coefficient

$$r_2^2 = 1 - \frac{\text{MSE}}{S_a^2} \tag{2.6}$$

compares the achievement of the forecaster with the root-mean-square-error that would have been achieved by a naive forecaster who always predicted $p_t = \bar{a}$. This will have no effect, of course, if the actual series is not subject to systematic trend. But for purposes of comparing the relative precision of different forecasters, it does recognize the fact that the forecaster of a series with a consistent upward or downward trend has an easier task. It will be identical to the correlation coefficient if the regression line of the predictions on actual realizations passes through the origin with a slope of unity. Furthermore, the difference $r^2 - r_2^2 = (\text{MSE} - S_e^2)/S_a^2$ constitutes a measure of the reduction in the mean-square-error obtainable by optimal

[5] The sampling distribution of U_1 has been investigated by Nagar [1962], but application of his tests requires unavailable knowledge of the parameter describing a tendency to systematically underestimate change.

correction for systematic linear bias, relative to the mean square error that would be obtained by naively forecasting $\bar{a}$.

When dealing with quarterly forecasts, it is also appropriate to consider the fact that a series with a systematic seasonal may be easier to forecast. For this reason another pseudo-partial r^2 constituting a more stringent measure of forecasting accuracy is of interest. We have computed

$$r_3^{\,2} = 1 - \frac{\text{MSE}}{S^2_{a.a}}. \tag{2.7}$$

Here the double subscript on the variance constituting the denominator indicates that it has been computed from seasonally adjusted realization data. Thus, $r_3^{\,2} = 0$ if the forecaster's mean square error is identical to that which would have been achieved by a hypothetical forecaster who used only his knowledge of his firm's trend and seasonal pattern in preparing a naive prediction. For computational reasons, it was most convenient to derive $S^2_{a.a}$ by subjecting actual realizations, the A_t, to seasonal adjustment by a procedure that equalizes quarterly means.

In summary, we observe that for perfect forecasts, MSE $= U_1 = 0$ and $r^2 = r_1^{\,2} = r_2^{\,2} = r_3^{\,2} = 1$. Furthermore, we may expect $r_1^{\,2} \geq r_2^{\,2} \geq r_3^{\,2}$, because these pseudo-$r^2$'s use successively more difficult naive benchmarks in measuring the degree of accuracy achieved by the forecaster.[6] Also, $r^2 \geq r_2^{\,2}$, because the standard coefficient of determination automatically adjusts for systematic linear bias. It is this attribute of the r^2 statistic that distinguishes it from the other measures of forecast accuracy. All the other yardsticks involve a comparison of the MSE actually achieved by the forecaster with that which would have been achieved by a naive forecaster of a specified degree of sophistication. This implies that the problem of evaluating forecasting prediction is greatly simplified when all forecasters are attempting to predict the same time series, for then the MSE, U_1, $r_1^{\,2}$, $r_2^{\,2}$, and $r_3^{\,2}$ criteria must of necessity rank the forecasters in the same order.[7]

Although the period we are studying was one of quite mild cyclical movement, all of the pseudo-correlation measures of forecast accuracy would probably assign a higher score to a sophisticated forecaster if his predictive ability were being appraised over a period characterized by more sizable cyclical fluctuations in economic activity. For example, if the forecaster derives his predictions from a well-designed econometric model, the standard error of estimate (his RMSE) will be insensitive to the degree of cyclical

[6] In a few exceptional cases the application of the additive seasonal adjustment procedure to the actual figures (rather than their relative changes) resulted in a larger RMSE than would have been obtained using $\bar{a}$ as the naive benchmark. In these circumstances we had $r_3^{\,2} > r_2^{\,2}$.

[7] The equivalent ranking follows from the fact that these measures involve the ratio of the MSE to a denominator that depends only on the actual series and not the forecasts.

volatility. Similarly, the MSE of predictions derived from a random customer poll will be insensitive to the degree of cyclical activity if sampling variation is the primary source of error. While the MSE constituting the numerator of the ratios used in the various pseudo-correlation measures will be unaffected, the denominators will tend to be large in periods of marked cyclical movement; but this means that the ratio to be subtracted from unity will be smaller, and the forecaster will have a higher score.

The seven alternative yardsticks for measuring forecast precision would more than suffice if it were not for the problem of comparing the accuracy of anticipations, as revealed by the new data, with the results of earlier studies. But Ferber [1953] and Modigliani and Sauerlander [1955] used an alternative measure involving a slightly more complicated naive projection in their pioneering evaluations of the accuracy of the carload shipments *ex ante* data collected by the American Railway Association. In order that the precision of the new Office of Business Economics *ex ante* data may be compared with their results, it is necessary to briefly review the yardstick that they employed in their investigations. Their approach was to compare the quarterly carload predictions with

$$E_t^* = A_{t-4}(A_{t-1}/A_{t-5}). \tag{2.8a}$$

Thus, the Ferber test elaborates on the simpler naive forecast of "same as current quarter of last year," A_{t-4}, by multiplying by the change observed last year; that is, A_{t-1}/A_{t-5} is an adjustment for recently observed trend. This procedure constitutes a crude adjustment for seasonal movements. For the purpose of testing the six-month anticipations, the Ferber naive forecast equation may be modified to

$$E_t^* = A_{t-4}(A_{t-2}/A_{t-6}) \tag{2.8b}$$

For both the naive forecast and the actual railroad anticipations data, Ferber and Modigliani-Sauerlander computed the average-absolute-error, defined as:[8]

$$\text{AAE}^* = \sum \frac{|E^* - A|}{n} \tag{2.9}$$

and

$$\text{AAE} = \sum \frac{|P - A|}{n}$$

For the prewar period, 1929–1941, Ferber found that the naive forecasts were more accurate than observed anticipations for the total nonfarm

[8] This is the appropriate measure if the forecaster's losses from erroneous prediction are proportional to the magnitude rather than the square of his forecast error.

aggregate and for each of the five component industries that he considered. For the period 1946–1950, the forecasts of the nonfarm aggregate had a 23 percent larger AAE than the naive forecast, although the anticipatory data were at least marginally superior to the naive forecasts in three industries—iron and steel, flour, and cement. We shall see that the new anticipatory data reveal that firms are now much more precise forecasters than the analysis of Ferber suggested.

3.3 FORECAST ACCURACY—INDUSTRY DATA

Let us now use these various indices of forecasting accuracy to appraise the predictive accuracy of the benchmark adjusted industry data. In addition to looking at the OBE aggregates, we shall also report on the more recent forecasting experience of the railroad shippers' forecast data over the comparable 1957–1964 period. Our study of aggregative *ex ante* data reveals the extent to which anticipation survey data may be used to forecast movements in the general level of economic activity; but aggregates provide only indirect evidence on the precision of the forecasts achieved by the typical business firm. We shall be examining evidence on the forecasting abilities of individual firms in Section 3.4.

3.3.1 *Turning-point Errors*

Errors in predicting the direction of sales movements are the exception rather than the rule, judging from Table 3.3.1a. Here the columns headed $\Delta p \, \Delta a < 0$ reveal the frequency of errors in predicting the direction of change, industry by industry, with both deseasonalized and unadjusted data.[9] Directional errors arise either by failing to predict a turning point or predicting a turning point that does not occur. It will be observed that the usual effect of seasonal adjustment is to increase the probability of a directional error; for example, the probability of a turning point error rises from 12 to 27 percent on the average for short durable anticipations when the data are adjusted for systematic seasonal movements. This is not surprising, for it is obvious that a forecaster knowing only the customary seasonal pattern might do fairly well at predicting the direction of change in the raw data. Moreover, the seasonally adjusted data may be quite hard for a forecaster to beat, for the adjustment procedure utilizes observations that are not available

[9] The raw data were subjected to an additive seasonal adjustment procedure that equalized quarterly means in advance of computing relative changes. The correction factors for anticipations were not identical to those for realizations.

TABLE 3.3.1a. TURNING-POINT ERRORS, AGGREGATE SALES DATA[a]

Industry	Short Anticipations				Long Anticipations			
			Deseasonalized				Deseasonalized	
	$\Delta p\ \Delta a < 0$	$\Delta a > 0$	$\Delta p\ \Delta a < 0$	$\Delta a > 0$	$\Delta p\ \Delta a < 0$	$\Delta a > 0$	$\Delta p\ \Delta a < 0$	$\Delta a > 0$
Durables								
Iron and steel	0.06	0.59	0.18	0.47	0.11	0.58	0.16	0.42
Nonferrous metals	0.24	0.47	0.12	0.65	0.32	0.53	0.37	0.63
Electrical machinery	0.12	0.59	0.41	0.47	0.21	0.63	0.21	0.79
Nonelectrical machinery	0.00	0.76	0.35	0.47	0.11	0.63	0.37	0.74
Motor vehicles	0.06	0.53	0.18	0.53	0.21	0.53	0.21	0.58
Transportation equipment	0.12	0.65	0.35	0.53	0.26	0.37	0.11	0.53
Other durables	0.24	0.53	0.29	0.47	0.21	0.53	0.37	0.53
Durable Average	0.12	0.59	0.27	0.51	0.20	0.54	0.26	0.60
Nondurables								
Food and beverages	0.12	0.71	0.35	0.47	0.21	0.63	0.26	0.79
Textiles	0.29	0.65	0.06	0.53	0.47	0.68	0.58	0.63
Paper	0.24	0.71	0.29	0.47	0.11	0.74	0.16	0.79
Chemicals	0.18	0.65	0.12	0.53	0.26	0.68	0.32	0.74
Petroleum	0.18	0.53	0.24	0.47	0.26	0.58	0.42	0.74
Rubber	0.12	0.53	0.35	0.47	0.26	0.63	0.42	0.74
Other nondurables	0.18	0.41	0.29	0.47	0.16	0.47	0.37	0.74
Nondurable Average	0.18	0.60	0.24	0.49	0.25	0.63	0.36	0.74

[a] The short anticipations are based on 17 observations; the long on 19 observations.

TABLE 3.3.1b. TURNING-POINT ERRORS, AGGREGATE INVENTORY DATA[a]

Industry	Short Anticipations				Long Anticipations			
			Deseasonalized				Deseasonalized	
	$\Delta p\ \Delta a < 0$	$\Delta a > 0$	$\Delta p\ \Delta a < 0$	$\Delta a > 0$	$\Delta p\ \Delta a < 0$	$\Delta a > 0$	$\Delta p\ \Delta a < 0$	$\Delta a > 0$
Durables								
Iron and steel	0.18	0.35	0.24	0.59	0.32	0.47	0.21	0.53
Nonferrous metals	0.47	0.53	0.29	0.59	0.47	0.63	0.58	0.58
Electrical machinery	0.12	0.59	0.18	0.53	0.21	0.58	0.42	0.79
Nonelectrical machinery	0.12	0.53	0.35	0.59	0.37	0.63	0.42	0.63
Motor vehicles	0.29	0.65	0.24	0.53	0.58	0.63	0.53	0.63
Transportation equipment	0.24	0.41	0.18	0.41	0.21	0.42	0.26	0.47
Other durables	0.12	0.59	0.18	0.53	0.26	0.68	0.37	0.68
Durable Average	0.22	0.52	0.24	0.54	0.35	0.58	0.40	0.62
Nondurables								
Food and beverages	0.06	0.47	0.29	0.47	0.05	0.47	0.68	0.79
Textiles	0.41	0.76	0.47	0.53	0.05	0.53	0.79	0.84
Paper	0.29	0.76	0.24	0.47	0.32	0.68	0.53	0.84
Chemicals	0.24	0.53	0.24	0.47	0.21	0.74	0.63	0.84
Petroleum	0.00	0.53	0.53	0.71	0.16	0.42	0.53	0.68
Rubber	0.00	0.47	0.41	0.71	0.26	0.58	0.42	0.68
Other nondurables	0.24	0.65	0.59	0.71	0.21	0.58	0.58	0.63
Nondurable Average	0.18	0.60	0.39	0.58	0.18	0.57	0.59	0.76

[a] The short anticipations are based on 17 observations; the long on 19 observations.

at the time the forecaster makes his prediction.[10] Note that the textile industry's long sales anticipation, after seasonal adjustment, involves a directional error more than 50 percent of the time! While there are no other instances of equally unsuccessful sales forecasts, we find that turning-point errors predominate in the long deseasonalized inventory anticipations data on Table 3.3.1b.

Since it is obviously easier to forecast the direction of change for a time series exhibiting a steady upward trend, we have also reported on the same table the proportion of the time that Δa is positive. Comparing a figure in the $\Delta a > 0$ column with the corresponding number in the $\Delta p\, \Delta a < 0$ column reveals that occasionally a naive sales forecaster might have done better than the aggregated firm anticipations by always forecasting an increase. For example, the fact that the seasonally adjusted three-month sales change is positive 74 percent of the time in nonelectrical machinery means that a naive optimist who always predicted an increase would have made direction-of-change errors 26 percent of the time, while the actual forecasts involved such errors 37 percent of the time. In a majority of the nondurable industries, a perennially optimistic six month forecast that seasonally adjusted sales will always increase would have generated fewer turning-point errors than our observations on seasonally adjusted anticipations. Table 3.3.1b reveals that inventory anticipations do not perform as well, in the majority of industries, as the naive forecaster. Both the transportation equipment and the iron and steel industries are distinguished by their ability to predict the direction of short-run and long run sales and inventory changes with greater precision than a naive forecaster.

Despite these shortcomings, however, the record at forecasting direction-of-change revealed by the OBE aggregate sales data is rather good relative to other data on expectations. Ferber's 1953 study of the railroad shippers' *ex ante* data for the 1927–1941 period had suggested a tendency to forecast precisely the wrong direction of movement practically all of the time; as Hart [1960, p. 209] complained, "it almost looks as if the shippers had followed the cheap but infallible rule for being right at turning-points (at the expense of being wrong all the rest of the time) by always predicting a turning opposite to the last turn observed . . . ." That the carload forecasts almost always involve a predicted change in the reverse of actual developments was indicated by a graph appearing in Hart's paper.[11] More than this, his graph also revealed that it often happened that when the shippers did succeed in forecasting the correct direction of change, they overstated the change by such

[10] This creates a problem even if the seasonal pattern is fixed rather than subject to shift, for the forecaster will have used a different sample of data than we have in estimating the seasonal.

[11] Hart [1960, p. 208] plotted forecast and actual carloadings for all manufactured products.

a large amount as to cause an error larger in magnitude than a no-change prediction! Clearly, we must consider the size as well as the direction of the forecast relative to the actual change.

3.3.2 *The Magnitude of Forecast Errors*

Mean-square-error and other measures of forecast accuracy are presented on Tables 3.3.2 through 3.3.4. Even a casual inspection of the evidence reveals that the answer to such a question as which industry is the best forecaster hinges upon the particular yardstick of forecast accuracy one chooses to employ. Thus, in terms of the RMSE criterion we see from Table 3.3.2a that the motor vehicle industry ranks eighth and the iron and steel industry stands last in terms of ability to forecast short-run sales movements. But in terms of all the other criteria, motor vehicles ranks at the top and iron and steel second or third.[12] Again, inspection of Table 3.3.2b reveals that these same two industries are scored as extremely inaccurate forecasters by the RMSE standard, although they generally rank among the top three industries in terms of the other yardsticks.

TABLE 3.3.2a. ACCURACY ANALYSIS, AGGREGATE DATA SHORT SALES ANTICIPATIONS

Industry	RMSE	U	U_1	r^2	r_1^2	r_2^2	r_3^2
Iron and Steel	0.079	0.128	0.235	0.969	0.945	0.943	0.916
Nonferrous metals	0.040	0.313	0.530	0.741	0.719	0.711	0.592
Electrical machinery	0.016	0.138	0.273	0.927	0.926	0.917	0.932
Nonelectrical machinery	0.022	0.165	0.303	0.924	0.908	0.899	0.900
Motor vehicles	0.034	0.066	0.132	0.982	0.983	0.982	0.945
Transportation equipment	0.037	0.296	0.542	0.703	0.706	0.694	0.544
Other durables	0.044	0.305	0.680	0.677	0.537	0.510	0.108
Durable Aggregate	0.022	0.112	0.212	0.964	0.955	0.953	0.900
Food and beverages	0.016	0.230	0.497	0.795	0.753	0.708	0.798
Textiles	0.039	0.489	0.971	0.325	0.058	−0.064	0.618
Paper	0.027	0.434	0.802	0.207	0.357	0.147	0.832
Chemicals	0.031	0.282	0.488	0.735	0.762	0.703	0.857
Petroleum	0.019	0.358	0.845	0.621	0.286	0.278	0.717
Rubber	0.042	0.293	0.654	0.724	0.572	0.550	0.116
Other nondurables	0.029	0.220	0.444	0.811	0.803	0.797	0.735
Nondurable Aggregate	0.012	0.265	0.529	0.643	0.720	0.600	0.936
Average of Industry Aggregates	0.034	0.265	0.528	0.724	0.665	0.627	0.686
Standard Deviation	(0.016)	(0.118)	(0.245)	(0.225)	(0.274)	(0.314)	(0.275)

[12] Remember that high values of RMSE, U and U_1 indicate inaccurate forecasting while the various correlation measures are scaled so that high values suggest precise forecasting.

TABLE 3.3.2b. ACCURACY ANALYSIS, AGGREGATE DATA LONG SALES ANTICIPATIONS

Industry	RMSE	U	U_1	r^2	r_1^2	r_2^2	r_3^2
Iron and steel	0.199	0.214	0.398	0.903	0.841	0.839	0.683
Nonferrous metals	0.073	0.497	0.859	0.330	0.262	0.250	−0.003
Electrical machinery	0.052	0.389	0.775	0.450	0.400	0.300	−0.158
Nonelectrical machinery	0.045	0.292	0.529	0.751	0.720	0.685	0.126
Motor vehicles	0.128	0.200	0.413	0.852	0.829	0.821	0.308
Transportation equipment	0.064	0.454	0.856	0.362	0.267	0.256	0.187
Other durables	0.068	0.373	0.854	0.562	0.270	0.244	−0.842
Durable Aggregate	0.065	0.324	0.608	0.752	0.631	0.616	0.263
Food and beverages	0.025	0.253	0.569	0.813	0.676	0.634	−1.105
Textiles	0.069	0.644	1.189	0.009	−0.415	−0.696	−0.722
Paper	0.025	0.292	0.589	0.483	0.653	0.426	0.325
Chemicals	0.050	0.360	0.601	0.583	0.639	0.538	−0.037
Petroleum	0.042	0.473	1.079	0.277	−0.164	−0.271	−1.176
Rubber	0.079	0.458	0.965	0.346	0.070	0.037	−0.740
Other nondurables	0.045	0.286	0.592	0.690	0.650	0.631	0.009
Nondurable aggregate	0.023	0.324	0.619	0.512	0.617	0.493	0.157
Average of Industry Aggregates	0.069	0.370	0.733	0.529	0.407	0.335	−0.225
Standard Deviation	(0.045)	(0.125)	(0.243)	(0.255)	(0.381)	(0.428)	(0.583)

TABLE 3.3.2c. ACCURACY ANALYSIS, AGGREGATE DATA SHORT INVENTORY ANTICIPATIONS

Industry	RMSE	U	U_1	r^2	r_1^2	r_2^2	r_3^2
Durables							
Iron and steel	0.037	0.391	0.623	0.667	0.612	0.611	0.416
Nonferrous metals	0.027	0.682	1.269	0.045	−0.610	−1.043	0.132
Electrical machinery	0.027	0.434	0.695	0·827	0.517	0.372	0.576
Nonelectrical machinery	0.026	0.518	0.881	0.689	0.224	0.106	−0.073
Motor vehicles	0.047	0.439	0.809	0.753	0.346	0.279	0.413
Transportation equipment	0.027	0.520	0.950	0.328	0.097	0.097	0.328
Other durables	0.024	0.362	0.658	0.740	0.567	0.472	0.712
Durable Aggregate	0.021	0.570	0.980	0.838	0.040	−0.231	0.334
Nondurables							
Food and beverages	0.029	0.289	0.607	0.917	0.631	0.623	−0.080
Textiles	0.029	0.345	0.607	0.804	0.632	0.610	−0.815
Paper	0.023	0.566	0.835	0.365	0.302	0.125	0.729
Chemicals	0.028	0.489	0.875	0.741	0.234	0.106	0.512
Petroleum	0.019	0.300	0.613	0.834	0.624	0.612	−3.086
Rubber	0.027	0.347	0.621	0.711	0.615	0.578	0.714
Other nondurables	0.036	0.291	0.551	0.745	0.696	0.676	−2.184
Nondurable Aggregate	0.021	0.863	1.569	0.157	−1.461	−4.027	0.171
Average of Industry Aggregates	0.029	0.427	0.757	0.655	0.302	0.392	−0.122
Standard Deviation	(0.007)	(0.117)	(0.195)	(0.241)	(0.447)	(0.346)	(1.156)

TABLE 3.3.2d. ACCURACY ANALYSIS, AGGREGATE DATA LONG INVENTORY ANTICIPATIONS

Industry	RMSE	U	U_1	r^2	r_1^2	r_2^2	r_3^2
Durables							
Iron and steel	0.056	0.439	0.722	0.552	0.479	0.465	0.298
Nonferrous metals	0.042	0.673	1.122	0.097	−0.259	−0.393	−0.510
Electrical machinery	0.043	0.464	0.723	0.691	0.478	0.401	−0.005
Nonelectrical machinery	0.044	0.484	0.826	0.731	0.318	0.288	−0.159
Motor vehicles	0.085	0.609	1.149	0.234	−0.319	−0.445	−0.680
Transportation equipment	0.033	0.374	0.657	0.582	0.568	0.547	0.524
Other durables	0.037	0.374	0.648	0.786	0.580	0.489	−0.092
Durable Aggregate	0.036	0.544	0.895	0.734	0.200	0.134	−0.028
Nondurables							
Food and beverages	0.037	0.267	0.557	0.897	0.690	0.678	−4.464
Textiles	0.051	0.429	0.740	0.767	0.453	0.418	−3.829
Paper	0.041	0.578	0.855	0.589	0.268	−0.005	−2.272
Chemicals	0.040	0.442	0.763	0.703	0.417	0.243	−1.290
Petroleum	0.028	0.289	0.629	0.771	0.604	0.603	−1.234
Rubber	0.048	0.363	0.632	0.708	0.601	0.532	0.079
Other nondurables	0.043	0.322	0.631	0.723	0.602	0.587	−0.781
Nondurable Aggregate	0.032	0.827	1.504	0.134	−1.262	−2.852	−2.415
Average of Industry Aggregates	0.045	0.436	0.761	0.631	0.315	0.392	−1.030
Standard Deviation	(0.013)	(0.120)	(0.178)	(0.218)	(0.356)	(0.311)	(1.515)

These discrepancies are in large part explained by the nature of the alternative measures of forecast accuracy. It will be remembered that the RMSE criterion constitutes a measure of absolute forecast accuracy while such measures as U_1 and the various correlation coefficients measure accuracy relative to the abilities of naive forecasters with varying degrees of sophistication. The high scores achieved by iron and steel and the transportation equipment industries in terms of these latter criteria suggest that the large RMSE for these industries arises because their shipments are inherently hard to predict. Relative to the abilities of naive forecasting procedures, the records of the iron and steel and the motor vehicle sectors are commendable.

Clearly, a host of dangers are inherent in any attempt at comparing the degree of forecasting precision achieved in different industries. Nonetheless, the following conclusions appear to stand out from an inspection of the statistics on aggregate forecasts presented in Table 3.3.2. First, forecasts that look quite good in terms of certain criteria do not stand up well in comparison with the more precise naive forecasting procedures. Thus, we observe on Table 3.3.2b that for eight industries and the nondurable aggregate, the long sales forecasts generate negative values of r_3^2, implying that a naive forecaster knowing the seasonal patterns and average change could achieve a smaller root-mean-square-error. Second, sales anticipations achieve a more accurate forecasting record than inventory expectations in terms of all the criteria other than RMSE. Furthermore, considerable accuracy, relative to other industries, in predicting sales does not imply that inventories can be forecast with precision. Witness the fact that while motor vehicles stands in second place at forecasting long sales in terms of all of the various correlation criteria, this industry does extremely poorly relative to others at forecasting inventory movements. We may also note that with the exception of positive r_3^2's for three industries, the longer run inventory forecasting records are worse relative to the record that a naive forecaster might achieve with a knowledge of seasonal movements and average change.

3.3.3 *Comparison With Alternative Estimates of Forecast Accuracy*

When Ferber correlated anticipated quarterly changes reported in the railroad shippers' survey for the 1927–1941 period with actual changes, the correlation coefficients were negative approximately half the time. In contrast, the correlation coefficients reported in the fourth column of Tables 3.3.2a and 3.3.2b for the OBE benchmark adjusted industry sales data are all positive.[13] Of course, Modigliani and Sauerlander [1955, p. 288–289] reported that the railroad shippers' forecasts were probably less accurate than certain other business forecasts. When they correlated predicted changes on actual changes using Dun and Bradstreet survey data, they obtained correlation coefficients of 0.03 for durables and 0.10 for nondurables; and with *ex ante* data collected by *Fortune* they obtained a correlation coefficient of 0.80 for durables and 0.54 for nondurables. But from Tables 3.3.2 and 3.3.3 we see that the new OBE data imply much more precise forecasting; the r^2's are 0.97 and 0.73 for short and long durable anticipations respectively.

Much the same story is revealed when the average-absolute-error is used to measure forecast accuracy. In the vast majority of cases, Table 3.3.3 reveals the sales anticipation data collected by the OBE have an average-absolute-error that is considerably smaller than that achieved with Ferber's naive extrapolative formula, equation 2.8a, which contains an explicit allowance for seasonal movements. For only one industry, petroleum, do the short anticipations reported by the OBE survey do worse than Ferber's naive extrapolation. Only for two industries, food and petroleum, does the Ferber extrapolation prove even marginally superior to the long OBE forecast.

In contrast, Ferber had found that his naive extrapolative formula was more precise than the shippers' expectations at predicting total nonfarm

[13] Since the carloading forecasts were prepared about six weeks before the beginning of the quarter to which they pertain, they involve a forecasting horizon almost equal in length to the long OBE anticipations.

TABLE 3.3.3. ACCURACY OF SALES ANTICIPATIONS RELATIVE TO FERBER'S NAIVE TEST, AGGREGATE DATA (RATIOS OF AVERAGE-ABSOLUTE-ERRORS)

	Short	Long
Durable		
Iron and steel	8%	36%
Nonferrous metals	45	54
Electrical machinery	49	48
Nonelectrical machinery	66	47
Motor vehicles	15	29
Transportation equipment	58	55
Other durables	96	89
Aggregate	15	42
Nondurable		
Food and beverages	87	115
Textiles	68	70
Paper	70	80
Chemicals	64	65
Petroleum	110	102
Rubber	83	71
Other nondurables	59	60
Aggregate	59	64

shipments, the average-absolute-error of the anticipations averaging 19 percent *larger* than the average-absolute-error for his naive extrapolative formula over the 1946–1950 period. Iron and steel constitutes the only industry for which a direct comparison between the precision of the shippers' forecasts and OBE *ex ante* data is possible. For this industry, the AAPE for the three-month sales forecast is only 8 percent of the AAPE of the naive projection; the longer forecast has an AAPE ratio of 36 percent. Contrast this with the iron and steel ratio of 74 percent reported by Ferber for the 1946–1950 period on the basis of the railroad shippers' forecast data. The new OBE forecasts, furthermore, are more accurate predictors of durable and nondurable manufacturing sales developments, relative to Ferber's naive model, than either the *Fortune* survey or the Dun and Bradstreet survey data for the 1947–1950 period analyzed by Modigliani and Sauerlander.[14]

[14] Modigliani and Sauerlander [1955, p. 288–289] reveal that the respondents to the *Fortune* Survey had an average-absolute-error only 78% as large as the Ferber naive benchmark for durable manufacturing and 92% as large for nondurables. The Dun and Bradstreet surveys did not do as well as the naive model.

There are at least two quite plausible explanations for the quite conflicting appraisals of business forecasting precision provided by the new OBE data and the earlier studies of the railroad shippers' forecasts. It is possible that the current generation of businessmen may be much better forecasters than their predecessors. But it is also conceivable that such writers as Hart [1960] were fully justified in questioning the validity of the shippers' carload anticipatory data.

In an attempt to resolve the issue we examined the recent performance of the shippers' forecasts over the comparable 1957–1964 period. The evidence, presented in Table 3.3.4, suggests that there is an element of truth in both

TABLE 3.3.4. RAILROAD SHIPPERS' FORECASTS, 1957–1964[a]

	RMSE	U	U_1	r^2	r_1^2	r_2^2	r_3^2	$\Delta p\, \Delta a < 0$
All commodities	0.082	0.34	0.77	0.74	0.33	0.425	−0.55	0.16
Iron and steel	0.228	0.48	1.03	0.44	−0.03	−0.076	−0.36	0.25

[a] Data from the *National Forecasts of the Regional Shippers Advisory Boards*, a quarterly publication of the Car Service Division of the Association of American Railroads.

explanations. The table reveals that the forecasts are much more accurate than earlier studies of the performance of the shippers' forecasts had suggested. Predicted and actual changes are quite highly correlated, although substantial error is introduced by a systematic tendency of shippers to overstate their carloading requirements.[15] Nonetheless, a comparison of Table 3.3.4 with the evidence presented on tables appearing earlier in this chapter reveals that the shippers' carload aggregates are not as precise as the sales forecasts provided by the OBE Inventory and Sales Anticipations Survey. In summary, businessmen now forecast with greater precision, but their predictive ability was probably not nearly as bad as studies of the railroad shippers' forecasts had suggested.

3.4 FIRM DATA AND AGGREGATION EFFECTS

How revealing are statistics derived from industry aggregates with regard to the forecasting abilities of the individual firm? "Not very" was the answer

[15] For all commodities, the predictions averaged out to a figure 3 or 4% larger than the actual average; this tendency was even more pronounced in iron and steel. This systematic tendency is not penalized by the correlation coefficient, but it does affect the magnitude of such measures of forecasting accuracy as the RMSE.

TABLE 3.4.1. TURNING-POINT ERRORS, FIRM SALES DATA[a]

	Short Anticipations					Long Anticipations				
				Deseasonalized					Deseasonalized	
Industry	n	$\Delta p\ \Delta a < 0$	$\Delta a > 0$	$\Delta p\ \Delta a < 0$	$\Delta a > 0$	n	$\Delta p\ \Delta a < 0$	$\Delta a > 0$	$\Delta p\ \Delta a < 0$	$\Delta a > 0$
Nonferrous metals	204	0.27	0.56	0.34	0.55	219	0.43	0.62	0.32	0.57
Electrical machinery	367	0.21	0.51	0.32	0.55	388	0.22	0.53	0.30	0.43
Nonelectrical machinery	355	0.25	0.54	0.29	0.53	381	0.28	0.60	0.33	0.61
Chemicals	445	0.14	0.52	0.22	0.54	468	0.18	0.68	0.36	0.67
Petroleum	485	0.26	0.55	0.28	0.53	516	0.27	0.58	0.34	0.60

[a] The columns on this table have identical headings to Table 3.3.1 discussed in Section 3.3.1, except that the additional column headed "n" indicates the total number of observations utilized in computing the fractions. Thus, the figure 0.27 for nonferrous metals in the $\Delta p\ \Delta a$ column indicates that 27% of a total of 204 quarters of short sales anticipations observed for the ten firms sampled from this industry involved an error in forecasting the direction of sales developments.

of many economists who argued that the gross inaccuracies relative to naive models displayed by the railroad shippers' forecasts data must be a consequence of aggregation distortions rather than a reflection of gross ineptness at the art of forecasting on the part of the typical business firm. We have concluded that the shippers' forecasts do exaggerate the seriousness of prediction errors at the industry level of aggregation. But the question of whether industry figures provide a reliable indicator of how well the typical firm can predict its own sales developments remains to be examined.

3.4.1 *Firm Turning-point Errors*

Examination of the summary evidence on firm turning-point errors presented in Table 3.4.1 reveals an overall picture of forecasting precision that is quite similar to that displayed by the industry aggregates. But there are some surprising differences in detail. Only one of the 83 firms in our sample could have achieved a better record in forecasting the direction of *both* short and long sales movements by always forecasting an increase. The chemical industry is the only one of the five industries we sampled in which the typical firm could have achieved a more precise record at forecasting the direction of seasonally adjusted long sales developments by always predicting an increase. In contrast, Table 3.3.1a revealed that for each of these five industries, fewer errors would have been made at predicting the direction of six-month industry sales movements by naively forecasting a continued rise rather than relying on the anticipation aggregates. In this respect, then, the aggregate data suggested less forecasting precision than that actually achieved by the firms in our sample. On the other hand, the aggregate *short* sales forecasts have a smaller probability of predicting the wrong direction of sales than the firm figures. Furthermore, the aggregate turning-point error statistics do not accurately rank industries in terms of the ability of sampled firms to forecast the direction in which their sales are moving. Thus, we conclude that the aggregate figures provide an imprecise but not grossly biased picture of the ability of firms to predict turning points.

3.4.2 *The Magnitude of Firm Errors*

Evidence on a variety of measures of forecast accuracy averaged over our sample of individual firms in five industries are presented in Tables 3.4.2a and 3.4.2b. The statistics were computed from the time series of predicted and actual relative change for each firm in our sample; then, the average value of

TABLE 3.4.2a. SALES ACCURACY ANALYSIS
FIRM DATA AVERAGES

	$\sqrt{MSE}$	RMSE	U	r^2	r_1^2	r_2^2	r_3^2
Short Sales Anticipations							
Nonferrous metals	0.11	0.10 s	0.32 s	0.64 s	0.59 s	0.56 s	0.30
Electrical machinery	0.20	0.17	0.37	0.59	0.32	0.29	−0.03
Nonelectrical machinery	0.10	0.09	0.36	0.57	0.46	0.43	0.29
Chemicals	0.10	0.09	0.28	0.72	0.64	0.59	0.51
Petroleum	0.11	0.10	0.43	0.43	0.23	0.18	0.00
Long Sales Anticipations							
Nonferrous metals	0.17	0.16	0.42 s*	0.43 s*	0.26 s	0.22 s	−0.14 s
Electrical machinery	0.22	0.20	0.39	0.54*	0.36	0.33*	−0.27
Nonelectrical machinery	0.14	0.13	0.41	0.45	0.32	0.26	−0.46 s
Chemicals	0.14	0.12	0.33 s	0.61 s*	0.54 s	0.45 s	−0.28
Petroleum	0.15	0.13	0.49 s	0.32 s	0.10 s*	0.01 s*	−1.29 s*

Note. The appearance of an "s" to the right of a figure indicates that the small firms achieved a more accurate predictive record than the large, on the average, in terms of that particular index of forecast accuracy.

The symbol $\sqrt{MSE}$ denotes the square root of the average of firm mean-square-errors. An asterisk by a figure indicates that the firm average reveals a higher degree of forecasting precision than was suggested by the aggregate data presented on earlier tables.

the accuracy statistics over all the firms in each industry were computed.[16] While the cross-section and time-series averages are necessarily the same for the mean-square-error, this is not true for the RMSE; this explains the

[16] The resulting averages of time-series statistics are not always the same as those that would be obtained by the cross-section approach of computing the measure of forecast accuracy over all firms in each year and then computing the average over all years. Our time-series approach, which is feasible only when data are available over several years, reveals how well the typical firm can predict its own sales developments over successive periods; in contrast, the cross-section approach reveals how well a firm's anticipated figure will serve at predicting how that firm's sales performance will depart from the average firm's performance in that period. A hypothetical example clarifies the distinction. Suppose that a_{tf} and p_{tf} denote the actual and predicted change for firm f at time t, and that the forecast error ϵ_{tf} is distributed independently of a_{tf}. Then if it were also true that $\epsilon_{tf} = \epsilon_{t.}$, but $\epsilon_{t.} \neq \epsilon_{t'}$ for some $t'' \neq t$ (so that all firms make the same prediction error in any one year but the prediction errors are not the same in every year), it would be found that the cross-section correlation over all firms in any one year of anticipated and actual sales is unity, but the correlation over time for any one firm is less than one. On the other hand, the situation would be precisely reversed if $\epsilon_{tf} = \epsilon_{.f}$ but $\epsilon_{.f} \neq \epsilon_{.f'}$ for some $f \neq f'$. In the latter time-series case, the perfect correlation indicates that each firm has a potential for perfect forecasting if it can learn the nature of its systematic tendency to over or underestimate change; in the former case, the perfect cross-section correlation does *not* reveal how well the typical firms can forecast future sales volume.

TABLE 3.4.2b. INVENTORY ACCURACY ANALYSIS
FIRM DATA AVERAGES

	RMSE	U	r^2	r_1^2	r_2^2	r_3^2
Total Inventory						
Short Anticipations						
Nonferrous metals	0.09	0.59 s*	0.19 s*	−0.53 s*	−0.65 s*	−0.06 s
Electrical machinery	0.12 s	0.61	0.17	−0.46	−0.55	−0.29
Nonelectrical	0.10	0.55	0.28	0.00 s	−0.07 s	0.16 s*
Chemicals	0.10	0.52	0.33	−0.11	−0.26	0.14 s
Petroleum	0.12	0.56	0.24	−0.17	−0.22	−0.17*
Long Anticipations						
Nonferrous metals	0.13	0.60 s	0.19 s*	−0.04 s	−0.14 s	−0.41 s
Electrical machinery	0.16 s	0.60	0.18	−0.28	−0.40	−0.82 s
Nonelectrical	0.16	0.59	0.22	−0.06	−0.16	−0.33 s
Chemicals	0.13	0.53	0.32	0.07	−0.17	−0.91*
Petroleum	0.19	0.56	0.24	0.02	−0.03	−0.52*
Finished Goods Inventory						
Short Anticipations						
Nonferrous metals	0.15	0.63 s	0.24 s	−0.66 s	−0.76 s	−2.92
Electrical machinery	0.14	0.59	0.25	−0.56 s	−0.98 s	−2.20 s
Nonelectrical	0.40	0.56	0.28	−0.13	−0.19	−0.59
Chemicals	0.16	0.53	0.32	−0.24	−0.45	−1.46
Petroleum	0.18	0.54 s	0.26	−0.14 s	−0.18 s	−0.64 s
Long Anticipations						
Nonferrous metals	0.17	0.57 s	0.28 s	−0.13 s	−0.17 s	−1.80
Electrical machinery	0.20	0.64	0.22	−0.35 s	−1.00 s	−1.43 s
Nonelectrical	0.43	0.56	0.31	−0.01	−0.10	−0.41 s
Chemicals	0.19	0.55	0.34	−0.68	−1.27	−2.35
Petroleum	0.32	0.57 s	0.23 s	−0.82	−0.90	−0.65

Note. The appearance of an "s" to the right of a figure indicates that the small firms achieved a more accurate predictive record than the large, on the average, in terms of that particular index of forecast accuracy.

An asterisk by a figure indicates that the firm average reveals a higher degree of precision than was suggested by the aggregate total inventory data presented on earlier tables.

discrepancy in the numbers reported in the first two columns of Table 3.4.2a.[17]

Comparing the figures reported on this table with the aggregates reported on Table 3.3.2, we find that the various measures almost invariably reveal, industry by industry, a lower level of firm forecasting accuracy than is

[17] For the same reason, our time-series averages are not comparable to the cross-section evidence presented by Modigliani and Sauerlander [1955, p. 305]. Using anticipated and actual changes in sales from the OBE-SEC Plant and Equipment Expenditure Survey for two years, 1948 and 1949, they report correlation coefficients ranging from 0.37 to 0.49 computed separately for each year among firms in a particular class size.

suggested by the corresponding industry aggregates. For example, the nonferrous metals aggregate RMSE for short sales anticipations is only about 40 percent as large as the RMSE for the average firm. There are occasional exceptions to the tendency for the process of aggregation to exaggerate the degree of forecasting precision actually achieved by the average firm—a total of 17 out of the 180 comparisons. Exceptions to the aggregation effect predominate only for the total inventory anticipation of the nonferrous metals industry.

This aggregation effect, if it is not a statistical illusion, has a number of implications. First, it means that the compilation of an industry forecast based on a survey of individual firms may result in an aggregate prediction that is considerably more precise, relative to naive extrapolative alternatives, than the prediction of the typical firm in the industry. Thus, a high degree of predictive ability by the individual firms participating in the survey is not a prerequisite for the attainment of an accurate forecast of aggregate activity. Second, it suggests that the comparison of aggregate industry *ex ante* data may not provide an accurate index of the relative forecasting ability of individual firms in various industries. Thus, Table 3.3.2 reveals that the electrical machinery industry has, relative to other industries, a remarkably accurate aggregate sales forecast in terms of the r_3^2 criteria, which involves comparison with a naive forecaster utilizing knowledge of seasonal movements. But we find on Table 3.4.2 that the average electrical machinery firm in our sample did slightly worse than the naive benchmark. Furthermore, the average firm in nonferrous metals, in nonelectrical machinery, and in chemicals clearly does better in terms of this criterion than the average firm in electrical machinery.

Is this aggregation distortion a simple statistical illusion? The errors of individual firms may be expected, more or less, to offset each other. The Law of Large Numbers might be invoked to explain why the industry aggregate RMSE's are smaller than those of the average firm.[18] But this argument does *not* explain why the aggregate *ex ante* data appear more accurate than the firm averages in terms of the other measures. It will be remembered that such criteria as U_1 and so forth could be interpreted as involving a comparison between the precision achieved by the forecaster with the abilities of alternative naive forecaster benchmarks. If the process of aggregating to the industry level increases the apparent accuracy of the anticipations data because of the tendency for offsetting errors to cancel out, it is difficult to see why the naive forecast procedures do not benefit in the same way. For some reason, the process of aggregation serves to reduce the errors of the actual forecasts *more* than it reduces the errors of the naive benchmarks.

[18] It will be remembered that the RMSE is computed from relative change data, which is independent of the units of measurement.

Is it possible that the aggregaton phenomenon revealed in the data constitutes a statistical illusion of a different kind? It will be remembered that the firm averages are derived from a subsample of firms selected on a systematic rather than a random basis.[19] Furthermore, in computing these averages the firm statistics were not weighted by size of firm. In addition, for every industry we have at least as many small as large firms in our sample. If small firms are both overrepresented and poor predictors, the firm average figures might well be distorted. In contrast, the aggregate benchmark adjusted industry figures discussed in Section 3.3 are constructed from a much larger sample in which the individual strata are appropriately weighted. But we shall argue that these factors do *not* explain the aggregation effect. While it is true that small firms are usually less accurate than large, an exception is provided by the nonferrous metals industry;[20] yet the aggregate effect that we have been observing manifests itself in this industry also. Furthermore, a closer examination of the data reveals that the differences in average ability between large and small firms are trivial relative to the size of the aggregation distortion. Indeed, the average statistic obtained by looking at only the large firms in each industry quite generally revealed a lower degree of average forecasting ability than the benchmark-adjusted industry aggregates suggested. Finally, we eliminated the sampling error explanation by looking at

TABLE 3.4.3. SALES ACCURACY ANALYSIS, AGGREGATE FIGURES FROM SAMPLED FIRMS

	RMSE	U	r^2	r_1^2	r_2^2	r_3^2
Short Sales Anticipations						
Electrical machinery	0.053	0.270	0.882	0.686	0.500	0.769
Nonelectrical machinery	0.017	0.142	0.922	0.916	0.914	0.844
Chemicals	0.013	0.141	0.928	0.926	0.924	0.833
Petroleum	0.029	0.462*	0.309*	0.208*	0.054*	0.530
Long Sales Anticipations						
Electrical machinery	0.023	0.102	0.967	0.958	0.958	0.902
Nonelectrical machinery	0.027	0.291	0.598	0.649	0.456	0.598
Chemicals	0.039	0.341*	0.619	0.603	0.597	−0.147
Petroleum	0.029	0.370	0.465	0.543	0.406	−0.160

Note. The asterisk indicates that the aggregate statistic implied a lower level of forecasting precision than is revealed by averaging individual firm statistics.

[19] For a discussion of sampling procedures, see Chapter 2.

[20] The appearance of the "s" to the right of a figure in Table 3.4.2 indicates that the small firms have a better prediction record than the large.

the degree of precision obtained with the aggregate unbenchmark adjusted data for four of our industries. The unbenchmark-adjusted aggregate is the time series obtained by summing the data for the individual firms we observe for our study.[21] Since we have, in effect, a complete census of firms constituting an aggregate, there can be no problem of sampling bias. Nonetheless, the aggregation effect shows up once more, as may be seen from examining the data on Table 3.4.3. We conclude that the greater predictive accuracy of the aggregates does not appear to be a simple statistical distortion.

3.5 CONCLUSIONS

Before it was possible for us to talk about the degree of precision obtained by respondents to the new OBE survey, it was necessary to define various statistics characterizing their accuracy. The arsenal of accuracy measures defined in Section 3.2 is embarrassingly large, but there exist two bases for cross-classification. The first concerns the issue of whether only directional errors, rather than either the magnitude or the square of the forecast error, should be tabulated. All three of these dimensions had to be considered for our results to be comparable with earlier studies, although in principal the number of measures could be greatly reduced if there were consensus within our profession as to the appropriate dimension for measuring forecast errors. The second basis of classification arises from the ambiguity involved in measuring the difficulty of the forecasting task. Invidious comparisons can be made with a wide variety of naive forecasts of varying degree of sophistication.

Prior to examining the data, it was impossible to tell how sensitive our conclusions would be to the choice of a particular yardstick of forecast accuracy. We would not have been surprised if we had found that all the measures told essentially the same story and that most of the yardsticks in our arsenal were redundant. But it turns out that the ranking of industries in terms of relative forecasting precision does hinge upon which measure one chooses to employ. We found, for example, that the motor vehicle and the iron and steel industries tie for second place in terms of ability to avoid turning-point errors in predicting short-run sales developments. But these two industries are the worst sales forecasters in terms of the RMSE criterion, which takes into account the magnitude of the forecast error. On the other hand, it turns out that sales in both these industries are inherently difficult to forecast, and their RMSE is small relative to that of the various naive benchmarks. For this reason, these two industries scored high relative to the others in terms of those measures that utilized a naive benchmark in rating

[21] Because of incomplete responses for the nonferrous metals industry, it was impossible for the computer to construct the aggregate series in the way we had specified in writing our program. See Chapter 2.

the difficulty of the forecasting task. So one moral to be drawn from our analysis is that "predictive ability" is indeed a nebulous concept; it is necessary to employ a variety of yardsticks.

More than a decade ago, Modigliani and Sauerlander [1955, p. 308] summarized the results of their investigation of the evidence then available on the forecasting abilities of business firms by admitting:

> When we first undertook the analysis . . . we had a strong *a priori* feeling that it would reveal business expectations to be of absolutely no forecasting value. Perhaps this expectation was partly prompted by the fact that the record of economists with regard to unconditional forecasting has been far from brilliant.

While the fragmentary evidence provided by the *Fortune* survey suggested to them that senior business executives might have considerable forecasting ability, the extensive data provided by the railroad shippers' forecasts implied that firms were almost totally unsuccessful at predicting future developments. The new evidence provided by the OBE survey reveals that businessmen are much more precise at forecasting the future than Modigliani and Sauerlander had expected. The forecasts are more precise than the simple assumption of "no change" sometimes invoked by economists in constructing models of the inventory cycle. The sales forecasts tend to dominate all but the most sophisticated naive model that we considered. The one naive model that consistently dominated actual sales forecasts exploited knowledge of the seasonal pattern for the entire sample period; obviously, this information is not available at the time the forecasts are formulated. While we suspect that the greater precision revealed by the OBE survey reflects, in part, an improvement in recent years in the forecasting ability of business firms, we feel that our results confirm the suspicion of these economists who objected that the railroad shippers' survey did not provide a reasonable measure of actual anticipations.

The question of whether the degree of forecasting precision revealed by the OBE should be regarded as reasonable or not may be, in part, a matter of individual judgment. However, it may be interesting to contrast with other types of error the mistakes made by firms in forecasting sales. It seems reasonable to suppose that the short sales forecasts of business firms would be less precise than the national income accountant's preliminary estimates of GNP. H. O. Stekler reports that from 1956 to 1964 the preliminary estimates of the quarterly change in aggregate inventory investment involved turning-point errors 15.6 percent of the time.[22] In contrast, Table 3.3.1b revealed that seasonally adjusted industry aggregates of inventory anticipations involve turning-point errors 24 percent of the time for durables and

[22] Stekler [1967, p. 474] presents evidence suggesting that the inventory component of the GNP accounts is particularly difficult to estimate. The preliminary estimates involved turning point errors in estimating GNP 3.2 percent of the time.

39 percent of the time for nondurables. Although the National Income Division revisions thus involve about half as many turning-point errors as the survey, their preliminary figures are published in the second month *after* the end of the quarter. It is also reasonable to suppose that the sales forecasts would be more precise than predictions of annual changes in macroeconomic variables. Theil [1966, p. 58] reveals that over the period 1953–1962 the Netherlands Central Planning Bureau's yearly forecasts of some 21 different macroeconomic variables generated errors with a median value of $r = 0.74$, RMSE $= 0.0363$ and $U_1 = 0.56$. A comparison of these figures with the aggregate industry short sales forecasting data of Table 3.3.2 reveals that the median RMSE statistics are comparable for short sales forecasting while the median r and U_1 are definitely higher for our OBE data. In contrast with the longer sales forecasts of Table 3.3.2, we see that the annual forecasts of the Central Planning Bureau indicate a slightly higher degree of precision. Comparing these Central Planning Bureau's figures with the *firm* data averages of Table 3.4.1 suggests that in terms of the correlation coefficient (which involves correction for systematic linear bias), the long sales forecasts are about as precise as the Central Planning Bureau's annual forecasts; in terms of U_1, however, the average firm does worse than the median performance of the Central Planning Bureau with the long sales anticipation and about equally well with its short sales forecast; finally, the average firm does worse at both long and short sales forecasting in terms of RMSE. Thus, it appears that the Central Planning Bureau's facility at annual prediction of Dutch macrovariables is roughly comparable in precision to the short-run predictions of business firms in the United States. All in all, it appears to us that the OBE data reveal a reasonable degree of precision in forecasting sales and inventory movements.

Theoretical models of the inventory cycle stress the importance of errors firms make when predicting future sales volume. Our analysis has revealed that sales forecasts are generally more precise than predictions of future inventory movement. Furthermore, industries with the most accurate aggregate sales forecasts are not necessarily characterized by a high degree of precision in planning their inventory movements. This phenomenon, which the inventory cycle literature had not led us to expect, manifests itself in the planned finished goods inventory as well as the total inventory data. We have also observed that the process of aggregation yields an industry sales forecast with a better prediction record than that obtained by the representative firm in the industry in predicting its own sales developments.[23] This suggests that a

[23] Since the effect shows up in r^2, as well as in the other statistics of forecast accuracy, it cannot be the result of a systematic tendency for certain firms to over estimate and others to underestimate sales.

survey of firms can yield quite useful predictions of aggregate industry movements even when the typical firm is not adept at forecasting its own future. It also raises a fundamental question, to which we shall return in subsequent chapters, as to whether, in the aggregate, errors in forecasting short-run sales volume are of sufficient magnitude to play the critical role in the development of economic fluctuations that is customarily attributed to them in the inventory cycle literature.

CHAPTER 4

The Composition of Forecast Errors

4.1 INTRODUCTION

To what extent are forecasting errors the product of systematic factors rather than purely random? One form of systematic error arises if firms are consistently conservative or optimistic in predicting the level of future demand; a related problem arises if forecasts have a variance that is quite different from the variance of actual realizations. These two types of systematic errors are analyzed in Section 4.2 with the aid of a decomposition procedure developed by Professor Theil. Then, in Section 4.3, we consider whether firms have a systematic tendency to underestimate the magnitude of changes, a phenomenon encountered by Modigliani and Sauerlander [1955] and by Theil [1959] in studies of aggregate forecasts. An attempt is made to decompose errors into market-share and industry components in Section 4.4. Finally, in Section 4.5 we subject to empirical test Pigou's proposition that waves of optimistic and pessimistic error play a critical role in the generation of business fluctuations. The entire argument is summarized in Section 4.6.

4.2 SYSTEMATIC ERRORS IN FORECASTING

Whether forecast errors are due to systematic factors may be visualized by considering graphically the scatter relating predicted (p) and actual changes (a). For example, Figure 4.1 suggests that aggregate manufacturing short

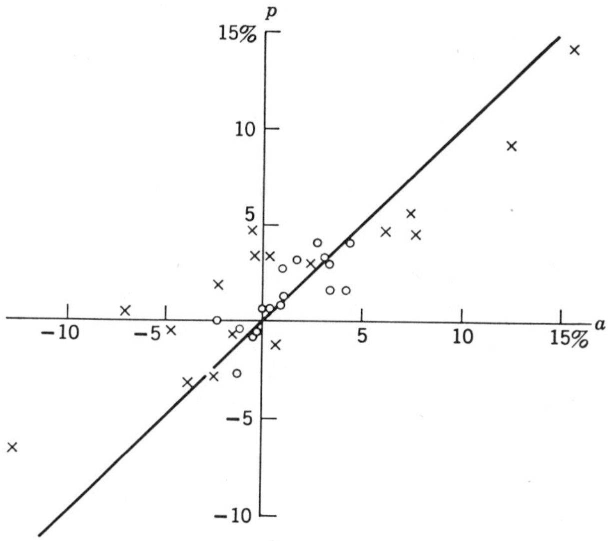

Figure 4.1 Predicted and realized three-month sales changes, 1957–1963. *Note:* "×" denotes durables and "○" denotes nondurables.

sales anticipations are more or less randomly distributed about the 45° "PF" line that denotes perfect forecasting.[1] However, caution is required in examining graphs of this type, for an optical illusion may arise from the arbitrary decision to plot one rather than the other variable on the ordinate. While the hypothetical observations on the three graphs of Figure 4.2 appear to be plotted at random about the "PF" line, we shall see that the points on the different graphs cannot possibly be generated by the same set of data!

Casual inspection of Figure 4.2 suggests that on all three graphs, the mean of the predicted change does equal the mean of the actual change. Indeed, one of the first issues we shall consider is whether actual expectations have this property rather than a systematic tendency toward either perennial optimism or pessimism. But a closer examination of the graphs also reveals that the variance of the predicted change is larger than the variance of the actual realizations on Figure 4.2*a*, while the reverse condition holds true in Figure 4.2*b*. We ask in Section 4.2.2 whether it is reasonable for either of these two conditions to hold true, or whether one should expect to find equality of the variances of a and p, as illustrated on Figure 4.2*c*.

The extent to which a tendency toward perennial optimism and pessimism or unequal variances can contribute to forecast errors is revealed by the

[1] The points scattered on the graph were obtained from time series covering the period 1958 to 1963.

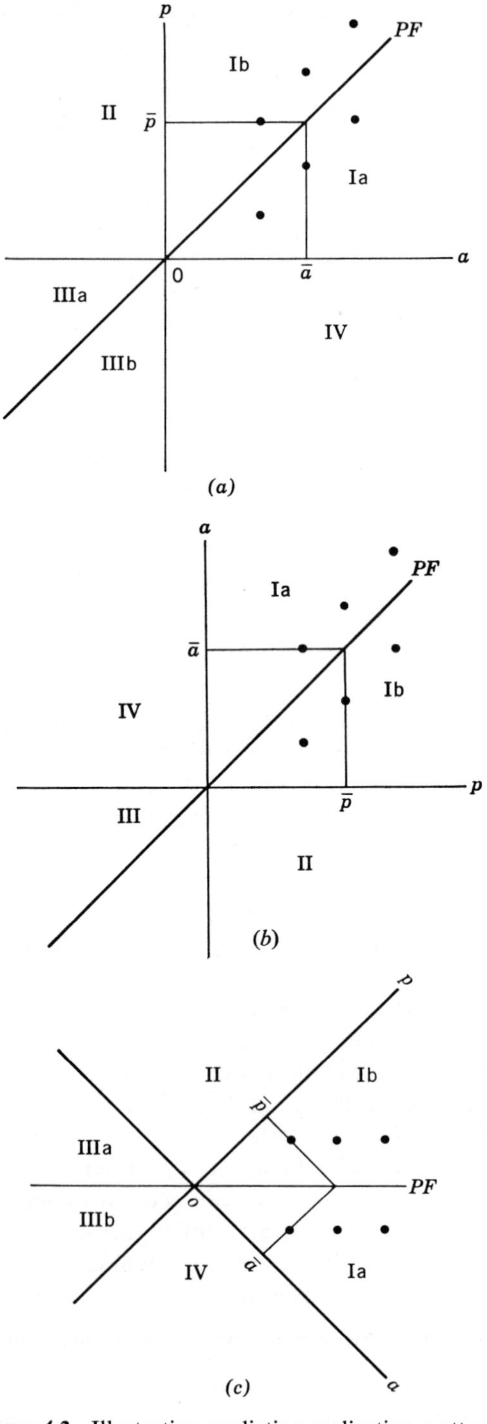

Figure 4.2 Illustrative prediction-realization scatters.

decomposition procedure developed by H. Theil [1958]. First, the mean-square-error (MSE) can be partitioned into two components:

$$\text{MSE} = \sum \frac{(p - a)^2}{n} = (\bar{p} - \bar{a})^2 + S_{p-a}^2 \tag{2.1}$$

where S_{p-a}^2 is the variance of the prediction errors.[2] The first term in this decomposition indicates the extent to which the magnitude of the MSE is the consequence of a systematic tendency to estimate too high or too low a level of sales volume, on the average. In other words, it shows how much the MSE could be reduced by adding the constant $\bar{a} - \bar{p}$ as a correction factor to the raw forecast. This phenomenon will be discussed in Section 4.2.1.

Theil has pointed out that a further decomposition of the MSE is possible. If we let r denote the correlation between a and p we have the identities:[3]

$$S_{p-a}^2 = S_p^{\ 2} + S_a^{\ 2} - 2 \operatorname{cov}(p, a) = S_p^{\ 2} + S_a^{\ 2} - 2rS_pS_a \tag{2.2}$$

$$= (S_p - S_a)^2 + 2(1 - r)S_pS_a \tag{2.3}$$

$$= (S_p - rS_a)^2 + (1 - r^2)S_a^{\ 2} \tag{2.4}$$

$$= (S_a - rS_p)^2 + (1 - r^2)S_p^{\ 2} \tag{2.5}$$

Dividing equation 2.1 by MSE, after eliminating S_{p-a}^2 with alternate expressions 2.3 and 2.4, yields Theil's two identities[4]

$$1 \equiv \text{BIASP} + \text{VARP} + \text{COVP} \tag{2.3'}$$

$$\equiv \text{BIASP} + \text{REGP} + \text{DISP} \tag{2.4'}$$

where BIASP $= (\bar{p} - \bar{a})^2/\text{MSE}$, the bias proportion

VARP $= (S_p - S_a)^2/\text{MSE}$, the variance proportion

COVP $= 2(1 - r)S_pS_a/\text{MSE}$, the covariance proportion

REGP $= (S_p - rS_a)^2/\text{MSE}$, the regression proportion

DISP $= (1 - r^2)S_a^{\ 2}/\text{MSE}$, the disturbance proportion.

[2] This follows at once if we let $e = p - a = (P - A)/A_{-1}$ and remember from elementary statistics that $S_{p-a}^2 = S_e^2 = \Sigma e^2/n - \bar{e}^2 = \text{MSE} - (\bar{p} - \bar{a})^2$.

[3] That identity 2.3 follows from 2.2 is obvious once it is observed that $(S_a - S_p)^2 = S_a^2 - 2S_aS_p + S_p^2$. Similarly, 2.4 follows once it is noted that $(S_p - rS_a)^2 = S_p^2 - 2rS_pS_a + r^2S_a^2$. Symmetry then yields 2.5.

[4] Theil originally developed his decomposition to partition the square of his inequality coefficient U, but in fact it serves to decompose any expression in which the numerator is the MSE; e.g., the decomposition of any measure of accuracy involving the ratio of MSE to any naive benchmark is identical to the decomposition of MSE because the denominator drops out.

The data on such concepts as BIASP, presented on tables discussed later in this section, permit us to identify various sources of the MSE.

The variance proportion term VARP in decomposition 2.3′ suggests that the magnitude of the MSE may be influenced by the extent to which the variance of predictions is larger or smaller than the variance of realizations. Although it is sometimes argued that VARP $= 0$ is a desirable property of forecasting procedures, we shall see in Section 4.3.2 that for various reasons the variance of predictions may either exceed or fall short of the variance of the realizations. Note also that the DISP term in 2.4′ concerns the variance of the residuals obtained by regressing the actual relative changes on the predicted changes, while the corresponding term of 2.5 concerns the variance of the residuals obtained when the regression is run in the opposite direction. These regressions are discussed in Section 4.3.2, where we consider the possibility of improving forecasts through systematic linear adjustment.

4.2.1 *Perennial Optimism*

Several alternative types of evidence can be mustered for the purpose of determining whether forecasters have either an optimistic or a pessimistic bias. Consider, first, the short sales forecasts. The data presented in the first two columns of Table 4.2.1a reveal that for eight of the fourteen industries, the average of short sales forecasts exceeds the average of the actual realized changes. This proportion (8/14) does not differ substantially from one half.[5] Specifically, if the predicted and actual changes are, in fact, symmetrically distributed with the same mean throughout the economy, the probability of $\bar{p} > \bar{a}$ for any given industry is one half; hence, the eight out of fourteen industries for which $\bar{p}$ exceeds $\bar{a}$ for short anticipations does not warrant the rejection of the hypothesis of equal means, as $P\ (\frac{3}{14} < k/14 < \frac{11}{14}) = 94$ percent if $\pi = 0.5$ and $n = 14$. Of course, the hypothesis that the discrepancy between anticipated and actual sales is zero may be tested separately for each industry. We find that for short anticipations there is not a single industry for which the absolute value of the discrepancy $\bar{d} = \bar{a} - \bar{p}$ exceeds twice its standard error.[6]

[5] A two tailed test is appropriate, for in advance of looking at the data there was no obvious reason for favoring the hypothesis of perennial optimism over perennial pessimism.

[6] Since the number of observations for each industry is small, it is necessary for $\bar{d}$ to be normally as well as independently distributed for this to constitute a reasonable test. In contrast to the proportion test, on the other hand, interindustry independence is not required.

TABLE 4.2.1a. STRUCTURE OF ANTICIPATION ERRORS, AGGREGATE DATA SHORT SALES ANTICIPATIONS[a]

Industry	$\bar{p}$	$\bar{a}$	S_p	S_a	BIASP	VARP	DISP	b_{ap}	b_{pa}
Iron and steel	0.066	0.060	0.273	0.331	0.005	0.539	0.548	1.193	0.812
Nonferrous metals	0.009	0.012	0.052	0.075	0.008	0.322	0.898	1.238	0.598
Electrical machinery	0.024	0.019	0.053	0.057	0.118	0.052	0.872	1.029	0.901
Nonelectrical machinery	0.024	0.022	0.056	0.069	0.010	0.371	0.753	1.193	0.775
Motor vehicles	0.041	0.046	0.254	0.255	0.020	0.000	0.977	0.993	0.990
Transportation equipment	0.019	0.014	0.054	0.068	0.022	0.128	0.973	1.047	0.672
Other durables	0.025	0.015	0.075	0.063	0.053	0.080	0.659	0.687	0.986
Durable Aggregate	0.023	0.019	0.089	0.100	0.036	0.281	0.765	1.109	0.869
Food and beverages	0.013	0.013	0.035	0.030	0.002	0.118	0.702	0.752	1.057
Textiles	−0.002	0.014	0.040	0.038	0.152	0.002	0.634	0.544	0.598
Paper	0.022	0.016	0.017	0.029	0.043	0.182	0.930	0.751	0.276
Chemicals	0.021	0.028	0.041	0.057	0.051	0.250	0.892	1.178	0.624
Petroleum	0.008	0.002	0.030	0.023	0.079	0.145	0.525	0.597	1.042
Rubber	0.032	0.014	0.073	0.063	0.176	0.057	0.611	0.734	0.986
Other nondurables	0.010	0.012	0.067	0.065	0.003	0.002	0.926	0.882	0.920
Nondurable Aggregate	0.012	0.013	0.019	0.019	0.000	0.000	0.902	0.804	0.800
Industry Average					0.05	0.16	0.78	0.92	
Standard Deviation					(0.06)	(0.16)	(0.16)	(0.24)	

[a] For none of the industries is the difference $\bar{d} = \bar{p} - \bar{a}$ more than twice its estimated standard error in magnitude.

TABLE 4.2.1b. STRUCTURE OF ANTICIPATION ERRORS, AGGREGATE DATA LONG SALES ANTICIPATIONS

Industry	$\bar{p}$	$\bar{a}$	S_p	S_a	BIASP	VARP	DISP	b_{ap}	b_{pa}
Iron and steel	0.168[a]	0.067	0.397	0.496	0.259	0.245	0.604	1.186	0.761
Nonferrous metals	0.034	0.011	0.051	0.084	0.104	0.204	0.894	0.942	0.350
Electrical machinery	0.050[a]	0.025	0.045	0.062	0.212	0.115	0.785	0.937	0.480
Nonelectrical machinery	0.042	0.028	0.054	0.080	0.100	0.328	0.788	1.276	0.589
Motor vehicles	0.111	0.069	0.310	0.301	0.112	0.005	0.826	0.897	0.950
Transportation equipment	0.028	0.009	0.060	0.074	0.085	0.048	0.857	0.743	0.488
Other durables	0.040	0.015	0.095	0.078	0.140	0.059	0.579	0.620	0.908
Durable Aggregate	0.056	0.020	0.075	0.105	0.294	0.208	0.647	1.209	0.622
Food and beverages	0.009	0.015	0.054	0.041	0.048	0.256	0.505	0.691	1.176
Textiles	0.011	0.024	0.048	0.053	0.032	0.005	0.583	0.106	0.087
Paper	0.034	0.027	0.028	0.033	0.068	0.049	0.899	0.833	0.579
Chemicals	0.038	0.039	0.041	0.074	0.000	0.431	0.904	1.381	0.422
Petroleum	0.019	0.011	0.045	0.037	0.040	0.042	0.570	0.427	0.648
Rubber	0.050[a]	0.015	0.076	0.081	0.197	0.004	0.679	0.629	0.550
Other nondurables	0.026	0.017	0.076	0.073	0.040	0.005	0.841	0.798	0.865
Nondurable Aggregate	0.021	0.019	0.028	0.033	0.007	0.051	0.962	0.853	0.600
Industry Average					0.10	0.13	0.74	0.82	
Standard Deviation					(0.08)	(0.14)	(0.14)	(0.33)	

[a] For these industries the observed difference $\bar{d} = \bar{p} - \bar{a}$ is more than twice its estimated standard error in magnitude.

TABLE 4.2.1c. STRUCTURE OF ANTICIPATION ERRORS, AGGREGATE DATA SHORT INVENTORY ANTICIPATION

Industry	$\bar{p}$	$\bar{a}$	S_p	S_a	BIASP	VARP	DISP	b_{ap}	b_{pa}
Iron and steel	−0.002[a]	0.003	0.035	0.059	0.019	0.421	0.855	1.370	0.487
Nonferrous metals	−0.004	0.010	0.018	0.019	0.274	0.002	0.465	0.226	0.201
Electrical machinery	−0.003	0.019	0.023	0.034	0.641	0.162	0.276	1.338	0.618
Nonelectrical machinery	−0.010	0.011	0.018	0.028	0.623	0.127	0.346	1.254	0.549
Motor vehicles	−0.020	0.018	0.045	0.056	0.652	0.053	0.343	1.080	0.697
Transportation equipment	−0.014	0.000	0.019	0.028	0.239	0.118	0.750	0.852	0.385
Other durables	−0.002[a]	0.016	0.030	0.033	0.505	0.017	0.491	0.954	0.776
Durable Aggregate	−0.009	0.010	0.013	0.019	0.821	0.093	0.127	1.382	0.606
Food and beverages	−0.018	0.007	0.049	0.047	0.755	0.006	0.224	0.914	1.004
Textiles	−0.008	0.011	0.035	0.047	0.449	0.148	0.503	1.180	0.681
Paper	−0.000	0.012	0.013	0.025	0.272	0.250	0.722	1.132	0.323
Chemicals	−0.011	0.012	0.023	0.029	0.696	0.062	0.293	1.124	0.660
Petroleum	−0.008	0.005	0.031	0.030	0.539	0.001	0.432	0.896	0.931
Rubber	−0.002	0.013	0.034	0.041	0.311	0.072	0.688	1.022	0.695
Other nondurables	0.000[a]	0.017	0.059	0.064	0.203	0.017	0.785	0.933	0.798
Nondurable Aggregate	−0.010	0.010	0.006	0.000	0.821	0.034	0.172	0.671	0.234
Industry Average					0.44	0.10	0.51	1.02	
Standard Deviation					(0.22)	(0.12)	(0.21)	(0.28)	

[a] For these industries the observed difference $\bar{d} = \bar{p} - \bar{a}$ is less than twice its estimated standard error in magnitude.

TABLE 4.2.1d. STRUCTURE OF ANTICIPATION ERRORS, AGGREGATE DATA
LONG INVENTORY ANTICIPATION

Industry	$\bar{p}$	$\bar{a}$	S_p	S_a	BIASP	VARP	DISP	b_{ap}	b_{pa}
Iron and steel	−0.009[a]	0.013	0.050	0.077	0.147	0.238	0.835	1.154	0.478
Nonferrous metals	−0.010	0.012	0.023	0.035	0.271	0.093	0.652	0.487	0.199
Electrical machinery	−0.005	0.021	0.033	0.056	0.384	0.282	0.518	1.414	0.489
Nonelectrical machinery	−0.021	0.011	0.031	0.052	0.530	0.229	0.377	1.432	0.510
Motor vehicles	−0.031	0.022	0.057	0.070	0.395	0.024	0.530	0.596	0.393
Transportation equipment	−0.019[a]	−0.011	0.033	0.049	0.058	0.233	0.925	1.131	0.514
Other durables	−0.004	0.024	0.042	0.052	0.568	0.076	0.419	1.104	0.712
Durable Aggregate	−0.016	0.011	0.021	0.039	0.570	0.257	0.306	1.627	0.451
Food and beverages	−0.017	0.013	0.071	0.066	0.626	0.018	0.322	0.881	1.019
Textiles	−0.020	0.017	0.046	0.067	0.536	0.175	0.399	1.286	0.596
Paper	−0.005	0.025	0.022	0.041	0.543	0.204	0.408	1.403	0.420
Chemicals	−0.006	0.025	0.038	0.046	0.605	0.043	0.394	1.025	0.687
Petroleum	−0.017	−0.002	0.049	0.045	0.289	0.030	0.576	0.791	0.975
Rubber	−0.000	0.029	0.056	0.070	0.374	0.082	0.623	1.045	0.678
Other nondurables	−0.011	0.013	0.065	0.068	0.299	0.003	0.670	0.883	0.819
Nondurable Aggregate	−0.014	0.013	0.010	0.016	0.757	0.037	0.226	0.588	0.228
Industry Average					0.40	0.12	0.55	1.05	
Standard Deviation					(0.06)	(0.10)	(0.18)	(0.29)	

[a] For these industries the observed difference $\bar{d} = \bar{p} - \bar{a}$ is less than twice its estimated standard error in magnitude.

Turning to the individual firm results reported on Table 4.2.2 we find that for short anticipations there are 40 out of 82 firms (49 percent) that have an average actual relative change exceeding the average predicted change. Since $P\left(\frac{32}{82} < k/82 < \frac{50}{82}\right) = 94$ percent for a sample of 82 firms if $\pi = 0.5$, the observed proportion of 40 out of 82 firms clearly constitutes an insignificant proportion; we accept the null hypothesis that a firm selected at random is equally likely to over- or underestimate change. Contrast this with the results we obtained when we looked at the firms individually; we found that for about 30 percent of the 82 firms, the discrepancy between anticipated and actual short sales is significant at the 5 percent level. The apparent inconsistency is easily reconciled; certain firms may be perennial optimists and others perennial pessimists, but on the average, the pessimistic and optimistic firms offset each other. It is reasonable to conclude that for the representative firm, if not for all firms, the means of short sales anticipations and actual realizations are identical; in this instance we should plot the point $\langle \bar{a}, \bar{p} \rangle$ on the 45° line of Figure 4.2.

Much the same story holds true for long sales anticipations, although we have 11 out of 14 industries for which $\bar{p} > \bar{a}$. Also, the industry aggregate data reveal significant discrepancies between the long anticipation and the actual realization means for three industries: iron and steel, electrical machinery, and rubber. However, the 37 out of 82 firms for which $\bar{p} > \bar{a}$ does not constitute a significant departure from 0.5. Again, we find that a substantial number of the individual firms, 30 percent, have a significant discrepancy. It is again clear that while some firms are perennial optimists and others perennial pessimists, these tendencies more or less cancel out in at least the majority of industries.

A rather different picture emerges when it comes to forecasting inventories, for there appears to be a systematic tendency for firms to underestimate the extent of inventory accumulation.[7] Thus, Table 4.2.1c reveals that in every industry the average predicted short inventory change was negative or zero, while in practice it turned out that the average change in inventories in every industry was positive. Furthermore, the individual firm data of Table 4.2.2 reveal that only 15 percent of the 83 firms in our sample overestimated in predicting short-run inventory movements. Essentially the same results hold true for long inventory anticipations. We see from Table 4.2.1d that $\bar{p}$ is negative for every industry aggregate. Although it is true that the actual average change was negative for transportation and petroleum, the average

[7] It should be noted that a perennially optimistic outlook with regard to sales is not a prerequisite for a consistent tendency to underestimate inventory movements. Total stocks may depart from plan as a result of unexpected fluctuations in the delivery of raw materials. Finished goods may depart from the anticipated level because production departs from plan as well as because of deviations between anticipated and realized sales volume.

TABLE 4.2.2. FORECAST DECOMPOSITION, FIRM DATA

	Proportion by Industry[a]					
	NFM	EM	NEM	CHEM	PET	All firms
Short Sales Anticipation						
$\bar{a} > \bar{p}$	0.55	0.47	0.68	0.40	0.40	0.49
$\bar{a} - \bar{p}$ more than twice its standard error	0	0.52	0.37	0.30	0.20	0.30
$S_p > S_a$	0.33	0.47	0.37	0.20	0.40	0.35
Long Sales Anticipations						
$\bar{a} > \bar{p}$	0.77	0.47	0.62	0.35	0.25	0.45
$\bar{a} - \bar{p}$ more than twice its standard error	0	0.23	0.25	0.25	0.10	0.18
$S_p > S_a$	0.33	0.41	0.31	0.10	0.25	0.36
Short Total Inventory						
$\bar{a} > \bar{p}$	0.20	0.11	0.25	0.10	0.15	0.15
$\bar{a} - \bar{p}$ more than twice its standard error	0.30	0.35	0.43	0.45	0.15	0.28
$S_p > S_a$	0.30	0.23	0.18	0.20	0.20	0.21
Long Total Inventory						
$\bar{a} > \bar{p}$	0.10	0.17	0.06	0.10	0.15	0.12
$\bar{a} - \bar{p}$ more than twice its standard error	0.40	0.35	0.50	0.65	0.25	0.31
$S_p > S_a$	0.10	0.35	0.18	0.20	0.05	0.18
Short Finished Inventory						
$\bar{a} > \bar{p}$	0.62	0.28	0.21	0.37	0.21	0.30
$\bar{a} - \bar{p}$ more than twice its standard error	0.12	0.21	0.14	0.25	0.05	0.15
$S_p > S_a$	0.37	0.28	0.14	0.25	0.36	0.28
Long Finished Inventory						
$\bar{a} > \bar{p}$	0.75	0.07	0.28	0.25	0.36	0.30
$\bar{a} - \bar{p}$ more than twice its standard error	0.37	0.21	0.14	0.18	0.05	0.16
$S_p > S_a$	0.12	0.14	0.28	0.25	0.31	0.23

[a] Note the approximate number of firms available by industry is revealed by Table 2.1.2. however, fewer firms were available in certain cells because of incomplete responses. Thus only 71 firms provided the information on finished goods inventories.

of predicted changes was even lower. Furthermore, only 10 out of 82 of the individual firms in our sample anticipated, on the average, a higher level of inventory increase than customarily occurred. The tendency of firms to underestimate inventory change manifests itself in finished goods inventory as well as in total stocks, for Table 4.2.2 reveals that for only 30 percent of the 71 firms is $\bar{p} > \bar{a}$ for short finished goods inventory. Long finished goods inventory yields precisely the same proportion.

It is hard to say whether this systematic tendency to understate inventory movements constitutes unwarranted "optimism" or "pessimism," although the tendency may arise from wishful thinking concerning the possibility of economizing by reducing inventory carrying costs. The phenomenon may well be a manifestation of Murray Foss's [1961] "controller effect"; i.e., a possible tendency of those who fill out the OBE questionnaire to be concerned with the carrying costs of inventory stocks. In contrast, those concerned with the physical aspects of the production and distribution process may appreciate the convenience yield of inventories and successfully push for larger than planned stocks. It is possible, however, that the downward bias in the inventory forecast is not the result of a divergence of viewpoints with regard to the appropriate magnitude of stocks. In many decision-making applications, it is appropriate to proceed under conditions of uncertainty by utilizing a "certainty equivalent" forecast in essentially the same way in which the actual magnitude would be used if it were known. Under certain conditions such forecasts *should* be biased.[8] Whatever its source, the tendency for inventory stocks to exceed, on the average, the anticipated change means that the point $\langle \bar{a}, \bar{p} \rangle$ would have to be placed in half-quadrant Ia of Figure 4.2.

4.2.2 *The Variance of Anticipated Change, Three Types of Forecasts*

Inspection of Table 4.2.1 reveals that in both the food and beverage industry and the petroleum industry the anticipated change is subject to considerably greater fluctuation than the actual realization; this is true whether we look at the short or long anticipation, and with either inventories or sales. Although this phenomenon is seen occasionally in certain other industries as well, we find in the majority of instances that the variance of the

[8] For example, if the loss from an inappropriate inventory level is strictly proportional to the gap between the target and realized level, it may be appropriate for the forecaster to employ as the point estimate the median rather than the mean of the probability distribution determining inventories as the point estimate; in these circumstances, the estimate will fall short of the realization on the average if the probability distribution is skewed to the left, Alternatively, with a symmetric probability distribution, a biased forecast may be appropriate if the cost of having inventories depart from their desired level is assymetric. For a discussion of certainty equivalents, see Holt, Modigliani, Muth, and Simon [1960] and Raiffa and Schlaifer [1961, Ch. 6].

actual change is larger than the variance of predictions. Indeed, we find that $S_p^2 < S_a^2$ for far more than half of the firms in every one of the five industries for which we have firm data. For only 29 out of 82 firms is this inequality reversed for short sales anticipations, and in all other instances the proportion is even smaller. Since $P(\frac{32}{82} < k/82 < \frac{50}{82}) = 94$ percent, if $\pi = 0.5$, it seems clear that the hypothesis of equality of variances should be rejected.

But shouldn't we expect to find $S_p^2 < S_a^2$; are there not simple logical factors that serve to explain the observed phenomenon and indeed imply that a one-tailed test of the hypothesis $\sigma_p^2 < \sigma_a^2$ is appropriate? The following rather involved analysis will reveal that while there are circumstances in which we might find $S_p^2 < S_a^2$, there are other conditions in which we might expect to find the condition reversed. Everything depends upon the way in which the forecast is calculated.

Suppose that a firm's market research department prepares its sales forecast on the basis of a customer survey. Suppose that while the customers are able to estimate quite precisely the quantity they will purchase, a rather small sample of customers is selected at random and polled each quarter. In these circumstances, we would expect to find that the sum of the demands anticipated by the polled customers (P_t), after being appropriately blown up by the reciprocal of the sampling rate, would constitute an unbiased estimate of actual sales, A_t. More precisely, we would have $P_t = A_t + \epsilon_t$, with the sampling error ϵ_t distributed independently of A_t. Furthermore, for each t, the expected value of the anticipated change, $P_t = (P_t - A_{t-1})/(A_{t-1})$, would be equal to the actual change $a_t = (A_t - A_{t-1})/(A_{t-1})$. But the variance of P_t would exceed the variance of A_t, when computed from time-series data, because of the presence of sampling error. Specifically, we would have $\sigma_P^2 = \sigma_A^2 + \sigma_\epsilon^2$, where σ_ϵ^2 denotes the sampling variance. The extent to which $\sigma_P^2 > \sigma_A^2$ depends upon both the variance at any point of time in the quantity demanded by the firm's various customers and the size of the sample used when inquiring about future demand.[9] The scatter of predictions on actual realizations would appear as in Figure 4.2*a*.

On the other hand, there are alternative circumstances in which the variance of the anticipated change will fall short of the actual variance in sales. To take a simple example, similar to one mentioned by Theil [1966, p. 32], suppose that the forecaster has correctly learned from past experience that sales tend to grow at a constant rate with a predictable seasonal movement; suppose in addition that he has also found that it is not profitable to attempt to forecast the pattern of other factors influencing the demand for his product. More precisely, the actual data is generated by $a_t = g_a + \epsilon_t$,

[9] In terms of relative changes, we have the conditional variances

$$\sigma^2_{p|A_{-1}} = \sigma_p^2/A_{-1}^2 = (\sigma_A^2 + \sigma_\epsilon^2)/A_{-1}^2 \quad \text{and} \quad \sigma^2_{a|A_{-1}} = \sigma_A^2/A_{-1}^2.$$

where g_q is the growth plus seasonal factor relevant for the qth quarter and ϵ_t is a random variable with zero expected value. If the forecaster predicts $p_t = g_q$, then the magnitude of σ_p^2 computed from time-series data will depend upon the extent of seasonal variation, while we will also have $\sigma_a^2 = \sigma_{g_q}^2 + \sigma_\epsilon^2$. Consequently, $\sigma_a^2 > \sigma_p^2$, as we observe with the OBE data in the majority of cases.

Forecasts prepared by a market research department with much more sophisticated techniques may also be characterized by $\sigma_a^2 > \sigma_p^2$. Suppose that the forecaster employs econometric techniques to estimate sales volume on the basis of certain exogenous variables, X_{it}. Suppose he has obtained with historical data quite precise estimates of a correctly specified linear model of the form $A_t = \sum_i \beta_i X_{it} + \epsilon_t$, where the stochastic disturbance ϵ_t, representing the effects of omitted variables, is distributed independently of X_{it}. In these circumstances the prediction $P_t = \sum_i b_i X_{it}$ will have a smaller variance than A_t, provided that the b_i calculated from historical data are reasonably precise estimates of the β_i. The scatter of points $\langle a, p\rangle$ will tend to appear in the form indicated on Figure 4.2*b*.

Let us now return to the market research department conducting the customer survey and ask whether it might not be possible to improve upon the raw sample prediction on the basis of knowledge gained from past experience concerning sales volume. Specifically, if P again denotes the survey prediction and A the actual realization we will have

$$P = A + \epsilon \tag{2.5}$$

with $E(\epsilon) = E(A\epsilon) = 0$. Furthermore, we have $\text{MSE}_P = \sigma_\epsilon^2$. We will consider the class of linearly adjusted forecasts:

$$\hat{P} = c + dP \tag{2.6}$$

Obviously, $E(\hat{P} \mid A) = c + dA$ and $\sigma^2_{\hat{P}|A} = d^2\sigma^2_{P|A} = d^2\sigma_\epsilon^2$. Furthermore, since the MSE is simply the sum of the variance and the squared bias, we will have

$$\begin{aligned}\text{MSE}_{\hat{P}|A} &= \sigma^2_{\hat{P}|A} + [E(\hat{P} \mid A) - A]^2 \\ &= d^2\sigma_\epsilon^2 + [c + (d-1)A]^2 = d^2\sigma_\epsilon^2 + c^2 + 2(d-1)cA + (d-1)^2A^2.\end{aligned} \tag{2.7}$$

What values of c and d are optimal depends upon the criterion utilized in making decisions under uncertainty. If, for example, our decision maker follows a minimax strategy of picking the values of c and d that minimize $\text{MSE}_{\hat{P}|A}$ for the worst possible value of A that a perverse Nature might generate, he would set $d = 1$ in order to eliminate A from 2.7; but then the forecaster should also make $c = 0$ and obtain:

$$\min_{c'd} \max_{A} \text{MSE}_{\hat{P}|A} = \sigma_\epsilon^2 \tag{2.8}$$

In other words, the raw survey forecast is optimal with this objective. On the other hand, the decision maker is more likely to want to minimize

$$\text{MSE}_{\hat{P}} = \int_{-\infty}^{\infty} \text{MSE}_{\hat{P}|A} f(A)\, dA$$

where $f(A)$ is the probability distribution summarizing the forecaster's prior judgement, derived from historical experience, concerning the likelihood of various values of A. Substituting from equation 2.7 reveals:

$$\text{MSE}_{\hat{P}} = d^2\sigma_\epsilon^2 + c^2 + 2(d-1)cE(A) + (d-1)^2[S_A^2 + E(A)^2] \tag{2.9}$$

Thus, only the mean and variance of the probability distribution are relevant because equation 2.6 is linear, the MSE criterion is quadratic in nature, and A and ϵ are independent. Differentiation of 2.9 with respect to c and d reveals that $\text{MSE}_{\hat{P}}$ is minimized with

$$d^0 = \frac{S_A^2}{S_A^2 + \sigma_\epsilon^2} \tag{2.10}$$

and

$$c^0 = (2 - d)\, E(A)$$

Since A and ϵ are distributed independently in 2.5 it follows that cov $(A, P) = S_A^2$ and $S_P^2 = S_A^2 + \sigma_\epsilon^2$.[10] Consequently, the optimal linear correction coefficient of equation 2.6 may be obtained by using historical data to estimate the regression of A on P; specifically, d^0 is the slope and c^0 the intercept of that regression.[11] This means that the error $\hat{P} - A$ is necessarily uncorrelated with $\hat{P}$.[12] A further point deserving emphasis is that running the regression in the reverse direction yields a slope of unity; i.e., $E(P \mid A) = A$. Consequently, the sampling error variance, σ_ϵ^2, is also the variance of the disturbances when P is regressed on A and we must have $r^2 = 1 - \sigma_\epsilon^2/S_p^2$, where σ_ϵ^2 is the disturbance of equation 2.5; but this means that $d_0 = r^2$.

[10] To obtain the covariance simply take the expected value of the expression obtained by multiplying both sides of 2.5 by A, noting that $E(A\epsilon) = 0$.

[11] That is, the slope of the regression of A on P is cov $(A, P)/S_p^2$, which is d^0. If the survey is a new operation the correction coefficient may still be calculated from 2.10 if information is available on sampling error σ_ϵ^2, and on the variance of actual sales.

[12] This is a property of Muth's [1961] "rational" expectations, a concept which we shall be discussing in Chapter 5.4.

Let us now consider the statistical properties of the sample survey forecast, after it has been subject to optimal correction. In the first place, it is clear from 2.5 and 2.6 that the linearly adjusted forecast will not be distributed independently of the realization. Indeed, the correlation between $\hat{P}$ and A must be identical to the correlation between P and A. However, the variance of $\hat{P}$ is of necessity less than the variance of either P or A. Specifically, we have from 2.10 and 2.6:

$$\sigma_{\hat{P}}^2 = \frac{S_A^{\ 4}}{(S_A^{\ 2} + \sigma_\epsilon^{\ 2})^2}\,\sigma_P^{\ 2} = \frac{S_A^{\ 4}}{S_A^{\ 2} + \sigma_\epsilon^{\ 2}} = S_A^{\ 2} - \frac{S_A^{\ 2}\sigma_\epsilon^{\ 2}}{S_A^{\ 2} + \sigma_\epsilon^{\ 2}} \leq S_A^{\ 2} \quad (2.11)$$

Note that $\sigma_{\hat{P}}^2$ approaches $S_A^{\ 2}$ from below as the forecast becomes more precise ($\sigma_\epsilon^{\ 2} \to 0$).

Except when dealing with raw forecasts obtained from sample surveys, then, we should expect to find the variance of the forecast less than the variance of the realizations. This means that in terms of Theil's decomposition, equation 2.3′, we should *not* expect to find that VARP $= [(S_p - S_a)^2/\text{MSE}] = 0$. Rather, with forecasts that are not subject to systematic linear bias we will have BIASP = REGP = 0, DISP = 1, and MSE $= (1 - r^2)S_a^{\ 2}$, as may be seen from equation 2.4′. Remember also that REGP = 0 implies $S_a - S_p = (1 - r)S_a$. We then find that VARP $= (1 - r)^2/(1 - r^2)$ must hold true for forecasts that have been corrected for systematic linear bias. This means, for example, that if $r = \frac{1}{2}$ for a forecast that cannot be improved in accuracy by systematic linear adjustment, we will have VARP $= \frac{1}{3}$; indeed, VARP is a monotonic decreasing function of r, and approaches a limit of zero as r approaches one. Clearly, VARP = 0 may not be a desideratum in its own right, but a small VARP is a characteristic of good forecasting.

This argument lends credence to a proposition that has been advanced concerning the composition of forecast errors. Theil [1958, p. 37] and Pashigian [1964, p. 403] have suggested that, other things being equal, we should expect to find empirically that BIASP and VARP are decreasing functions of forecasting accuracy. While we might expect to find a large value of BIASP associated with a large U and a small correlation between actual and predicted sales, the cross-sectional evidence on Table 4.2.3 reveals that this hope is not fulfilled with much regularity. For example, we note that for short sales anticipations in two out of the five industries U and BIASP are negatively rather than positively correlated. Furthermore, the magnitude of DISP is negatively rather than positively correlated with the RMSE in four out of ten cases. We do find, however, that with the single exception of short chemical anticipations, VARP is positively correlated with RMSE. With but one exception, then, this aspect of the Theil-Pashigian hypothesis is fulfilled.

TABLE 4.2.3. FORECAST ACCURACY VERSUS BIASP, VARP, AND DISP COEFFICIENTS OF CORRELATION—FIRM DATA

	Short Sales					Long Sales				
	r^2 with	U with	RMSE with			r^2 with	U with	RMSE with		
	DISP	BIASP	BIASP	VARP	DISP	DISP	BIASP	BIASP	VARP	DISP
Nonferrous metals	−0.46	0.09	0.42	0.51	−0.35	0.74	0.80	−0.34	0.35	0.05
Electrical machinery	0.13	0.34	0.44	0.18	−0.42	0	0.37	0.23	0.57	−0.41
Nonelectrical machinery	−0.24	−0.45	−0.44	0.61	0.57	0.03	0.14	−0.27	0.50	0.38
Chemicals	0.39	0.45	−0.10	−0.21	0.06	0.56	0.41	0.08	0.20	0.18
Petroleum	0.05	−0.44	−0.27	0.03	−0.20	0.11	−0.16	−0.36	0.25	0

Note. The entries in this table were derived by correlating various concepts developed by Theil for decomposing forecast errors with three alternative measures of forecast accuracy. Each sampled firm constituted an observation.

4.3 UNDERESTIMATION OF CHANGE

Perhaps the most controversial characteristic of anticipations encountered in studies of the railroad shippers' forecast data by Ferber [1953] and Modigliani and Sauerlander [1955, p. 278] was the apparent tendency of firms to underestimate change systematically. Underestimation of change is the tendency to underestimate changes in sales, regardless of direction. Thus, it involves overestimation of sales when business is declining and understatement when conditions are improving. It is not a systematic tendency to underestimate sales volume, which is perennial pessimism. In those quarters throughout the period 1927 to 1950 in which shipments were rising, the aggregate forecasts underestimated total carload utilization by 5 percent on the average; but when shipments were falling they overestimated by 16 percent on the average.[13] Also, Theil [1958, 1966, p. 52] found that macroeconomic forecasters habitually underestimate change. Thus, of 210 separate forecasts of various macroeconomic variables made annually from 1953 to 1962 by the Netherlands Central Planning Bureau, 59 percent involved underestimation of change and 26 percent overestimation, while 15 percent were turning-point errors. Again, Zarnowitz [1967, p. 49] reports that over the period 1952–1963, forecasters of the Gross National Product of the United States underestimated change 59 percent of the time and overestimated only 32 percent of the time; 9 percent of the forecasts involved turning-point errors.[14]

4.3.1 *The Probability of Underestimating Change*

There are four possible outcomes deserving consideration—overestimation of change (OEC), underestimation of change (UEC), turning-point errors (TPE), and no change (NC). We are particularly interested in the probability that the event UEC will occur. If we visualize the problem in terms of Figure 4.2*a*, where predicted changes are plotted against realizations, we observe that points in half-quadrant Ia indicate that the firm has underestimated an increase. Similarly, points in half-quadrant IIIa indicate that the firm predicted a much smaller drop than actually occurred. The proportion of points in the union of these two half-quadrants indicates the probability that

[13] The prevalence of change underestimation in the railroad shippers' data is apparent when the data are plotted. See, particularly, the graphical presentation of Albert G. Hart [1960, p. 208].

[14] The phenomenon of change underestimation is the subject of a major study now under way at the National Bureau under the direction of Jacob Mincer [1966], but his approach is quite different from ours.

the firm underestimates change.[15] On the other hand, points in half-quadrants Ib and IIIb denote OEC while points in II and IV constitute TPE.[16]

Now the probability of change underestimation will depend upon the type of forecaster we are observing and the characteristics of the series being predicted. Suppose that Nature and her forecaster draw "realizations" and "predictions" from separate urns that are uniformly distributed with zero mean. Then a glance at Figure 4.2*a* will confirm that the probability of OEC will be 1/4 if the urns have identical variances; OEC and UEC will be equally likely events. However, the probability of overestimation will be less than 1/4 and the probability of underestimation greater than 1/4 if the variance of the forecaster's urn is less than the variance of Nature's urn. Furthermore, the forecaster who wishes to minimize his mean-square-prediction-error would always predict the mean of Nature's urn, if known, rather than draw a random number.[17] Thus, we should not be surprised if underestimation of change tends to prevail.[18] In practice, of course, neither Nature nor her forecasters draw randomly from urns. Nonetheless, the analogy does serve to suggest that underestimation of change should hardly be regarded as an unexpected phenomenon. In common sense terms, the forecaster who shoots for average tendencies makes predictions that may tend to track actual developments, but with rather less variance.

Evidence on the frequency with which aggregate anticipations data over- and underestimate change is presented on Table 4.3.1. In contrast to the railroad shippers' forecast data analyzed by Ferber, overestimation of change is *not* a rare phenomenon. Quite the contrary, we observe that for both short and long sales anticipations, unadjusted for seasonal variation, over- and underestimation of change occur with approximately equal frequency. Indeed, overestimation predominates for most of the nondurable industries and in several durables, including electrical machinery. Once the data are adjusted for seasonal variation, however, the likelihood of observing change underestimation increases at the expense of a reduction in change

[15] It will be noted that the figures reported by Modigliani and Sauerlander, which we referred to in our preceding paragraph, might be generated by a preponderance of turning point errors rather than points in half-quadrants Ia and IIIa.

[16] It should also be observed that the firm can predict no change, which may indeed be a reasonable course of action in the fact of extreme ignorance; indeed, it has sometimes been suggested that aggregate *ex ante* data display a tendency toward change underestimation because many sampled firms respond with a no-change prediction.

[17] See Chapter 3.2.

[18] Admittedly, if the mean of Nature's urn is not zero, the likelihood of overestimating change will rise above 1/4 if the forecaster draws from an urn with the same mean and variance as Nature's. Also, if the forecaster is a perennial optimist who overestimates the mean of Nature's urn, and if Nature's urn has a positive mean, the probability of over-estimation will exceed the probability of underestimation.

overestimation.[19] Although the preponderance of change underestimation revealed by the unadjusted data is not sufficient to enable us to reject the hypothesis that over- and underestimation of change are equally likely events, the shift in relative frequencies generated by seasonal adjustment suggests that a significant difference exists for both durable and nondurable short sales anticipations.[20] The discrepancy for seasonally adjusted long sales anticipations is also significant at the five percent level for the durable industries.

Rather similar effects prevail with regard to inventory anticipations. Note, however, that while firms tend to underestimate change when inventories are rising, they habitually overestimate when inventories are falling. This tendency, which prevails with both short and long inventory anticipations, is obviously the consequence of the tendency of firms to consistently anticipate a smaller level of inventories than is actually realized, a phenomenon that we considered in Section 4.2.1.

The individual firm data on over- and underestimation of sales changes appears on Table 4.3.2. More often than not, firms underestimate rather than overestimate change when forecasting future sales movements, but the effect is not universal. As with the aggregate sales forecasts, the extent to which underestimation prevails is not particularly sensitive to whether actual sales are rising or falling. A comparison of these figures with those of Zarnowitz's study suggests that firms do not underestimate in predicting their sales developments with nearly the same frequency with which the typical forecaster of business conditions understates change.[21]

[19] The *ex ante* and *ex post* data were adjusted separately. That is, the anticipations data were not adjusted by the same seasonal factors generated in adjusting the actual realizations.

[20] The experiment involved in forecasting is characterized by the multinomial distribution, for there are n independent repeated trials with four possible outcomes. But we are interested in the null hypothesis $P(\text{OEC}) = P(\text{UEC})$, which may be tested by considering the conditional probability of OEC given that either OEC or UEC has occurred. This conditional probability is $\frac{1}{2}$ under the null hypothesis, and the k times that OEC occurs out of n' occurrences of either OEC or UEC is binomial. That is, for short unadjusted sales expectations, OEC occurred 38 percent and UEC 50 percent in a total of 119 trials; thus, there were a total of $n' = 105$ times in which either OEC or UEC occurred and OEC occurred 43 percent of the time in which there was either over- or underestimation of change. Tables of the binomial distribution reveal that the hypothesis of $\pi = 0.5$ should not be rejected for an observed proportion of 43 percent successes in 105 trials. This conditional use of the binomial distribution is appropriate, even though n' is a random variable, for the unconditional probability of rejecting the null hypothesis, when true with this approach is

$$\sum_{n'=1}^{n} P(\text{rejecting } H_0 \mid n')P(n') = 5\%\left[\sum_{n'=0}^{n} P(n')\right] = 5\%$$

[21] As explained in more detail in Section 4.3, Theil and Zarnowitz found that change underestimation occurs about 60% of the time in forecasts of annual change in macroeconomic variables.

TABLE 4.3.1a. OVER- AND UNDERESTIMATION OF CHANGE PROBABILITIES INDUSTRY SHORT SALES ANTICIPATIONS

	$a > 0$			$a < 0$				
	OEC	UEC	TPE	OEC	UEC	TPE	OEC	UEC
Short Sales Anticipations								
Durables								
Iron and steel	0.60*	0.40	0	0	0.86	0.14	0.35	0.59
Nonferrous metals	0.13	0.75	0.13	0.11	0.56	0.33	0.12	0.65
Electrical machinery	0.70*	0.30	0	0.29	0.43	0.29	0.53*	0.35
Nonelectrical machinery	0.31	0.69	0	0	1.00	0	0.24	0.76
Motor vehicles	0.44	0.56	0	0.38	0.50	0.13	0.41	0.53
Transportation equipment	0.64*	0.27	0.09	0	0.67	0.17	0.41t	0.41
Other durables	0.78*	0.22	0	0.38*	0.13	0.50	0.59*	0.18
All	0.51*	0.46	0.03	0.18	0.55	0.24	0.38	0.50
Nondurables								
Food and beverages	0.50*	0.33	0.17	0.60*	0.40	0	0.53*	0.35
Textiles	0.45*	0.18	0.27	0.50*	0.17	0.33	0.47*	0.18
Paper	0.42	0.50	0.08	0t	0	0.60	0.29	0.35
Chemicals	0.09	0.73	0.09	0.33t	0.33	0.33	0.18	0.59
Petroleum	0.67*	0.33	0	0.50*	0.13	0.38	0.59*	0.24
Rubber	0.67*	0.22	0	0.38*	0.25	0.25	0.53*	0.24
Other nondurables	0.43t	0.43	0.14	0.40t	0.40	0.20	0.41t	0.41
All	0.45*	0.39	0.11	0.40*	0.25	0.29	0.43*	0.34
Short Sales Anticipations, Seasonally Adjusted								
Durables								
Iron and steel	0.50t	0.50	0	0.22	0.44	0.33	0.35	0.47

Nonferrous metals	0.36	0.55	0.09	0.17	0.67	0.17	0.29	0.59
Electrical machinery	0.13	0.88	0	0t	0.22	0.78	0.06	0.53
Nonelectrical machinery	0	1.00	0	0t	0.33	0.67	0	0.65
Motor vehicles	0.44	0.56	0	0.25	0.38	0.38	0.35	0.47
Transportation equipment	0.44t	0.44	0.11	0.13	0.25	0.63	0.29	0.35
Other durables	0.13	0.88	0	0.22	0.22	0.56	0.18	0.53
All	0.30	0.67	0.03	0.14	0.34	0.52	0.22	0.51
Nondurables								
Food and beverages	0	1.00	0	0	0.33	0.67	0	0.65
Textiles	0.22	0.78	0	0.13	0.75	0.13	0.18	0.76
Paper	0.13	0.88	0	0	0.44	0.56	0.06	0.65
Chemicals	0.11	0.89	0	0	0.75	0.25	0.06	0.82
Petroleum	0.38	0.63	0	0	0.56	0.44	0.18	0.59
Rubber	0.50*	0.38	0.13	0.11	0.33	0.56	0.29	0.35
Other nondurables	0.13	0.75	0.13	0	0.56	0.44	0.06	0.65
All	0.21	0.76	0.03	0.03	0.52	0.44	0.12	0.64

Note. OEC denotes overestimation of change; the symbol "$a > 0$" indicates that the first data column yields the conditional probability of overestimating change, given that the actual change was positive; the notation "$a < 0$" reveals that the second OEC column reports the conditional probability of overestimation given $a < 0$; the final OEC column is the unconditional probability of overestimation of change. Similarly, UEC concerns underestimation of change and TPE turning point errors. Subtracting the sum of the proportions OEC + UEC + TPE from unity reveals the proportion of no change predictions.

An asterisk indicates that the probability of overestimating change exceeds the probability of underestimating change; a "t" indicates a tie.

For short sales and inventories there are 17 observations for each industry and for long anticipations there are 19; consequently, the *All* durables and *All* nondurables are based on 119 observations for short and 133 observations for long anticipations respectively.

TABLE 4.3.1b. OVER- AND UNDERESTIMATION OF CHANGE PROBABILITIES INDUSTRY LONG SALES ANTICIPATIONS

	$a > 0$			$a < 0$				
	OEC	UEC	TPE	OEC	UEC	TPE	OEC	UEC
Long Sales Anticipations								
Durables								
Iron and steel	0.27	0.73	0	0	0.75	0.25	0.16	0.74
Nonferrous metals	0.40t	0.40	0.10	0.22t	0.22	0.56	0.32t	0.32
Electrical machinery	0.67*	0.33	0	0.29*	0.14	0.57	0.53*	0.26
Nonelectrical machinery	0.50t	0.50	0	0.14	0.57	0.29	0.37	0.53
Motor vehicles	0.40	0.50	0.10	0.33t	0.33	0.33	0.37	0.42
Transportation equipment	0.43	0.57	0	0.25	0.33	0.42	0.32	0.42
Other durables	0.70*	0.10	0.20	0.33t	0.33	0.22	0.53*	0.21
All	0.49t	0.44	0.06	0.23	0.38	0.38	0.37	0.41
Nondurables								
Food and beverages	0.33	0.42	0.25	0.57*	0.29	0.14	0.42*	0.37
Textiles	0.15	0.38	0.46	0.33*	0.17	0.50	0.21	0.32
Paper	0.57*	0.43	0	0.40*	0.20	0.40	0.53*	0.37
Chemicals	0.31	0.62	0.08	0	0.33	0.67	0.21	0.53
Petroleum	0.64*	0.18	0.18	0.50*	0.13	0.38	0.58*	0.16
Rubber	0.75*	0.08	0.17	0.14	0.43	0.43	0.53*	0.21

Other nondurables	0.67*	0.22	0.11	0.40t	0.40	0.20	0.53*	0.32
All	0.48*	0.35	0.18	0.35*	0.29	0.37	0.43*	0.32
Long Sales Anticipations, Seasonally Adjusted								
Durables								
Iron and steel	0.13	0.75	0.13	0.09	0.73	0.18	0.11	0.74
Nonferrous metals	0.17	0.58	0.25	0	0.43	0.57	0.11	0.53
Electrical machinery	0.53*	0.47	0	0t	0	1.00	0.42*	0.37
Nonelectrical machinery	0.36	0.50	0.14	0t	0	1.00	0.26	0.37
Motor vehicles	0.55*	0.36	0.09	0.13	0.50	0.38	0.37	0.42
Transportation equipment	0.50t	0.50	0	0.22	0.56	0.22	0.37	0.53
Other durables	0.50*	0.40	0.10	0	0.33	0.67	0.26	0.37
All	0.40	0.50	0.10	0.08	0.43	0.49	0.27	0.47
Nondurables								
Food and beverages	0.40t	0.40	0.20	0.25t	0.25	0.50	0.37t	0.37
Textiles	0.08	0.50	0.42	0	0.14	0.86	0.05	0.37
Paper	0.53*	0.47	0	0	0.25	0.75	0.42t	0.42
Chemicals	0.21	0.71	0.07	0t	0	1.00	0.16	0.53
Petroleum	0.50*	0.29	0.21	0t	0	1.00	0.37*	0.21
Rubber	0.43*	0.36	0.21	0t	0	1.00	0.32*	0.26
Other nondurables	0.43*	0.36	0.21	0	0.20	0.80	0.32t	0.32
All	0.38	0.44	0.18	0.03	0.11	0.86	0.29	0.35

TABLE 4.3.1c. OVER- AND UNDERESTIMATION OF CHANGE PROBABILITIES
INDUSTRY SHORT INVENTORY ANTICIPATIONS

	$a > 0$			$a < 0$				
	OEC	UEC	TPE	OEC	UEC	TPE	OEC	UEC
Short Inventory Anticipations								
Durables								
Iron and steel	0.17	0.83	0	0.45*	0.27	0.27	0.35	0.47
Nonferrous metals	0.11*	0	0.67	0.25*	0.13	0.25	0.18*	0.06
Electrical machinery	0	0.80	0.20	0.86*	0.14	0	0.35	0.53
Nonelectrical machinery	0	0.44	0.22	0.88*	0.13	0	0.41*	0.29
Motor vehicles	0	0.55	0.45	0.67*	0.33	0	0.24	0.47
Transportation equipment	0	0.43	0.43	0.60*	0.30	0.10	0.35t	0.35
Other durables	0.10	0.70	0.20	0.71*	0.14	0	0.35	0.47
All	0.05	0.53	0.32	0.61*	0.21	0.11	0.32	0.38
Nondurables								
Food and beverages	0.13	0.75	0.13	0.89*	0.11	0	0.53*	0.41
Textiles	0.08	0.38	0.54	0.50t	0.50	0	0.18	0.41
Paper	0	0.38	0.31	0	0.75	0.25	0	0.47
Chemicals	0	0.56	0.44	0.88*	0.13	0	0.41*	0.35
Petroleum	0.11	0.89	0	0.88*	0.13	0	0.47	0.53
Rubber	0.25	0.75	0	0.67*	0.33	0	0.47	0.53

Other nondurables	0.09	0.64	0.27	0.50*	0.33	0.17	0.24	0.53
All	0.08	0.59	0.27	0.69*	0.27	0.04	0.33	0.46
Short Inventory Anticipations, Seasonally Adjusted								
Durables								
Iron and steel	0.20	0.50	0.30	0.29	0.57	0.14	0.24	0.53
Nonferrous metals	0.20	0.50	0.30	0.43*	0.29	0.29	0.29	0.41
Electrical machinery	0	0.78	0.22	0.25	0.63	0.13	0.12	0.71
Nonelectrical machinery	0	0.40	0.60	0.57*	0.43	0	0.24	0.41
Motor vehicles	0.11	0.44	0.44	0.50t	0.50	0	0.29	0.47
Transportation equipment	0	0.57	0.43	0.80*	0.20	0	0.47*	0.35
Other durables	0.11	0.78	0.11	0.25	0.50	0.25	0.18	0.65
All	0.09	0.56	0.34	0.45*	0.44	0.11	0.26	0.50
Nondurables								
Food and beverages	0	0.38	0.63	0.67*	0.33	0	0.35t	0.35
Textiles	0	0.33	0.67	0.63*	0.13	0.25	0.29*	0.24
Paper	0	0.75	0.13	0	0.67	0.33	0	0.71
Chemicals	0	0.63	0.38	0.33	0.56	0.11	0.18	0.59
Petroleum	0.08	0.25	0.67	0.80*	0	0.20	0.29*	0.18
Rubber	0.17	0.42	0.42	0	0.60	0.40	0.12	0.47
Other nondurables	0.08	0.42	0.50	0.20*	0	0.80	0.12	0.29
All	0.06	0.43	0.49	0.38*	0.36	0.26	0.19	0.40

TABLE 4.3.1d. OVER- AND UNDERESTIMATION OF CHANGE PROBABILITIES INDUSTRY LONG INVENTORY ANTICIPATIONS

	$a > 0$			$a < 0$				
	OEC	UEC	TPE	OEC	UEC	TPE	OEC	UEC
Long Inventory Anticipations								
Durables								
Iron and steel	0	0.56	0.44	0.40t	0.40	0.20	0.21	0.47
Nonferrous metals	0.17t	0.17	0.58	0.43*	0.29	0.29	0.26*	0.21
Electrical machinery	0	0.73	0.27	0.63*	0.25	0.13	0.26	0.53
Nonelectrical machinery	0	0.33	0.58	0.71*	0.29	0	0.26	0.32
Motor vehicles	0.08	0.17	0.75	0.43*	0.29	0.29	0.21t	0.21
Transportation equipment	0.13	0.38	0.50	0.55*	0.45	0	0.37	0.42
Other durables	0.08	0.62	0.31	0.50*	0.33	0.17	0.21	0.53
All	0.06	0.42	0.49	0.52*	0.34	0.14	0.26	0.38
Nondurables								
Food and beverages	0.11	0.78	0.11	0.90*	0.10	0	0.53*	0.42
Textiles	0.10	0.70	0.10	0.67*	0.33	0	0.37	0.53
Paper	0	0.46	0.46	0.33	0.67	0	0.11	0.53
Chemicals	0.07	0.64	0.29	0.80*	0.20	0	0.26	0.53
Petroleum	0.13	0.63	0.25	0.73*	0.18	0.09	0.47*	0.37
Rubber	0.09	0.64	0.27	0.38t	0.38	0.25	0.21	0.53

Other nondurables	0.09	0.55	0.27	0.50*	0.38	0.13	0.26	0.47
All	0.08	0.62	0.26	0.63*	0.30	0.07	0.32	0.48
Long Inventory Anticipations, Seasonally Adjusted								
Durables								
Iron and steel	0	0.80	0.20	0.33	0.44	0.22	0.16	0.63
Nonferrous metals	0	0.18	0.82	0.38t	0.38	0.25	0.16	0.26
Electrical machinery	0.07	0.40	0.53	0.25	0.75	0	0.11	0.47
Nonelectrical machinery	0	0.33	0.67	0.57*	0.43	0	0.21	0.37
Motor vehicles	0	0.33	0.67	0.57*	0.14	0.29	0.21	0.26
Transportation equipment	0.11	0.33	0.56	0.50t	0.50	0	0.32	0.42
Other durables	0	0.46	0.54	0.50t	0.50	0	0.16	0.47
All	0.02	0.40	0.57	0.45*	0.43	0.12	0.19	0.41
Nondurables								
Food and beverages	0	0.20	0.80	0.75*	0	0.25	0.16t	0.16
Textiles	0	0.06	0.94	0.67*	0.33	0	0.11t	0.11
Paper	0.06	0.31	0.63	0.67*	0.33	0	0.16	0.32
Chemicals	0	0.31	0.69	0.67*	0	0.33	0.11	0.26
Petroleum	0.15*	0.08	0.77	0.83*	0.17	0	0.37*	0.11
Rubber	0	0.46	0.54	0.17	0.67	0.17	0.05	0.53
Other nondurables	0.08	0.17	0.75	0.43*	0.29	0.29	0.21t	0.21
All	0.04	0.23	0.73	0.56*	0.28	0.16	0.17	0.24

TABLE 4.3.2. OVER- AND UNDERESTIMATION OF CHANGE, INDIVIDUAL FIRM SALES PROBABILITIES

		$a > 0$			$a < 0$			
	OEC	UEC	TPE	OEC	UEC	TPE	OEC	UEC
Short sales anticipations								
Nonferrous metals	0.32	0.42	0.26	0.30	0.40	0.28	0.31	0.41
Electrical machinery	0.42	0.43	0.16	0.36	0.38	0.26	0.39	0.40
Nonelectrical machinery	0.42*	0.40	0.17	0.33t	0.33	0.35	0.38*	0.37
Chemicals	0.38	0.49	0.13	0.45*	0.40	0.16	0.41	0.44
Petroleum	0.33	0.43	0.23	0.31	0.37	0.30	0.32	0.41
Short sales anticipations, seasonally adjusted								
Nonferrous metals	0.36*	0.35	0.29	0.25	0.35	0.40	0.31	0.35
Electrical machinery	0.40*	0.33	0.27	0.30	0.32	0.38	0.36*	0.32
Nonelectrical machinery	0.31	0.51	0.18	0.21	0.37	0.42	0.26	0.45
Chemicals	0.30	0.51	0.19	0.28	0.46	0.25	0.29	0.49
Petroleum	0.31	0.47	0.22	0.27	0.38	0.35	0.29	0.43
Long sales anticipations								
Nonferrous metals	0.33	0.39	0.26	0.27	0.34	0.39	0.30	0.37
Electrical machinery	0.45*	0.41	0.15	0.33	0.36	0.30	0.39t	0.39
Nonelectrical machinery	0.46*	0.36	0.17	0.25	0.31	0.44	0.38	0.34
Chemicals	0.34	0.49	0.17	0.40*	0.38	0.21	0.37	0.44
Petroleum	0.32	0.44	0.24	0.28	0.41	0.31	0.30	0.43
Long sales anticipations, seasonally adjusted								
Nonferrous metals	0.30	0.36	0.34	0.15	0.27	0.57	0.25	0.32
Electrical machinery	0.45*	0.32	0.23	0.36*	0.25	0.39	0.41*	0.29
Nonelectrical machinery	0.44*	0.36	0.21	0.21	0.26	0.53	0.35*	0.32
Chemicals	0.32	0.38	0.31	0.31*	0.24	0.46	0.31	0.33
Petroleum	0.31	0.40	0.29	0.23	0.35	0.42	0.28	0.38

Note. Symbols * and "t" are defined on Table 4.3.1. For short anticipations, a total of 204 forecasts were examined for nonferrous metals, 367 for electrical machinery, 355 for nonelectrical machinery, 445 for chemicals and 485 for petroleum. Approximately 5% more observations were available on long forecasts.

Several additional points stand out when the characteristics of firm forecasts are compared with the summary industry statistics. First, the relative frequency of over- and underestimation of change in the individual industry aggregates does not constitute an accurate reflection of the extent to which firms in that industry actually err in either direction. Thus, the statistics compiled from the industry aggregates suggest that the highest incidence of change overestimation occurs in the short run sales forecasts of petroleum, unadjusted for seasonal movements; specifically, we estimate that $P(\text{OEC}) = 0.59$. Contrast this figure with our finding that the individual petroleum firm typically overestimates 32 percent of the time, which is not an exceptional record relative to the performance of individual firms in the four other industries for which data are available. Second, we note that in contrast to the aggregate industry level data, the process of seasonal adjustment does not have a consistent tendency to accentuate the tendency toward change underestimation. Perhaps this strange tendency of the aggregate figures can be dismissed as a mere statistical artifact.

4.3.2 Regression Analysis of Change Underestimation

Let us consider the nature of the line of regression relating predicted and actual change. If we denote the relative prediction error by $\Psi_t = (P_t - A_t)/A_{t-1}$, while p_t and a_t are again the predicted and actual relative change, we have

$$p_t - a_t = \Psi_t \tag{3.1}$$

Now suppose that $\Psi_t = \beta_0 + (\beta_1 - 1)a_t + \epsilon_t$, where $E(\epsilon_t) = 0$. Then we may write

$$p_t = \beta_0 + \beta_1 a_t + \epsilon_t \tag{3.2}$$

If it turns out that $\beta_0 = (1 - \beta_1)\bar{a}$, the mean of the time series of predictions will equal the mean of actual changes (i.e., $\bar{p} = \bar{a}$) and it will seem reasonable to conclude that forecasters are neither perennially optimistic nor pessimistic. Also, it seems reasonable to define underestimation of change as the condition $0 \leq \beta_1 < 1$. Note that this concept of change underestimation is not identical to the frequency concept employed in the preceding section; thus, if $\beta_0 = 0$ and $\beta_1 = 1$, we might find an excessive number of points on one side or the other of the perfect forecasting line if ϵ_t is not symmetrically distributed.

Now consider the regression:

$$p_t = b_0 + b_1 a_t + e_t \tag{3.3}$$

It is tempting to conclude that underestimation is present when we observe the least squares regression coefficient b_1 to be less than unity. This is indeed reasonable for one particular specification of the stochastic properties of the disturbance ϵ_t; that is, *if* ϵ_t is distributed independently of a_t, then $\beta = 1$ implies $E(b_1) = 1$.[22]

While we shall see that the required independence condition may conceivably be satisfied if the forecasts are derived from a market survey, it is essential to recognize the circumstances in which the independence condition will be violated. Suppose, for example, that the raw market survey data is subjected to linear adjustment in accordance with the procedure described in Section 4.2.2. From equations 2.5 and 2.6 we note that $\text{cov}(\hat{p}a) = d\sigma_a^2$. Then we obviously have:

$$\text{plim}\,(b_1) = \text{plim}\left[\frac{\text{cov}\,(\hat{p}a)}{\sigma_a^{\;2}}\right] = d \tag{3.4}$$

Observe that with the raw sample survey data d is unity and regression equation 3.3 may be used to test for change underestimation. But if the raw forecasts are subject to optimal linear correction we will have, by 2.10, $d = d^0 = \sigma_a^2/(\sigma_a^2 + \sigma_\epsilon^2) < 1$. In this situation, the application of regression 3.3 will be likely to suggest change overestimation.

Now consider a forecast that is derived with the aid of an appropriately specified econometric model rather than from a customer survey. Under this alternative specification of the distribution of ϵ_t, it is appropriate to consider the actual realization as the dependent variable:

$$a_t = b_0' + b_1'p_t + e_t' \tag{3.5}$$

In terms of this regression, it is tempting to state that underestimation of change is occurring whenever $b_1' > 1$. Since $1/b_1'$ is a consistent estimate of β_1 under this alternative specification of the stochastic properties of ϵ_t, this is a reasonable interpretation.[23]

A serious ambiguity arises, however, if the actual realizations are regressed on a sample survey forecast subjected to optimal correction. We will have

$$\text{plim}\,(b_1') = \frac{\text{cov}(pa)}{\sigma_p^{\;2}} = \frac{d^0\sigma_a^{\;2}}{\sigma_a^{\;2} + \sigma_\epsilon^{\;2}} = d^{0^2} < 1 \tag{3.6}$$

This suggests *over*estimation of change.

[22] If $\beta_0 = 0$ because $\bar{p} = \bar{a}$ as well as $\beta_1 = 1$, then the regression may be run without the intercept and it will still be true that $E(b_1) = 1$.

[23] We note that $E(b_1') = 1/\beta_1$ if ϵ_t is distributed independently of $p_{t'}$ for all t and t'; this condition would not be satisfied if the predictions were generated by a model utilizing lagged values of actual realizations. Even if this condition is satisfied, however, we do not have $E(1/b_1') = \beta_1$; after all, harmonic and arithmetic averages are not identical. But it is nonetheless true that $\text{plim}\,(1/b_1') = \beta_1$.

The appropriate test for underestimation of change would be obvious if there existed *a priori* information establishing that either regression 3.3 or 3.5 is specified correctly. Unfortunately, either extreme seems plausible and there is no obvious way of resolving the issue empirically. We shall see, however, that in the absence of such information, something may still be said concerning the phenomenon of change underestimation, although a certain ambiguity remains. Consider the empirical evidence on short sales anticipations for aggregate data presented in the last two columns of Table 4.2.1a. We see that for the iron and steel industry, $b_1' = 1.193$ and $b_1 = 0.812$. Since $b_1' > 1$ and $b_1 < 1$, both suggest underestimation of change; the sample evidence unambiguously implies that this phenomenon characterizes short sales expectations in this industry.[24] In contrast, we find that for the food and beverage industry $b_1' = 0.752$ and $b_1 = 1.057$; again the evidence is unambiguous, although this time it points in the direction of change overestimation. But ambiguities can and do arise when both b_1' and b_1 are less than unity, as is the case for short term aggregate motor vehicle forecasts ($b_1' = 0.993$ and $b_1 = 0.990$). What we have here is $S_p \doteq S_a$, so that Theil's VARP $\doteq 0$ and we necessarily have the ambiguous case of $b_1' \doteq b_1 < 1$.

The evidence at both the firm and the industry level of aggregation is summarized on Table 4.3.3. In columns headed "$b_1' > 1$" we report the number of instances in which change is unambiguously underestimated. Columns headed "$b_1 > 1$" indicate unambiguous change overestimation. The columns headed by a "?" reveal the extent to which the answer to the issue of change underestimation is ambiguous because both regression coefficients are less than unity. Ambiguities obviously predominate, particularly at the firm level. Although, for seven out of fourteen industries, the evidence points toward change underestimation in the aggregate predictions of short-run sales developments, the vast majority of the individual firms yielded ambiguous results.

Since aggregation appears to suppress the degree of ambiguity displayed by the predictions of individual firms, it is conceivable that this aggregation effect partially explains the contrast between our results and the more decisive suggestion of change underestimation reported by earlier investigators who studied forecasts of macroeconomic variables and aggregate *ex ante* data derived from summing individual firm forecasts. For example, Theil [1961, p. 179] concluded:

> [W]hether there is any tendency towards underestimation of changes depends on the criterion chosen; but . . . we have observed this bias even under the "strongest" of the criteria which we considered, viz., in the sense of the regression of actual on predicted changes.

[24] Since $b_1' b_1 = r^2 \leq 1$, $b_1' > 1$ implies $b_1 < 1$.

TABLE 4.3.3. UNDERESTIMATION OF CHANGE—REGRESSION RESULTS

	Short Anticipations			Long Anticipations		
	$b_1' > 1$	$b_1 > 1$	?	$b_1' > 1$	$b_1 > 1$	?
Aggregate data						
Sales anticipations	7	2	5	4	1	9
Inventory anticipations	9	1	4	10	1	3
Individual firm data—sales anticipations						
Nonferrous metals	1	2	6	1	0	8
Electrical machinery	2	5	10	0	1	16
Nonelectrical machinery	2	1	13	3	0	13
Chemicals	7	1	12	4	0	16
Petroleum	2	1	17	4	2	14
Total	14	10	58	12	3	67
Individual firm data—total inventories						
Nonferrous metals	1	0	9	1	0	9
Electrical machinery	0	0	17	1	0	16
Nonelectrical machinery	1	0	15	1	0	15
Chemicals	1	0	19	4	0	16
Petroleum	1	1	18	2	0	18
Total	4	1	78	9	0	74
Individual firm data—finished goods inventory						
Nonferrous metals	0	0	8	2	0	6
Electrical machinery	1	1	12	2	1	11
Nonelectrical machinery	2	0	12	2	1	11
Chemicals	2	1	13	6	0	10
Petroleum	1	1	17	1	1	17
Total	6	3	62	13	3	55

Note. Columns headed "$b_1' > 1$" unambiguously indicate change underestimation while "$b_1 > 1$" indicate unambiguous overestimation; the "?" columns reveal the extent of ambiguity.

Since our sample does not yield decisive results, the question of whether firms typically over- or underestimate change may now be said to depend upon how one elects to define the concept; alternatively, it may be viewed as hinging upon certain unknown properties of the distribution of ϵ.

It is necessary to concede that the results reported in Table 4.3.3 are subject to sampling error. Unfortunately, the distributions of the two regression coefficients, b_1 and b_1', depend critically upon the properties of the random variable ϵ_t. If it is indeed permissible to assume, as part of the maintained hypothesis, that ϵ is distributed independently of p_t, a simple F test can be utilized to investigate the null hypothesis that $\beta_0 = 0$ and $\beta_1 = 1$ in equation 3.2. Our application of this test at the 5 percent level to individual firm data led to the rejection of the null hypothesis at least one third of the time. While this result casts suspicion on the conjecture that firms neither over- nor underestimate change, it is quite possible that the much too frequent rejection of the null hypothesis arises from a failure of ϵ to be distributed independently of p_t. Note also that the evidence presented on Table 4.3.3 suggests that it is not reasonable to assume that $\beta = 1$ *and* ϵ is distributed independently of either a_t or p_t. If $\beta = 1$ and if ϵ were distributed independently of a_t, we would find $b_1 > 1$ approximately half the time; in fact, this is rather a rare event. Similarly, the phenomenon $b_1' > 1$ is sufficiently rare to lead us to reject the hypothesis that $\beta = 1$ *and* ϵ is distributed independently of p_t. In fact, it is quite conceivable that $\beta = 1$ but that the presence of random measurement errors in observing both a and p mean that ϵ_t is not distributed independently of either the realization or the prediction.

4.4 MARKET SHARE DECOMPOSITION

Business firms concerned about their performance relative to that of other firms in their industry often focus attention upon their share-of-market as well as sales volume.[25] Fluctuations in a firm's market-share may reveal the extent to which changes in fortune result from the strengths and limitations of the firm's marketing strategy and to what extent they result from factors external to the firm that are buffeting the entire industry. Furthermore, a popular forecasting strategy is first to attempt to forecast what the future has in store for the industry and then to estimate the fraction of this total market that the firm can expect to corner. It is natural, therefore, to inquire to what extent the errors made by a firm in forecasting its sales volume arise from difficulties in predicting industry volume and to what extent they stem from the problems involved in determining market-share.

[25] Trends in market share held by the dominant firms in an industry are often regarded by economists as a measure of the extent of market imperfection. Obviously, such considerations are outside the scope of this study. Furthermore, we are not concerned with the "market-shares solution" of the oligopoly problem; according to this model, a "following" firm may attempt to preserve a fixed share of total sales of a differentiated product regardless of the effects of its actions on short-run profits. While it is sometimes said that fear of antitrust action constrains efficient firms from attempting to increase market share, the concern then is obviously with trends rather than with short-run fluctuations.

Market-share forecasting is a topic of particular interest for our study because it is conceivable that this type of predictive strategy might explain certain characteristics of sales forecast errors. It will be remembered that we found in Chapter 3.4.2 that company sales predictions are not as precise as aggregate industry forecasts obtained by summing the predictions made by individual firms, even when adjustment is made for the difficulty of the forecasting task by utilizing naive forecasts as a standard of comparison. It seems reasonable to conjecture that this phenomenon occurs because firms are quite sophisticated at forecasting industry developments but resort to forecasting same-share-as-last-period in predicting movements in company sales; in other words, the representative firm may simply predict that sales volume will change proportionately to the change it anticipates in total industry sales. This approach, or any simple technique for projecting market-share, is likely to yield substantial errors in the firm's forecast because market-shares are subject to violent fluctuation.[26] Nonetheless, the summing of the individual firm forecasts may still yield a quite precise predictor of industry developments because the errors in forecasting share may roughly offset each other. That is, the resulting industry forecast will be a weighted average of the industry sales forecasts made by the individual firms, with each firm's forecast of industry developments being weighted by its anticipated market share.[27]

The question of market share decomposition is also of interest with regard to the issue of change underestimation. It will be recalled from Table 4.3.3 that the regression of predicted on actual change almost always yields a slope coefficient less than unity. As mentioned in Section 4.3, this phenomenon may arise because of a lack of statistical independence between the forecast error and the actual realization. But another conjecture deserves consideration. The regression of the firm's anticipated sales change on its actual sales change may have yielded a slope coefficient less than unity because firms resort to predicting no change in their market share.

These two conjectures are interesting, but the argument is hardly conclusive. There are circumstances in which market-share can be forecast with greater precision than industry output. For example, automobile manufacturers sometimes contract to buy a specified percentage of their requirements for certain inputs from a particular supplier, although they cannot

[26] Our data for the nonelectrical machinery, nonferrous metals, and petroleum industries revealed that the standard deviations of firm shares are generally two to seven times as large as the standard deviations of aggregate industry sales; the market-shares of all except two or three firms were subject to greater fluctuation than industry sales. A programming error prevented us from obtaining evidence on the other two industries.

[27] The weights will necessarily sum to unity if each firm predicts no change in market share; with more sophisticated market share prediction procedures, this consistency requirement may not necessarily be satisfied.

predict precisely what the value of their total requirements will be. Obviously, it would be useful to resolve these issues but, unfortunately, data by firm on anticipated market share are not available.

We have found it possible to develop a procedure for testing indirectly whether the systematic prediction errors made by firms arise primarily from bias in forecasting market share or from bias in forecasting total demand for the industry's output. It will become apparent when we describe this technique that its validity rests upon the assumption that firms apply the market share procedure to the rather global (essentially 2 digit SIC) industry concepts for which we have data, rather than to smaller market segments; for example, in our application we considered data on nonelectrical machinery when, in practice, some firms who use the market-share procedure may be concerned with the aggregate sales of turret lathes while others may be concerned about their share of the market for milling machines. Furthermore, our evidence is not as extensive as we would like because part of our output was lost due to a mistake in computer programming. But we shall see that what evidence we do have suggests that, in practice, the errors made by firms do not tend to arise primarily from systematic mistakes in forecasting changes in market share.

In considering the problem of decomposing a firm's observed sales forecast into a market share and an industry aggregate forecast, it is convenient to temporarily adopt a special notation. Let $\hat{S}$ and S denote the forecast and realized industry sales, $\hat{s}$ and s the forecast and realized market share, and $\hat{S}^f$ and S^f the forecast and realized firm sales. Then we obviously have:

$$\hat{S}^f = \hat{s}\hat{S} \tag{4.1}$$

and

$$S^f = sS \tag{4.1'}$$

We do not observe $\hat{s}$ or $\hat{S}$. Now let us define the first-difference operator Δ to indicate anticipated and realized *relative* change; for example, $\Delta\hat{s} = (\hat{s} - s_{-1})/s_{-1}$ while $\Delta s = (s - s_{-1})/s_{-1}$. We then have:[28]

$$\Delta S^f = \Delta s + \Delta S + \Delta s \, \Delta S \tag{4.2}$$

and

$$\Delta \hat{S}^f = \Delta \hat{s} + \Delta \hat{S} + \Delta \hat{s} \, \Delta \hat{S} \tag{4.2'}$$

In order to decompose the forecast change into its unobserved components, let us assume that the forecast changes in industry sales and in market share

[28] To verify the first of these expressions note that

$$\Delta S^f S_{-1}{}^f = S^f - S_{-1}{}^f = sS - s_{-1}S_{-1} - (s - s_{-1})S_{-1} + s_{-1}(S - S_{-1}) + (s - s_{-1})(S - S_{-1});$$

dividing through by $S_{-1}{}^f$ now yields 4.2. To obtain the second expression, involving expectations, repeat the procedure with carets over all the nonlagged terms.

are proportional to the actual realized changes specifically, we suppose

$$\Delta\hat{S} = \alpha\,\Delta S + \epsilon \tag{4.3}$$

and

$$\Delta\hat{s} = \alpha'\,\Delta s + \epsilon' \tag{4.3'}$$

where $E(\epsilon) = E(\epsilon') = 0$. In other words, we are assuming as part of the maintained hypothesis that the systematic errors a firm makes in forecasting the change in industry sales and its market share are proportional by factors $1 - \alpha$ and $1 - \alpha'$ to the actual changes. The accuracy with which industry sales and share are predicted then depends upon α and α' and the variances of the stochastic disturbances. This procedure, similar to that used by Lovell [1961] in a study of inventory behavior, is related to the concepts of "rational" and "implicit" expectations advanced by Muth [1961] and Mills [1962]; all of these approaches will be examined in detail in Chapter 5. It is important to note now that for purposes of determining whether systematic errors occur in predicting either industry sales or market share, we can obtain an equation involving only observed variables and stochastic disturbances by substituting 4.3 and 4.3′ into 4.2′. We have:

$$\Delta\hat{S}^f = \alpha\,\Delta s + \alpha'\,\Delta S + \alpha'\alpha\,\Delta s\,\Delta S + \epsilon'' \tag{4.4}$$

where

$$\epsilon'' = (1 + \alpha\,\Delta S)\epsilon' + (1 + \alpha'\,\Delta s)\epsilon + \epsilon\epsilon'$$

Note that if firms typically predict no change in their market share, $\alpha' = \epsilon' = 0$ and the equation reduces to

$$\Delta\hat{S}^f = \alpha\,\Delta S + \epsilon \tag{4.4'}$$

The problem of estimating parameters α and α' of 4.4 is greatly simplified if the disturbances of 4.3 and 4.3′ are assumed to be distributed independently of the actual realizations, as specified by Edwin Mills in developing the concept of implicit expectations.[29]

The evidence presented on Tables 4.4.1 and 4.4.2 suggests that we should reject the hypothesis that firms typically predict no change in their market share. Quite the contrary, we observe for both short and long anticipations that, if anything, firms are more likely to understate the change in industry sales than to understate changes in their market share! Similar results were obtained when the interaction term was deleted from the regression[30] and also

[29] Obviously, Mill's hypothesis will not assure that ϵ'' of 4.4 is homoscedastic, but it will be uncorrelated with the explanatory variables.

[30] This approach is frequently invoked by econometricians on the grounds that the interaction effect is of a second order of magnitude. We also planned to run regressions in logarithms, an approach that eliminates the interaction term, but these results as well as those for the electrical machinery and chemical industry were lost as a result of programming errors; a rerun was not feasible.

TABLE 4.4.1. SHARE AND INDUSTRY DECOMPOSITION, POOLED REGRESSIONS, SHORT SALES

$\Delta SAS = \alpha_0 + \alpha' \,\Delta INDB + \alpha \,\Delta Share + \alpha\alpha' \,\Delta IND\,\Delta SHARE + \epsilon$

	Nonferrous Metals	Nonelectrical Machinery	Petroleum
$\bar{R}_2$	0.8381	0.5544	0.3718
$\bar{S}_{est}$	0.10	0.09	0.11
df	146	256	343
F	2.32	2.38	2.44
Number of firms	9	16	20
Variables			
α_0	0.015	0.020	0.012
	(0.008)	(0.007)	(0.006)
$\hat{\alpha}'$	0.634	0.597	−0.037
	(0.107)	(0.093)	(0.282)
$\hat{\alpha}$	1.026	0.677	0.631
	(0.038)	(0.038)	(0.045)
$\widehat{\alpha\alpha}'$	−0.268	0.278	−2.359
	(0.904)	(0.519)	(1.967)

TABLE 4.4.2. SHARE AND INDUSTRY DECOMPOSITION, POOLED REGRESSIONS, LONG SALES

$\Delta SAL = \alpha_0 + \alpha' \,\Delta INDB + \alpha \,\Delta Share + \alpha\alpha' \,\Delta IND\,\Delta SHARE + \epsilon$

	Nonferrous Metals	Nonelectrical Machinery	Petroleum
$\bar{R}^2$	0.6506	0.5000	0.4752
$\bar{S}_{est}$	0.14	0.12	0.15
df	161	282	363
F	1.10	1.73	2.70
Number of firms	9	16	20
Variables			
$\hat{\alpha}_0$	0.046	0.045	0.009
	(0.011)	(0.008)	(0.008)
$\hat{\alpha}'$	0.342	0.265	0.030
	(0.135)	(0.096)	(0.209)
$\hat{\alpha}$	0.600	0.599	0.688
	(0.065)	(0.037)	(0.040)
$\widehat{\alpha\alpha}'$	3.576	−0.000	−0.564
	(0.656)	(0.392)	(0.976)

when the sum of the sampled firms' sales rather than the benchmark adjusted industry aggregates were used in the regression. While it must be admitted that, at best, problems of heteroscedasticity and collinearity are present with our approach,[31] the tentative evidence suggests that there is no tendency for firms to underestimate changes in market share to a greater extent than changes in industry sales volume.

A further inference concerning the market share decomposition of sales forecasts is provided in the next section. If firms in a given industry generally tend to form their expectations by adjusting with a projected market-share factor a forecast of industry developments, we would expect to find that their forecast errors might be quite highly correlated. The tendency would be particularly strong if all the firms usually derived the industry component of their sales volume forecast from the same source. We shall see, however, that the errors that different firms make in forecasting sales are not highly correlated with each other.

4.5 WAVES OF OPTIMISM AND PESSIMISM

To the extent that managers of firms in the same industry read the same trade journals and listen to the same business analysts, they may well be induced to form the same opinions and possibly to make similar errors in judging business prospects. Furthermore, conventional wisdom may lead to like interpretations of the economic implications of political events, stock market movements, and so forth. Clearly, Pigou's proposition [1929] concerning the importance of synchronized movements in business expectations deserves empirical investigation.

The new data of the Office of Business Economics sales and inventory expectations survey now provide us with observations on short-run anticipations that permit a closer appraisal of the role that Pigou assigned to expectational errors as a major factor in the generation of cyclical fluctuations. Admittedly, the data for our study pertain only to the short-run planning horizon relevant to inventory rather than fixed investment spending. But it would seem that the short horizon errors involved in the formation of production and inventory decisions are more likely than long-run expectations to constitute a key factor in the generation of business cycles; after all, the evidence presented in Chapter 1 indicated that inventory investment is the most volatile component of total investment spending.

[31] The "implicit expectations" approach of Edwin Mills involves the assumption that the expectations error is distributed independently of the actual realization, which is convenient when the expectations variable is dependent, as in the present application. Obvious difficulties are raised if the prediction error is distributed independently of the prediction, as Muth specified in developing his concept of rational expectations.

We have already seen that expectations are rather accurate. Indeed, the degree of precision is sufficiently high to suggest that expectations data must mirror quite closely the fluctuations displayed by actual realizations; this means that sales expectations must move in waves of optimism and pessimism. Whether the *errors* in forecasting move in waves is a question deserving consideration. We noted in Chapter 3 that the effect of aggregation is to increase the apparent accuracy of forecasts relative to the precision of various naive benchmark prediction procedures. This in itself suggests that expectational errors may largely offset each other rather than move in waves. Now we shall investigate more directly the extent to which expectational errors are synchronized. First, in Section 4.5.1 we report on the extent of the correlation among the forecast errors made by different firms and industries. Then, in Section 4.5.2 we apply the technique of principal components in order to estimate the maximum extent to which a common psychological element could account for forecast errors. Our analysis is quite similar in approach to that of T. Kloek and R. Bannick [1961], who pioneered the application of principal components techniques in analyzing Munich Business Test diffusion indices on anticipated changes.[32]

4.5.1 Correlation Matrices

Some insight into the extent to which expectational errors are synchronized is provided by the matrix of correlation coefficients relating the relative forecast errors made in each industry. We correlated all 91 possible pairs of the 14 time series $x_{ti} = (\mathrm{SAS}_{ti} - \mathrm{SA}_{ti})/\mathrm{SA}_{ti}$, where i indicates the industry. Again, we computed a second 14×14 correlation matrix for long anticipations from the 14 time series $x_{ti}' = (\mathrm{SAL}_{ti} - \mathrm{SA}_{ti})/\mathrm{SA}_{ti}$. Similarly, for each of the five industries for which we had firm data, we computed the matrices of correlation coefficients revealing the relationship between the forecast errors made by each pair of firms in that industry. Thus, we computed a total of twelve matrices of correlation coefficients from our sales expectations data.

Now it is obvious that the hypothesis of waves of expectational errors implies that these correlation coefficients should be large. But large relative to what? The null hypothesis of zero correlation might be tested. However, rejection of the null hypothesis would not suffice to establish that waves of optimistic and pessimistic errors constitute an essential element of the business cycle. Since the business cycle is characterized by the common experience of periods of prosperity and slump, actual sales are correlated. This means that even if businessmen were to form their expectations in complete isolation from each other and without consulting common news media, we would not

[32] The motivation we present in the following section for the use of principal components is quite different from that of Kloek and Bannick.

find a complete absence of any relationship among their forecasts. And if businessmen form their expectations by simple projections from past experience, one would find, as a consequence of the cycle rather than a cause, that their forecast errors are highly correlated. The essential question, then, is whether the observed correlation among forecast errors is higher than one would expect to be generated as a result of the common cyclical experience of actual sales. In order to analyze this issue, we computed a second set of twelve correlation matrices, replacing the anticipatory variable with a naive projection of no change that is, SAS_i was replaced with $SA_{i,-1}$ and SAL_i with $SA_{i,-2}$. In other words, the fundamental question to be answered is whether the interfirm and the interindustry correlation among forecast errors is substantially larger than the correlation among actual changes in economic activity; or to put it another way, would prediction errors be more highly synchronized if firms always resorted to a no-change forecast?

TABLE 4.5.1. MEAN AND FREQUENCY DISTRIBUTION OF CORRELATION COEFFICIENTS, BENCHMARK ADJUSTED INDUSTRY AGGREGATES

		Interval Midpoint[a]									
	$\bar{R}$	−0.9	−0.7	−0.5	−0.3	−0.1	0.1	0.3	0.5	0.7	0.9
Short sales anticipation	0.202	0	0	0	8	14	21	24	16	8	0
Naive comparison	0.224	1	6	5	5	9	8	21	16	13	7
Long sales anticipation	0.338	0	0	0	7	7	13	22	21	19	2
Naive comparison	0.231	0	1	4	6	15	15	20	14	10	6
Short inventory anticipation	0.050	0	1	5	13	22	20	18	10	2	0
Naive comparison	0.091	2	9	6	8	15	6	15	7	9	4
Long inventory anticipation	0.235	0	0	0	5	12	23	24	20	7	0
Naive comparison	0.223	1	7	4	7	12	5	13	18	18	6
Inventory condition	0.443	0	0	1	2	6	8	12	30	30	2

[a] All intervals are closed on the left; all except the "0.9" interval are open on the right; thus the interval "−0.7" is [−0.8, −0.6).

Summary statistics characterizing these correlation matrices are presented on Tables 4.5.1 and 4.5.2. Table 4.5.1 reveals the frequency distribution of the correlation coefficients derived from the benchmark adjusted industry data. In addition, the first column reports the average correlation between industry pairs. Observe that the naive projection procedure of predicting the same-as-last-period would lead to more closely correlated forecast errors, on the average, than the actual short sales and short inventory anticipations. Only for long sales anticipations is a higher degree of correlation provided by the actual anticipations. This suggests that with the exception of long sales anticipations, expectational errors are less highly correlated across industries than are actual sales developments. We note also, from the last row of Table

4.5.1, that the index of excess stocks provided by the inventory condition variable is much more highly correlated across industries than are either anticipations or actual sales and inventory changes.

TABLE 4.5.2. AVERAGE VALUE OF CORRELATION COEFFICIENTS, INDIVIDUAL FIRM DATA

	NFM[a]	EM	NEM	CHEM	PET
Short sales anticipation		0.062	0.040	0.041	0.078
Naive comparison		0.012	0.096	0.114	0.058
Anticipation *sa*[b]		0.012	0.218	0.210	0.102
Actual—*sa*		0.123	0.347	0.342	0.195
Long sales anticipation		0.115[a]	0.094	0.149	0.042
Naive comparison		0	0.116	0.118	0.079
Anticipation *sa*		0.084	0.077	0.166	0.024
Actual—*sa*		0.064	0.243		0.026
Short inventory anticipation	0.083	0.017	0.037	0.028	0.017
Naive comparison		0.028	0.105	0.062	0.013
Anticipation *sa*		0.074	0.145	0.094	0.014
Actual—*sa*		0.195	0.279	0.364	0.037
Long inventory anticipation	−0.005	−0.029	−0.005	0.009	0.043
Naive comparison		0.002	0.095	0.069	0.038
Anticipation *sa*		0.028[a]	0.085	—[a]	0.011
Actual—*sa*		0.012	0.117	0.067	0.041
Number of firms	10	17	16	20	20

[a] Very few observations were available for these categories.
[b] *sa* denotes adjustment in advance of performing the computations with a constant additive seasonal correction procedure.

Table 4.5.2 shows that much the same holds true within each industry. Here the average correlation coefficients are reported for all firms in the five industries whenever we had sufficient data.[33] Because of the possibility

[33] Our program deleted the observations for any quarter in which any sampled firm failed to respond with the required expectational variable. In retrospect, we found that we might have obtained more complete results by deleting poor respondents from our sample entirely or computing correlation coefficients with different numbers of observations depending on the response record of only the particular pair of firms involved. But we were processing data "blind," had not fully anticipated the extent of the nonresponse problem, and did not build a sufficiently sophisticated data inspection routine into our program.

that many firms might be subject to divergent seasonal movements, which might mask the expectational relationships, we also report the results obtained with data subject to prior seasonal adjustments; in essence, the resulting statistics, denoted *sa* on the table, are partial correlation coefficients net of the effect of seasonal movements.[34]

Note that the interfirm correlations of expectations errors within the five industries are smaller than the average interindustry correlations reported on the preceding table. Most of the time, in 21 out of the 30 cases in which the data suffice to permit comparisons, we find that actual sales are more closely related than firm anticipation errors. Exceptions to this rule predominate among firms in the petroleum industry; thus, the errors of the short sales anticipation and both the short and long inventory expectations are more closely correlated than the expectational errors that would be generated by a naive forecast of no change. In electrical machinery, we find exceptions for short sales anticipations, long sales anticipations, and seasonally adjusted long inventory anticipations. However, in nonelectrical machinery the association among actual realizations is in every case stronger than the association among anticipations. In chemicals there is one exception, that of long sales anticipations.

In sum, inspection of the correlation matrices suggests that if a psychological element does play a role in explaining the generation of waves of optimistic and pessimistic error, it does not result in a much higher degree of synchronization of forecast errors than would be generated if entrepreneurs relied on a simple projection of no change.[35] Furthermore, the degree of synchronization of forecast errors is less than the interfirm and interindustry association of the discrepancies between desired and actual inventory as measured by the COND variable.

4.5.2 *Principal Components*

Since the waves of optimistic and pessimistic error are not directly observable, obvious difficulties are involved in attempting to test Pigou's proposition that this factor plays a major role in the business cycle. At best, only a limited amount of light can be shed on this problem by a purely descriptive comparison of correlation matrices. In this section, we shall show

[34] This would be precisely so if the adjustment procedure had been applied to relative changes in order to eliminate a multiplicative seasonal. In practice, however, it was more convenient to adjust for an additive seasonal by processing the raw data and computing changes from a seasonally adjusted series obtained in this way.

[35] We have not attempted to test the significance of this proposition, which would be a difficult task because the correlation coefficients, both interindustry and intraindustry interfirm, are obviously not independently distributed.

that the method of principal components can be employed to estimate the *maximum* extent to which a single psychological factor can be invoked to explain the occurrence of forecast errors. We shall confine our analysis to the industry benchmark data.

In order to state our problem more precisely, let $x_{ti} = (\text{SAS}_{ti} - \text{SA}_{ti})/\text{SA}_{ti}$ again denote the relative forecast error made in industry i at time t, and let $z_{ti} = (x_{ti} - \bar{x}_i)/S_i$ denote the normalized error, where S_i is the standard deviation of actual sales. Now let u_t denote an unobservable index of the common psychological element contributing to the generation of expectational error. If we suppose that the relation is linear we may write

$$z_{ti} = \beta_i u_t + \epsilon_{ti} \qquad \begin{matrix} t = 1, 2, \ldots T \\ i = 1, 2, \ldots N \end{matrix} \qquad (4.1)$$

where ϵ_{ti} denotes the influence of *non*psychological factors, possibly specific to industry i, that contribute to the generation of expectational errors. Note that even if u_t could be observed, there would be difficulty in estimating the coefficients β_i because of the possibility that the other determinants of expectational errors might be correlated with u_t. Nonetheless, it is interesting to speculate on the question of how much forecast errors could be reduced if each industry's β_i were made equal to zero through a magical elimination of the common psychological factor u_t.

Our estimates of the maximum proportion of the errors of forecast that may conceivably be attributed to a common psychological factor generating erroneous waves of optimism and pessimism are reported in the first column on Table 4.5.3.[36] These are upper bounds, and we see that no more than 46 percent of the variance of the long sales anticipations forecast errors can be attributed to a common factor. The corresponding figure for short sales is only 32 percent. We note that the inventory anticipations are not as well explained by a single factor. Furthermore, the "naive comparison" figures calculated from the actual sales change correlation matrices discussed in Section 4.5.1 reveal that the degree of concordance in the movement of actual sales changes is as high as that which we can attribute, as a maximum, to the sales forecast error figures.

As a first step in explaining the nature of these estimates, let $S_i{*}$ denote the variance of the forecast errors for industry i that would result, other things being equal, *if* β_i were zero in equation 4.1. We note that without this magical reduction, the variance of z_{ti} is unity in each industry. Thus, the average over n industries of the proportion of the variance of the errors that

[36] As explained below the second column indicates the maximum contribution that can be attributed to expectational waves if the major factor explaining simultaneous waves is some other factor.

TABLE 4.5.3. PRINCIPAL COMPONENT ANALYSIS, BENCHMARK ADJUSTED INDUSTRY AGGREGATES

	Proportion of Variance Accounted for by Components			
	(1)	(2)	(3)	(4)
Short sales anticipation	0.3206	0.1649	0.1357	0.0570
Naive comparison	0.4814	0.1882	0.1608	0.0570
Long sales anticipation	0.4621	0.1484	0.1087	0.0672
Naive comparison	0.3524	0.2764	0.1755	0.0888
Short inventory anticipation	0.1624	0.1797	0.1381	0.1189
Naive comparison	0.4687	0.2008	0.1355	0.0676
Long inventory anticipation	0.3483	0.1515	0.1250	0.1104
Naive comparison	0.5019	0.1809	0.1532	0.0649
Inventory condition	0.5309	0.1845	0.0717	0.0465

result from the psychological waves is simply $\delta = (n - \sum S_i^*)/n$. The figures presented in the first column of Table 4.5.3 are simply the maximum value of δ attainable over all possible time series u_t and slope coefficients β_i. Note that our measure "δ" of the maximum contribution of a psychological element to the generation of concordance in the occurrence of forecast errors weights all industries equally; for example, a 10 percent reduction in the variance of the forecast error in the other nondurable industry is just as important as a 10 percent reduction in the forecast error variance for iron and steel.[37]

The estimates, reported in the first column of Table 4.5.3, are derived under the assumption that waves of optimism and pessimism constitute the dominant factor in explaining the degree of coincidence in the timing of forecast errors, and that other influences are uncorrelated with the psychological element. If either of these conditions is not true, our estimate of the importance of the psychological factor is too high. Thus, the second column of data reveals the extent to which a common psychological influence contributes to forecast errors if the major part of the concordance in timing is explained by some other factor, such as the simultaneous movements of actual sales during the course of the business cycle.[38]

Because a time series measuring the influence of a common psychological stimulus upon economic forecasters is not obtainable, it is obviously not

[37] A more detailed explanation appears in the appendix to this chapter.

[38] The influence of the second factor is computed so as to maximize its ability to explain the total variance, subject to the condition that it be uncorrelated with the first factor.

possible to establish precisely how important a role such a psychological component plays in the generation of simultaneous waves of errors. But our analysis does suggest that if waves of optimistic and pessimistic error do play a role, their contribution cannot be large. At a maximum, the common psychological influence, the unobserved time series u_t, could account for less than half of the variance of the errors made in forecasting long sales movements. We note an interesting fact from the naive comparisons based on the correlations of actual changes across firms and industries; the degree of synchronization among forecast errors, whatever its cause, is no greater, and indeed usually less, than would occur if entrepreneurs ignored all external stimuli and always projected as their forecast the continuation of current developments.

4.6 SUMMARY AND CONCLUSIONS

Certain systematic elements have been found to characterize forecast errors. To some extent, these elements are offsetting. Thus, we found that while some firms are perennial optimists in forecasting sales developments, others are perennial pessimists and the two tendencies appear to cancel out in the aggregate. Because of this tendency of the peculiarities of individual firms to offset each other, our inspection of aggregate figures for the fourteen industries did not reveal any significant tendency toward either perennial optimism or pessimism with short sales anticipations. For long anticipations, however, the industry aggregates suggest a significant degree of perennial optimism in iron and steel, electrical machinery, and rubber. However, the tendency to underestimate inventories appears as an almost universal characteristic of business forecasting that manifests itself in the aggregate as well as in the data of individual firms. This bias may be a manifestation of Foss's controller effect: the questionnaire may typically be filled out by accounting personnel who are overly optimistic in hoping that lower carrying costs can be realized by reducing inventories.

Another systematic characteristic concerns a tendency for the variance of forecasts to be less than the variance of sales. We found that for only about one third of the firms did the variance of the anticipations exceed the variance of realizations. Examination of the aggregate data revealed that only for the food and beverage and the petroleum industries are the variances of the forecasts greater than the variances of the realizations. There are several reasons why expectations may fluctuate less than reality. For example, forecasts made with an appropriate econometric model will have a smaller variance than actual realizations. We did note, however, that forecasts derived from market surveys may have a variance greater than the realization. But again, if the predictions obtained from a market survey are subjected to optimal linear correction in order to incorporate historical information, the corrected market survey forecast will also have a variance less than that of actual realizations. For these reasons, we were not surprised to find, in terms of one of Theil's procedures for decomposing forecast errors (equation 2.3′), that his VARP term is generally not zero.

A third systematic tendency, discussed in Section 4.3, involves underestimation of changes. More often than not, firms predict too small an increase when the market for their product is improving and overestimate sales volume when the market is falling off. The frequency of change underestimation is particularly pronounced in seasonally adjusted electrical machinery and chemical aggregates. While it is true that change underestimation characterizes the sales forecasts of individual firms, the process of aggregation serves to exaggerate the effect. It has sometimes been suggested, particularly with reference to the Railroad Shippers' Forecast data, that change underestimation in aggregate data manifests itself because many firms provide a "no-change" response, but this is not the case with our data. We find that the "no-change" response is indeed a rare phenomenon.

The phenomenon of change underestimation was also studied with linear regression. In the majority of applications, the regression of the predicted change on the realization yielded a coefficient less than unity. This type of evidence has sometimes been regarded as indicative of change underestimation. In fact, however, the situation is ambiguous. Indeed, we found that when the realizations were regressed on the predicted changes, the slopes were usually less than unity, suggesting over- rather than underestimation of change. Unfortunately this ambiguity could not be resolved because of difficulties involved in specifying the stochastic properties of the error term. We noted, however, that if VARP is small, this type of ambiguity is almost certain to occur.

A quite different type of systematic error was considered in Section 4.4. There we investigated the possibility that firms derive their sales forecasts by multiplying predictions of total industry sales by their current market share. We pointed out that an aggregate of such forecasts might be quite precise even if inherent difficulties in forecasting market share meant that the firm forecasts were very inaccurate. This effect would be particularly pronounced if firms presumed that their market-share would remain constant. If it were true that firms typically formed their sales anticipations in this way, it would mean that a quite different approach from that employed in the next chapter would be required in analyzing the way in which sales anticipations are generated. Unfortunately, anticipated market-share cannot be observed directly. The proxy procedure we employed suggested that, in practice, firms do not suffer from a systematic tendency to underestimate changes in market-share by a greater extent than they underestimate total industry sales changes. In particular, the evidence suggested that firms do not simply project the maintenance of current market-share.

A final type of systematic error concerned the phenomenon of waves of optimism and pessimism discussed by members of the psychological school of business cycle theorists. Such waves would be quite likely to be generated if firms break aggregate industry forecasts down into a prediction of their own sales on the basis of an extrapolation of market share. Our application of the technique of principal components suggested that a single psychological element could explain as much as 32 percent of the variance of short sales anticipation errors and 46 percent of long sales anticipation errors. These are fairly large proportions, but we showed that they are no larger than might be expected from the degree of concordance in the movement of actual sales in different industries. That is to say, if expectations were simply a naive projection of same-sales-as-last-period, the resulting expectational errors made by different firms would be as closely related as actual prediction errors are in practice. This result casts serious doubt upon the Pigouvian notion concerning the critical nature of simultaneous waves of optimistic and pessimistic forecasting errors.

Statistical Appendix

The procedure for finding $\max_{u_t, \beta_i} \delta$ of Table 4.5.3 is that of principal components, although the application is quite different from the way it is customarily employed in econometric analysis.[39] The first thing to note is that the unobserved time series u_t measuring the common psychological element of expectational error may be taken without loss of generality to have unit variance and zero mean.[40]

Next, observe that given any time series u_t, its role in explaining the movements of z_{ti} will be maximized if we estimate β_i by the method of least squares, for this minimizes the contribution of the ϵ_{ti} to the variance of the errors. To the extent that the two unobserved time series u_t and ϵ_{ti} are, in fact, correlated, this procedure will overstate the contribution of the u_t. With this qualification in mind, we are using

$$\hat{\beta}_i = \sum_t u_t z_{ti} / \sum u_t^2 = \sum_t u_t z_{ti},$$

where the second equality follows from the normalization of u_t; in matrix notation we can write $\hat{\beta}' = \text{row}\,(\hat{\beta}_i) = u'Z$, where $u' = \text{row}\,(u_t)$ and $Z = [z_{ti}]$. The contribution of the psychological factor u_t to $S_{z_i}^2$, the variance of forecast errors in the ith industry, is $\hat{\beta}_i^2 \sigma_{u_i}^2 = \hat{\beta}_i^2$, and the total contribution of u_t to the variance of forecasts is simply $\sum_i \hat{\beta}_i^2 = \hat{\beta}'\hat{\beta} = u'ZZ'u$. We wish, then, to find the T component time series vector u that maximizes $\hat{\beta}'\hat{\beta} = u'ZZ'u$ subject to the constraint $u'u = 1$; so we construct the Lagrangian expression $L = u'(ZZ')u - \lambda(u'u - 1)$ and obtain by the rules of matrix

[39] For a discussion of a variety of alternative interpretations of the principal components technique see Tintner [1952, pp 102–14]; also T. W. Anderson [1958]. The usual econometric application involves the mechanical replacement of a set of explanatory variables with a smaller set of orthogonal components in advance of running a regression; the implications of this *ad hoc* approach with respect to problems of parameter estimation and hypothesis testing have not been fully investigated.

[40] For example, if $\sum u_t = 0$ but $\sum u_t^2 = \sigma_u^2 \neq 1$, we simply use the normalized series $u_t^* = u_t/\sigma_u$ and replace β_i with $\beta_i^* = \beta_i \sigma_u$.

differentiation the requirement

$$\frac{\partial L}{\partial u} = 2ZZ'u - 2\lambda u = 0 \tag{4.2}$$

as a necessary condition for a maximum. But this implies

$$[ZZ' - \lambda I]u = 0 \tag{4.3}$$

That is, the time series u is one of the characteristic vectors and λ the corresponding root of the $T \times T$ matrix ZZ'. Furthermore, premultiplying by u' reveals that since $u'u = 1$ the latent root λ is actually $\beta'\beta$, the expression to be maximized, as well as the Lagrangian coefficient. Obviously, we are interested in the largest root λ of 4.3. While this could in principle be calculated from the $T \times T$ singular matrix ZZ', we note that if we premultiply 4.3 by Z' we have

$$Z'[ZZ' - \lambda I]u = [Z'Z - \lambda I]Z'u = [Z'Z - \lambda I]\hat{\beta}, \tag{4.4}$$

since $Z'u = \hat{\beta}$.[41] Thus, λ is the largest latent root and $\hat{\beta}$ the corresponding latent vector of the $n \times n$ matrix $Z'Z$, which is the $n \times n$ correlation matrix analyzed in Section 4.5.1.

[41] This exploits a duality aspect of the principal component approach linking the time-series and cross-sectioned aspects of the problem of explaining variations in forecast errors.

CHAPTER 5

The structure of expectations

5.1 INTRODUCTION

How anticipations are generated has been a topic of continued speculation and debate. Assumptions concerning the structure explaining the generation of expectations are frequently invoked in constructing dynamic models. Thus, in the familiar cobweb cycle model of price adjustment, it is assumed that producers expect the current price to prevail in the next period. Again, in elementary models of the inventory cycle it is assumed that producers expect to be able to market the same quantity as was actually sold in the preceding period. The effects of alternative assumptions concerning the way in which expectations are generated upon the stability of such models has been the subject of intensive theoretical analysis.[1]

A number of case studies describe the procedures actually used by business firms in forecasting demand conditions.[2] Wide variations in business practice rather than a single law of expectations formation are suggested by these studies. Some firms say they rely upon a jury of executive opinion in deriving their sales forecast. Other firms use a detailed survey of customer plans, either

[1] For example, Nerlove [1958a] and Mills [1961] have analyzed the implications of adaptive expectations in elaborating upon the cobweb model of price determination. Mills [1962] and Muth [1961] have considered the role of "implicit" and "rational" expectations within the same context. Enthoven and Arrow [1956] and Arrow and Nerlove [1958] have considered the implications of alternative price expectations formulation assumptions within the context of general equilibrium models. Lovell [1962] and Foster [1963] have considered the effects of alternative assumptions concerning the structure generating sales expectations upon the stability of multisector models of the inventory cycle.

[2] See National Industrial Conference Board [1963] or Butler and Kavesh [1966] for discussions of sales forecasting techniques.

as reported by a random sample survey or as compiled from reports prepared by the firm's own salesmen. Brand managers are often expected to provide useful predictions. The more sophisticated firm may consider a variety of measures of general economic conditions in predicting demand for its own product; many firms use quite mechanical procedures to extrapolate apparent trends in recent sales volume. The National Industrial Conference Board reports that many firms prefer to average a variety of approaches rather than to rely upon any single technique. Obviously, it can at best be only as a first approximation that any model sufficiently simple to be employed in dynamic model construction can be said to capture the essence of the forecasting process.

Given the complexity of the phenomenon, one might hope that prior empirical investigations would have served to eliminate a number of likely models from further consideration. But in practice, empirical studies have not served to contract the range of admissible assumptions, in part because of the difficulties involved in observing *ex ante* variables. Consequently, econometricians are frequently compelled to invoke as part of the maintained hypothesis an explicit assumption as to how anticipations are generated. This approach underlies much of the recent empirical work on consumption, fixed investment, and inventory behavior.[3] Although a large variety of alternative hypotheses concerning the generation of anticipations have been employed, both in the construction of dynamic models and in econometric investigations, the data on actual expectations required for the direct testing of alternative models explaining the generation of anticipations have been hard to come by.

The new expectations data provided by the OBE survey offers an opportunity to investigate a number of controversial issues that have not been exhaustively tested against appropriate evidence. We shall consider first, in Section 5.2, the extrapolative expectations framework used in models of the inventory cycle, as elaborated upon by Robert Ferber [1953] in his empirical analysis of the railroad shippers' carload anticipation data. In addition to replicating on new data Ferber's tests of his original model, we shall also inquire whether the property of regressivity that he observed manifests itself also in our new data. Then, in Section 5.3, we shall confront Nerlove's [1958a] adaptive (exponential smoothing) hypotheses of expectation formation with the new observations on actual anticipations. In addition, we must

[3] Watts [1958], Ando and Modigliani [1963], and Zellner, Huang, and Chau [1965] invoked explicit assumptions about the formulation of income expectations in analyzing consumption behavior. Cagan [1956] used the adaptive expectations model in his classic study of inflation. Dale Jorgenson [1963] assumed static expectations about future sales volume and price levels in his empirical studies of fixed investment. Enthoven [1956], Lovell [1962, 1968], Johnston [1962], Ladd [1963], and Ball and Drake [1963] are but a few of the investigators who made explicit assumptions about the formulation of expectations in analyzing inventory investment.

consider conjectures of Eisner [1958] and Meiselman [1962] concerning the way in which surprise leads to the revision of initial expectations.

Whether expectations possess the "rational" or "implicit" properties attributed to them by Muth [1961] and Mills [1959, 1962] will be considered in Section 5.4. Although neither Muth's "rational" nor Mills' "implicit" expectations concepts constitute hypotheses concerning the structure by which expectations are generated, they do suggest that actual realizations might be employed appropriately by the econometrician as proxies for anticipations when *ex ante* concepts cannot be directly observed. Because of its simplicity, the validity of this proxy procedure will receive careful consideration. Since the analysis of all these issues proves rather involved, in part because of the availability of evidence at a number of different levels of aggregation, a convenient summary of the main implications that we have derived from the empirical investigations is presented in Section 5.5.

Before proceeding to this sequence of topics, we must note a common feature underlying the behavioral models we shall be considering. All attribute to the forecaster a "technical" strategy of attempting to predict the firm's future sales in terms of its own past sales history. This permits a much simpler model than might otherwise be required, and from a purely econometric point of view, it is convenient research strategy to be able to assume that whatever correlation exists between the forecasts of any pair of firms arises because of similarities in sales history; this assures that the stochastic disturbances for different firms are independently distributed with both the Ferber and the adaptive expectations model. The assumption might be open to question if we had found in Chapter 4.5.1 that there exists a stronger relationship among the forecast errors made by different firms than might arise from a same-as-last-period projection. Obviously, doubt concerning the validity of our research strategy would appear fully justified if we had found strong evidence in Chapter 4.5.2 that individual firm forecasts are influenced by a common psychological element, as might be generated by the general acceptance of the same forecast of general business activity. Also, doubt about the appropriateness of this approach would have been created if we had found evidence that firms form their sales forecasts by preparing separate projections of market-share and aggregate industry movements. However, the evidence of the preceding chapter does not serve to cast doubt upon the conjecture that firms prepare their sales forecasts independently by projecting from their own individual experience. We do regret, however, that it has not proved feasible for us to consider the alternative possibility that producers of intermediate products generally employ an "end-use" forecasting procedure of attempting to forecast, possibly with an input-output table, the demand for their own output on the basis of information on the rate of final consumption of finished products.[4] In addition, it was not possible for us to investigate, for firms producing primarily to order, the effect of the rate of new order accumulation upon sales expectations.

5.2 FERBER'S LAW OF EXPECTATIONS FORMATION

The most elementary version of the extrapolative model states that events in the coming period will be the same as today's. In his model of the inventory cycle, Metzler [1941] elaborated upon this approach by allowing an adjustment for recently observed change. Because of the complications presented by seasonal movements, such simple models will not suffice for the empirical analysis of the structure generating short-run expectations. One possible approach would be to use seasonally adjusted data. An alternative procedure was employed by Robert Ferber [1953, 1960] in analyzing the railroad shippers' anticipations data. On the basis of interviews with a number of firms, Ferber concluded that in making forecasts, firms typically attempt to allow for seasonal movements by modifying the figure for the corresponding quarter of the previous year in the light of recently observed trend. Thus, in his empirical studies of the railroad shippers' carload *ex ante* data, Ferber attempted to exploit this knowledge of the structure of expectations rather than use seasonally adjusted data. Specifically, he tested models of the form

$$\begin{aligned} P &= \alpha + A_{-4}[\beta + \gamma(A_{-1} - A_{-5})/A_{-5}] + \epsilon \\ &= \alpha + \beta A_{-4} + \gamma A_{-4}(A_{-1} - A_{-5})/A_{-5} + \epsilon \qquad (2.1) \end{aligned}$$

where P denotes anticipated carloadings of quarter t, the exogenous variable A is actual carloadings, and ϵ is a random variable with zero expected value. Obviously, if $\alpha = \gamma = 0$ and $\beta = 1$, the equation degenerates to the prediction of no change from the corresponding quarter of the preceding year. On the other hand, if $\beta = \gamma = 1$ while $\alpha = 0$, we have $P = A_{-1}(A_{-4}/A_{-5})$, which is a static forecast of same-as-last-quarter, adjusted for the actual seasonal of last year. When Ferber [1953, p. 70] fitted equation 2.2 to the railroad shippers' forecast data, aggregated over all commodities other than farm products, he obtained for the 1927–1941 period:

$$P = 0.09 + 0.986A_{-4} + 0.43A_{-4}\frac{A_{-1} - A_{-5}}{A_{-5}} + e, \qquad R^2 = 0.972 \quad (2.2)$$

[4] For example, a steel firm may attempt to predict its sales on the basis of demand projections for automobiles, household appliances, etc. Edward Foster [1963] utilized this approach in constructing a multisector model of the inventory cycle.

On the basis of this evidence and the results of an extremely thorough application of his model to data for several individual industries,[5] Ferber [1953, p. 77] concluded that equation 2.1 constitutes "a good approximation to the law of formation of aggregate expectations."

Ferber's provocative results have not been accepted as conclusive, primarily because of the limitations of the *ex ante* data used in his study. As mentioned in Chapter 3, many economists, notably Albert G. Hart [1960], regarded the extremely inaccurate nature of the railroad shippers' forecasts as evidence that they could not constitute a valid measure of actual expectations. Our analysis of the OBE data has confirmed that the railroad shippers' forecasts grossly understate the precision with which entrepreneurs forecast sales volume. Nonetheless, we shall see that the OBE data yield results remarkably similar to those obtained by Ferber. We shall consider first the results obtained with the short anticipations; then, in Section 5.2.2 we shall report results from the long anticipation data. Finally, in Section 5.2.3, we consider the phenomenon of regressivity.

5.2.1 *Short Anticipations*

The results of running equation 2.1 on the OBE three-month anticipations data are reported on Table 5.2.1. We observe that the Ferber model does considerably better at predicting aggregate short sales anticipations for nondurable than for durable industries. Indeed, the negative value for $\bar{R}^2$ reported on the table for iron and steel reveals that for this industry the standard error of the estimate, adjusted for degrees of freedom, is larger than the variance of the dependent variable. The unsatisfactory result for steel may result from the limitations of any simple extrapolative formula in an industry that is subject to extreme disruptions from strikes. The fit is grossly unsatisfactory for both nonferrous metals and transportation equipment. On the other hand, the equation yields quite impressive results for all of the nondurable industries and is particularly strong for the aggregate nondurable series. Furthermore, interindustry differences are not marked among the nondurable industries, and the small value of the F statistic suggests that the equation obtained by pooling the data over nondurable industries is to be preferred, at least given the small number of degrees of freedom available for individual industries, to the parameter estimates obtained by treating each industry separately.

The Ferber model of expectations generation was used by Johnston [1961] in his econometric investigation of the determinants of the short-run

[5] We report certain of these industry results later in Table 5.2.5.

production decision. Because Johnston could not observe expectations directly, he substituted equation 2.1 into his behavioral equation for production in order to obtain an expression involving only observable variables. He hypothesized that $\alpha = 0$ and $\beta = 1$, but obtained implied estimates of γ from the coefficients of his production regressions. Inspection of Table 5.2.1 suggests that for those industries in which the model yields tight fits, Johnston's hypothesis that $\alpha = 0$ and $\beta = 1$ is not to be rejected. For nondurables, and for several durable industries as well, this evidence suggests that firms may simply expect the same level of sales as last year, plus about 50 to 60 percent of the change that has been observed over the immediately preceding year.

The five separate intercept regressions pooled over firms within industries are also of interest,[6] for the rather small values of the F statistics lend credence to the hypothesis that all firms within each industry have essentially the same coefficients for their expectations formation equation. The results are generally quite satisfactory. As might be expected from the regressions obtained from the aggregate industry benchmark adjusted data, nonferrous metals has the lowest value of $\bar{R}^2$. But even for this industry, Ferber's model does not appear grossly unsatisfactory.

More information was provided by computer output on the 82 individual firm regressions. The tables are too detailed to be reproduced here, but we can report that with the exception of two firms, one in electrical machinery and one in nonelectrical machinery, all the estimates of β are positive. For four firms, the estimated value of β is greater than unity. But in no case do any of the individual firm coefficients depart significantly (at the 5 percent level) from the range of zero to one. Eight firms yield a negative estimate of γ, implying that an extreme reversal of trend is typically expected; but again none of these coefficients is significant. Furthermore, a total of 65 out of 82 estimates of β are more than twice their standard error. While for the parameter γ only a minority of 36 t coefficients are greater than two, the null hypothesis that $\gamma = 0$ would have yielded only about four t statistics of this magnitude.[7] Although this suggests that the Ferber model does fairly well at the level of the individual firm, we shall see later that the Nerlove model is more satisfactory.

[6] When the intercepts are constrained to be identical for all firms in an industry the estimated value of β is very close to one. Obviously, this distortion arises because, given firms of quite different size, a β of unity emphasizes the usefulness of last period's sales in explaining interfirm differences in the current sales anticipation. The pooled regression with separate firm intercepts eliminates this distortion.

[7] More precisely, if one tests the null hypothesis at the 5% level on 100 different samples, one should expect to commit about 5 times the type I error of rejecting the null hypothesis when in fact the null hypothesis is true.

TABLE 5.2.1. FERBER EXTRAPOLATION—SHORT SALES

$$\text{ASSALE} = \alpha + \beta\,\text{SALE}_{-4} + \gamma\,\text{SALE}_{-4}\left(\frac{\text{SALE}_{-1} - \text{SALE}_{-5}}{\text{SALE}_{-5}}\right) + \epsilon$$

Durable Manufacturing Regressions

Industry	1	2	3	4	5	6	7	Aggregate	Pooled	Pooled With Separate Intercept
df	11	11	11	11	11	11	11	11	95	89
$\bar{R}^2$	−0.1752	0.1918	0.7824	0.7593	0.3049	0.0892	0.7395	0.4070	0.9335	0.9557
$\bar{S}_{est}$	491.98	48.14	189.40	324.38	1015.33	222.54	166.49	2072.00	612.49	500.28
d	1.386	2.137	1.103	1.150	2.303	1.358	2.057	1.688	1.910	1.911
Variables										
α	3812.432	1546.420	599.124	1151.702	2645.169	2735.711	248.470	17773.12	103.059	2080.265
	(525.081)	(248.335)	(852.866)	(1336.405)	(1766.320)	(1151.975)	(707.148)	(7269.967)	(148.683)	(315.734)
β	0.025	0.019	0.921	0.895	0.614	0.337	0.956	0.500	1.011	0.438
	(0.129)	(0.159)	(0.140)	(0.157)	(0.286)	(0.285)	(0.206)	(0.216)	(0.029)	(0.084)
γ	0.021	0.280	0.652	0.538	0.322	0.333	0.666	0.431	0.271	0.249
	(0.118)	(0.124)	(0.172)	(0.245)	(0.268)	(0.197)	(0.167)	(0.207)	(0.098)	(0.081)

$F = 5.00$ with 18, 77 degrees of freedom if all coefficients identical
$F = 2.28$ with 12, 77 degrees of freedom if all coefficients identical except intercepts

Nondurable Manufacturing Regressions

Industry	1	2	3	4	5	6	7	Aggregate	Pooled	Pooled With Separate Intercept
df	11	11	11	11	11	11	11	11	95	89
$\bar{R}^2$	0.8694	0.6942	0.7372	0.8509	0.7259	0.5973	0.7763	0.9150	0.9979	0.9979
$\bar{S}_{est}$	247.58	167.87	129.55	279.54	109.68	92.20	261.35	708.47	191.34	192.49
d	1.804	1.619	1.181	1.608	3.401	1.776	2.417	1.302	2.028	2.055
Variables										
α	42.713	557.102	98.622	311.573	−352.208	124.549	−732.001	−4979.581	23.481	−35.818
	(2087.766)	(808.018)	(562.356)	(875.886)	(1697.495)	(440.730)	(1217.591)	(4897.213)	(37.697)	(381.832)
β	1.005	0.855	1.014	0.980	1.050	0.953	1.132	1.123	1.013	1.021
	(0.150)	(0.215)	(0.171)	(0.117)	(0.177)	(0.284)	(0.169)	(0.105)	(0.005)	(0.053)
γ	0.833	0.626	0.411	0.659	0.510	0.770	0.202	0.626	0.649	0.581
	(0.283)	(0.162)	(0.373)	(0.199)	(0.212)	(0.228)	(0.245)	(0.190)	(0.068)	(0.080)

$F = 0.67$ with 18, 77 degrees of freedom if all coefficients identical
$F = 0.62$ with 12, 77 degrees of freedom if all coefficients identical except intercepts

(*continued*)

TABLE 5.2.1 (*continued*). FERBER EXTRAPOLATION—SHORT SALES

$$\text{ASSALE} = \alpha_f + \beta\,\text{SALE}_{-4} + \gamma\,\text{SALE}_{-4}\left(\frac{\text{SALE}_{-1} - \text{SALE}_{-5}}{\text{SALE}_{-5}}\right) + \epsilon$$

Pooled Firm Data (Separate Intercepts)

	Nonferrous Metals	Electrical Machinery	Nonelectrical Machinery	Chemicals	Petroleum
Partial $\bar{R}^2$	0.2906	0.6186	0.7632	0.7877	0.7371
$\bar{S}_{est}$	7737.6	7677.9	10139.	10713.	8598.2
df	158	282	278	347	389
F	1.18	1.77	0.98	0.96	1.27
$\bar{d}$	1.55	1.79	1.85	1.84	1.71
Number of firms	9	17	16	20	20
Variables					
β	0.489	0.756	0.879	0.902	0.877
	(0.075)	(0.043)	(0.030)	(0.029)	(0.031)
γ	0.266	0.364	0.485	0.355	0.594
	(0.062)	(0.039)	(0.040)	(0.038)	(0.042)

An alternative ratio form of equation 2.1 was also considered by Ferber [1953, p. 77]:

$$\frac{P - A_{-1}}{A_{-1}} = \beta - 1 + (\beta - \gamma)\left(\frac{A_{-4} - A_{-1}}{A_{-1}}\right) + \gamma\left(\frac{A_{-4} - A_{-5}}{A_{-5}}\right) + \frac{\epsilon}{A_{-1}} \quad (2.3)$$

If the coefficient α in equation 2.2 is zero, the two forms are equivalent. Of course, the presence of trend may well mean that this second equation will yield a smaller coefficient of multiple correlation than the first. But from the point of view of parameter estimation and hypothesis testing, it is to be preferred if, as seems likely, it satisfies the homoscedasticity requirement of the regression model; that is, the disturbance ϵ/A_{-1} rather than ϵ may have constant variance. For this reason we also consider regressions in ratio form.[8]

The results of fitting the ratio form of Ferber's model to the micro data are reported on Table 5.2.2. Ferber [1953, p. 77] obtained an $\bar{R}^2$ of 0.83 when he fitted this model to his aggregate railroad shippers' forecast data.[9] Only for the petroleum industry aggregates do we obtain an $\bar{R}^2$ of this order of magnitude from the benchmark adjusted industry aggregate data. We found that the individual firm regressions were rather unsatisfactory. Six of the nine estimated values of γ are negative for nonferrous metals, seven of seventeen for electrical machinery, ten of sixteen for nonelectrical machinery, eight of twenty for chemicals, and nine of twenty for petroleum. A total of fifteen of the estimated γ's are more than twice their standard errors, and one of these is negative. The pooled regressions, on the other hand, are reasonably satisfactory, with the obvious exception of the negative valued γ for nonferrous metals.

5.2.2 *Long Anticipations*

For purposes of explaining the anticipation series involving the longer forecast horizon, a slight modification of equations 2.1 and 2.3 is required.

[8] The problem of determining the form for which the homoscedasticity requirement will be satisfied is a difficult one that we have not attempted to surmount. In any case, however, the presence of heteroscedasticity does not in itself serve to generate biased parameter estimates; but it will distort tests of significance. Fortunately, much of our analysis is insensitive to this issue. The reader may note that while equation 2.3 contains only two parameters, we did not constrain the intercept to $\beta - 1$ in order to take advantage of this restriction and save a degree of freedom.

[9] Ferber reported only the coefficient of multiple determination, not the estimates of β and γ. While the equation he fitted differed slightly in form from our equation 2.3, a comparison of the two reveals that they yield identical $\bar{R}^2$'s.

TABLE 5.2.2. FERBER EXTRAPOLATIONS—SHORT RATIO

$$\frac{\text{ASSALE} - \text{SALE}_{-1}}{\text{SALE}_{-1}} = \beta - 1 + (\beta - \gamma)\left(\frac{\text{SALE}_{-4} - \text{SALE}_{-1}}{\text{SALE}_{-1}}\right) + \gamma\left(\frac{\text{SALE}_{-4} - \text{SALE}_{-5}}{\text{SALE}_{-5}}\right) + \frac{\epsilon}{\text{SALE}_{-1}}$$

Durable Manufacturing Regressions

Industry	1	2	3	4	5	6	7	Aggregate	Pooled	Pooled With Separate Intercept
df	11	11	11	11	11	11	11	11	95	89
$\bar{R}^2$	0.0071	0.3076	0.7002	0.7242	0.6352	0.2239	0.6659	0.4613	0.3434	0.3169
$\bar{S}_{est}$	0.1443	0.0385	0.0292	0.0309	0.1689	0.0491	0.0459	0.0639	0.1018	0.1038
d	1.733	2.147	1.623	1.768	2.267	2.429	1.683	2.217		
Variables										
$\beta - 1$	0.004	0.009	0.020	0.027	0.047	0.020	0.028	0.025	0.025	0.042
	(0.039)	(0.011)	(0.011)	(0.013)	(0.049)	(0.014)	(0.014)	(0.019)	(0.011)	(0.028)
$\beta - \gamma$	0.228	0.350	0.281	0.367	0.730	0.341	0.392	0.444	0.436	0.450
	(0.159)	(0.169)	(0.170)	(0.218)	(0.286)	(0.182)	(0.173)	(0.241)	(0.083)	(0.086)
γ	−0.084	0.011	0.554	0.361	0.215	0.088	0.741	0.210	0.046	0.041
	(0.129)	(0.174)	(0.182)	(0.211)	(0.272)	(0.211)	(0.232)	(0.229)	(0.074)	(0.076)

$F = 2.42$ with 18, 77 degrees of freedom if all coefficients identical
$F = 3.37$ with 12, 77 degrees of freedom if all coefficients identical except intercepts

Nondurable Manufacturing Regressions

Industry	1	2	3	4	5	6	7	Aggregate	Pooled	Pooled With Separate Intercept
df	11	11	11	11	11	11	11	11	95	89
$\bar{R}^2$	0.7776	0.0908	−0.1455	0.5611	0.8419	0.4458	0.7873	0.4954	0.5120	0.5268
$\bar{S}_{est}$	0.0165	0.0412	0.0196	0.0305	0.0110	0.0576	0.0361	0.0152	0.0354	0.0349
d	1.769	1.954	0.959	2.413	3.548	1.842	2.261	1.405		
Variables										
$\beta - 1$	0.009	0.004	0.022	0.023	0.013	0.033	0.031	0.016	0.019	0.016
	(0.010)	(0.012)	(0.012)	(0.015)	(0.004)	(0.017)	(0.013)	(0.008)	(0.005)	(0.010)
$\beta - \gamma$	0.254	0.255	−0.105	0.257	0.563	0.209	0.846	0.350	0.298	0.324
	(0.279)	(0.178)	(0.240)	(0.170)	(0.170)	(0.225)	(0.259)	(0.216)	(0.075)	(0.079)
γ	0.912	0.307	−0.014	0.405	0.582	0.658	0.218	0.600	0.515	0.491
	(0.269)	(0.286)	(0.208)	(0.199)	(0.196)	(0.291)	(0.245)	(0.247)	(0.089)	(0.092)

$F = 1.50$ with 18, 77 degrees of freedom if all coefficients identical
$F = 1.46$ with, 12, 77 degrees of freedom if all coefficients identical except intercepts

(continued)

TABLE 5.2.2 (*continued*). FERBER EXTRAPOLATIONS—SHORT RATIO

$$\frac{\text{ASSALE} - \text{SALE}_{-1}}{\text{SALE}_{-1}} = \beta - 1 + (\beta - \gamma)\left(\frac{\text{SALE}_{-4} - \text{SALE}_{-1}}{\text{SALE}_{-1}}\right) + \gamma\left(\frac{\text{SALE}_{-4} - \text{SALE}_{-5}}{\text{SALE}_{-5}}\right) + \frac{\epsilon}{\text{SALE}_{-1}}$$

Pooled Firm Data

	Nonferrous Metals	Electrical Machinery	Nonelectrical Machinery	Chemicals	Petroleum
$\bar{R}^2$	0.6555	0.5017	0.3700	0.7072	0.2907
$\bar{S}_{est}$	0.14	0.21	0.10	0.11	0.11
df	166	298	293	366	408
F	1.03	3.95	3.68	2.43	2.13
$\bar{d}$	1.84	1.80	1.95	1.95	1.63
Number of firms	9	17	16	20	20
Variables					
$\beta - 1$	0.045	0.055	0.042	0.051	0.025
	(0.011)	(0.013)	(0.006)	(0.007)	(0.006)
$\beta - \gamma$	0.645	0.656	0.444	0.701	0.417
	(0.036)	(0.054)	(0.041)	(0.044)	(0.043)
γ	−0.094	0.146	0.098	0.166	0.164
	(0.046)	(0.056)	(0.045)	(0.042)	(0.047)

Specifically, we consider

$$\text{ALSALE} = \alpha + \beta\text{SALE}_{-4} + \gamma\text{SALE}_{-4}\left(\frac{\text{SALE}_{-2} - \text{SALE}_{-6}}{\text{SALE}_{-6}}\right) + \epsilon \quad (2.1')$$

and

$$\frac{\text{ALSALE} - \text{SALE}_{-2}}{\text{SALE}_{-2}} = \beta - 1 + (\beta - \gamma)\frac{(\text{SALE}_{-4} - \text{SALE}_{-2})}{\text{SALE}_{-2}} + \frac{\gamma(\text{SALE}_{-4} - \text{SALE}_{-6})}{\text{SALE}_{-6}} + \frac{\epsilon}{\text{SALE}_{-2}} \quad (2.3')$$

Regressions obtained with equation 2.1′ are reported on Table 5.2.3. Inspection of industry aggregate regressions reported on this table reveals that perhaps for a majority of industries the Ferber model yields a somewhat tighter fit in explaining long anticipations than it does in explaining three-month anticipations. Again, the equation is grossly unsatisfactory for iron and steel. For nondurables, the regression obtained by pooling the data over industries, with separate intercepts, suggests that firms predict the same as the corresponding quarter of last year plus approximately 50 percent of the trend increase observed over the past year. For durables, however, interindustry differences appear more marked, and the extremely small coefficient for the trend adjustment factor is insignificant in the pooled regression.

Turning to the data for individual firms, we observe that the pooled regressions with separate intercepts yield quite satisfactory results, although γ is insignificant for nonferrous metals. Eighteen out of 82 estimated values of γ obtained in individual firm regressions were found to be more than twice their standard error in magnitude. Some 12 of the 82 γ coefficients were negative, but none of these was more than twice its standard error. Only one firm yielded a negative β. These results do not serve to cast serious doubt upon the validity of Ferber's law as an explanation of how longer sales anticipations are generated.

Regressions obtained with the ratio form of Ferber's model, equation 2.3′, are reported on Table 5.2.4. The results are somewhat more impressive than those obtained when the ratio form of Ferber's model was applied to the short anticipations data. With the exception of one nonelectrical firm, all the estimated values of γ are positive. It is, however, rather surprising to find that the implied estimate of β (that is, the sum of the second and third regression coefficients) is generally greater than one. In terms of equation 2.3′ it is seen that this may be interpreted as a perennially optimistic expectation of trend that prevails regardless of the rate of growth that has occurred in the immediately preceding year. But with this one anomaly, the results certainly serve to lend support to Ferber's law of expectations formation.

TABLE 5.2.3. FERBER EXTRAPOLATION—LONG SALES

$$\text{ALSALE} = \alpha + \beta\,\text{SALE}_{-4} + \gamma\,\text{SALE}_{-4}\left(\frac{\text{SALE}_{-2} - \text{SALE}_{-6}}{\text{SALE}_{-6}}\right) + \epsilon$$

Durable Manufacturing Regressions

Industry	1	2	3	4	5	6	7	Aggregate	Pooled	Pooled with Separate Intercept
df	14	14	14	14	14	14	14	14	116	110
$\bar{R}^2$	−0.0909	0.3559	0.8649	0.8983	0.5608	0.1997	0.6194	0.6875	0.9485	0.9647
$\bar{S}_{est}$	474.57	67.81	211.57	252.67	780.69	306.09	236.95	1506.47	531.37	439.80
d	1.685	1.650	1.146	1.604	1.692	1.281	2.088	1.178	1.434	1.706
Variables										
α	4029.863	946.287	1467.883	2420.453	2360.992	2270.340	489.979	15739.02	188.985	1501.559
	(605.024)	(198.432)	(503.363)	(566.627)	(977.501)	(836.706)	(659.169)	(3549.670)	(116.040)	(222.924)
β	0.039	0.420	0.806	0.767	0.711	0.467	0.920	0.592	1.042	0.633
	(0.158)	(0.131)	(0.086)	(0.068)	(0.161)	(0.213)	(0.196)	(0.108)	(0.023)	(0.058)
γ	−0.065	0.120	0.358	0.293	0.051	0.201	0.276	0.200	−0.035	0.006
	(0.079)	(0.129)	(0.141)	(0.109)	(0.178)	(0.185)	(0.226)	(0.130)	(0.064)	(0.053)

$F = 6.16$ with 18, 98 degrees of freedom if all coefficients identical
$F = 3.14$ with 12, 98 degrees of freedom if all coefficients identical except intercepts

Nondurable Manufacturing Regressions

Industry	1	2	3	4	5	6	7	Aggregate	Pooled	Pooled with Separate Intercept
df	14	14	14	14	14	14	14	14	116	110
$\bar{R}^2$	0.9116	0.8111	0.8628	0.8394	0.6700	0.4415	0.7753	0.9256	0.9965	0.9967
$\bar{S}_{est}$	298.04	164.75	115.92	342.77	246.49	102.48	294.98	895.23	245.67	238.07
d	1.767	1.708	1.639	1.546	2.495	1.716	1.656	1.553	1.687	1.827
Variables										
α	−27.224	186.508	288.825	1321.371	1647.668	610.964	1000.865	3008.221	95.481	677.987
	(1483.461)	(461.002)	(317.039)	(704.084)	(1362.966)	(327.170)	(922.777)	(3280.023)	(43.708)	(294.308)
β	1.007	0.970	0.980	0.863	0.843	0.664	0.899	0.967	1.012	0.943
	(0.110)	(0.125)	(0.097)	(0.100)	(0.144)	(0.216)	(0.130)	(0.071)	(0.006)	(0.041)
γ	0.854	0.338	0.062	0.390	0.345	0.352	0.380	0.362	0.483	0.427
	(0.325)	(0.136)	(0.291)	(0.226)	(0.168)	(0.212)	(0.177)	(0.160)	(0.070)	(0.074)

$F = 1.28$ with 18, 98 degrees of freedom if all coefficients identical

$F = 0.81$ with 12, 98 degrees of freedom if all coefficients identical except intercepts

(*continued*)

TABLE 5.2.3 (*continued*). FERBER EXTRAPOLATION—LONG SALES

$$\text{ALSALE} = \alpha_f + \beta\,\text{SALE}_{-4} + \gamma\,\text{SALE}_{-4}\left(\frac{\text{SALE}_{-2} - \text{SALE}_{-6}}{\text{SALE}_{-6}}\right) + \epsilon$$

Pooled Firm Data (Separate Intercepts)

	Nonferrous Metals	Electrical Machinery	Nonelectrical Machinery	Chemicals	Petroleum
Partial $\bar{R}^2$	0.3771	0.6324	0.7156	0.8662	0.3257
$\bar{S}_{est}$	7065.3	6518.1	11956.	8844.2	20358
df	173	304	302	371	419
F	1.05	5.61	2.17	1.95	0.99
$\bar{d}$	1.23	1.80	1.54	1.87	1.77
Number of firms	9	17	16	20	20
Variables					
β	0.588	0.755	0.725	0.883	0.866
	(0.061)	(0.036)	(0.028)	(0.020)	(0.065)
γ	0.088	0.142	0.245	0.282	0.348
	(0.054)	(0.031)	(0.041)	(0.032)	(0.103)

5.2.3 Regressivity of Expectations

Perhaps the most provocative aspect of Ferber's investigation concerned his observation that forecasters have a tendency to predict a return toward the situation of the corresponding quarter of the previous year rather than extrapolate recently observed trend. The nature of this regressive characteristic is most easily appreciated by rewriting Ferber's law, equation 2.1, as:

$$P = \alpha + \beta A_{-1}\frac{A_{-4}}{A_{-5}} - (\beta - \gamma)(A_{-1} - A_{-5})\frac{A_{-4}}{A_{-5}} + \epsilon \qquad (2.4)$$

where the ratio A_{-4}/A_{-5} constitutes a crude form of allowance for seasonal movements. It is clear from this formulation that expectations would be essentially a static forecast of no change, other than seasonal, from the current level if $\alpha = 0$ and $\beta = \gamma = 1$. In fact, Ferber's aggregate railroad shippers' data yielded a figure of 0.986 for β and 0.43 for γ. Thus, the coefficient of the second term of equation 2.4 is indeed negative, implying a tendency in forming expectations to regress toward the situation of the corresponding quarter of the previous year; in other words, forecasters expect a reversal of the recently observed trend, as measured by the change $A_{-1} - A_{-5}$. Ferber referred to $\beta - \gamma$ as the "reversal coefficient" in his discussions of this regressivity phenomenon.[10] In the upper left-hand panel of Table 5.2.5 it will be observed that the reversal coefficients he obtained for individual industries ranged from 0.47 to 0.73, which confirms the extreme regressivity characteristic he observed in the aggregate.

Ferber's "regressive" property also characterizes the new *ex ante* data provided by the Office of Business Economics for an entirely new sample period. This may be seen by perusing the estimates of β and γ presented in earlier tables and summarized in the lower left-hand panels of Table 5.2.5. Whatever the limitations of Ferber's data, his observation that expectations are regressive appears to be confirmed.

These findings may be interesting, but they also raise several puzzling questions. In particular, a number of investigators have argued that it was this regressive characteristic of expectations that explained the notorious inaccuracies of the railroad shippers' forecasts. But as shown in Chapter 3, the *ex ante* data provided by the new OBE survey constitute quite good forecasts of actual developments. Clearly, a tendency to discount recently observed trend, a sizable reversal coefficient, does not necessarily imply that the resulting forecasts are inaccurate. Perhaps the regressive anticipations are quite accurate because actual sales are also regressive.

[10] The provocative concept of regressivity has been a subject of continued discussion and refinement. See, in particular, the papers of Bossons and Modigliani [1960, 1966].

TABLE 5.2.4. FERBER EXTRAPOLATIONS—LONG RATIO

$$\frac{\text{ALSALE} - \text{SALE}_{-2}}{\text{SALE}_{-2}} = \beta - 1 + (\beta - \gamma)\left(\frac{\text{SALE}_{-4} - \text{SALE}_{-2}}{\text{SALE}_{-2}}\right) + \gamma\left(\frac{\text{SALE}_{-4} - \text{SALE}_{-6}}{\text{SALE}_{-6}}\right) + \frac{\epsilon}{\text{SALE}_{-2}}$$

Durable Manufacturing Regressions

Industry	1	2	3	4	5	6	7	Aggregate	Pooled	Pooled with Separate Intercept
df	14	14	14	14	14	14	14	14	116	110
$\bar{R}^2$	0.6401	0.1743	0.2408	0.6341	0.6947	0.3637	0.6018	0.5545	0.6130	0.6024
S_{est}	0.2566	0.0443	0.0396	0.0324	0.1798	0.0440	0.0643	0.0521	0.1297	0.1315
d	1.426	1.337	1.270	1.161	1.400	2.491	1.961	1.013		
Variables										
$\beta - 1$	0.049	0.036	0.054	0.055	0.095	0.051	0.066	0.067	0.070	0.080
	(0.065)	(0.011)	(0.012)	(0.010)	(0.045)	(0.011)	(0.018)	(0.013)	(0.012)	(0.032)
$\beta - \gamma$	1.015	0.410	0.375	0.534	1.009	0.021	0.973	0.640	0.923	0.940
	(0.191)	(0.177)	(0.223)	(0.133)	(0.213)	(0.149)	(0.272)	(0.157)	(0.073)	(0.077)
γ	0.431	0.258	0.565	0.579	0.816	−0.446	1.237	0.557	0.532	0.533
	(0.129)	(0.172)	(0.214)	(0.111)	(0.150)	(0.195)	(0.244)	(0.135)	(0.054)	(0.055)

$F = 1.53$ with 18, 98 degrees of freedom if all coefficients identical
$F = 2.03$ with 12, 98 degrees of freedom if all coefficients identical except intercepts

Nondurable Manufacturing Regressions

Industry	1	2	3	4	5	6	7	Aggregate	Pooled	Pooled with Separate Intercept
df	14	14	14	14	14	14	14	14	116	110
$\bar{R}^2$	0.8392	0.2577	0.0434	0.5394	0.6029	0.1400	0.6665	0.5749	0.3866	0.4509
$\bar{S}_{est}$	0.0203	0.0412	0.0252	0.0261	0.0271	0.0624	0.0439	0.0184	0.0414	0.0391
d	1.767	1.885	1.402	1.833	2.111	1.975	1.696	1.620		
Variables										
$\beta - 1$	0.005	0.018	0.058	0.051	0.018	0.060	0.040	0.031	0.036	0.041
	(0.011)	(0.012)	(0.014)	(0.012)	(0.007)	(0.017)	(0.013)	(0.008)	(0.005)	(0.010)
$\beta - \gamma$	0.213	0.528	0.448	0.404	0.734	0.416	0.670	0.566	0.462	0.508
	(0.321)	(0.205)	(0.276)	(0.153)	(0.218)	(0.260)	(0.222)	(0.210)	(0.085)	(0.083)
γ	1.102	0.702	0.252	0.406	1.138	0.522	1.018	0.856	0.672	0.691
	(0.126)	(0.273)	(0.214)	(0.093)	(0.222)	(0.245)	(0.175)	(0.178)	(0.077)	(0.073)

$F = 2.29$ with 18, 98 degrees of freedom if all coefficients identical
$F = 1.68$ with 12, 98 degrees of freedom if all coefficients identical except intercepts

(continued)

TABLE 5.2.4 (*continued*). FERBER EXTRAPOLATIONS—LONG SALES RATIO

$$\frac{\text{ALSALE} - \text{SALE}_{-2}}{\text{SALE}_{-2}} = \beta - 1 + (\beta - \gamma)\left(\frac{\text{SALE}_{-4} - \text{SALE}_{-2}}{\text{SALE}_{-2}}\right) + \gamma\left(\frac{\text{SALE}_{-4} - \text{SALE}_{-6}}{\text{SALE}_{-6}}\right) + \frac{\epsilon}{\text{SALE}_{-2}}$$

Pooled Firm Data

	Nonferrous Metals	Electrical Machinery	Nonelectrical Machinery	Chemicals	Petroleum
$\bar{R}^2$	0.6886	0.4680	0.2744	0.7927	0.4661
$\bar{S}_{est}$	0.13	0.22	0.13	0.11	0.12
df	181	320	317	390	438
F	3.75	3.43	4.68	3.29	2.04
$\bar{d}$	1.42	1.96	1.50	1.86	1.82
Number of firms	9	17	16	20	20
Variables					
$\beta - 1$	0.063	0.056	0.065	0.044	0.018
	(0.010)	(0.013)	(0.007)	(0.006)	(0.006)
$\beta - \gamma$	0.845	0.727	0.513	0.769	0.539
	(0.042)	(0.055)	(0.052)	(0.043)	(0.044)
γ	0.335	0.684	0.434	0.846	0.623
	(0.037)	(0.046)	(0.045)	(0.022)	(0.032)

TABLE 5.2.5. REGRESSIVITY OF EXPECTATIONS

	Anticipated as Dependent Variable				Actual as Dependent Variable			
	β	γ	$\beta - \gamma$	$\bar{R}^2$	β	γ	$\beta - \gamma$	$\bar{R}^2$
Ferber's Data[a]								
Aggregate	0.986	0.43	0.56	0.972	0.886	0.823	0.063	0.90
Iron and steel	0.917	0.448	0.47	0.907	0.746	0.752	−0.006	0.771
Cement	1.077	0.490	0.59	0.979	0.957	0.799	0.158	0.942
Flour	1.042	0.311	0.73	0.947	0.821	0.484	0.337	0.714
Lumber	0.989	0.406	0.58	0.986	0.909	0.844	0.065	0.923
Ag. Imple.	1.003	0.444	0.56	0.943	0.782	0.653	0.129	0.773
Benchmark Aggregates								
OBE data—short sale								
Durable aggregate	0.500	0.431	0.069	0.407	0.554	0.418	0.136	0.350
Sepincep	0.438	0.249	0.189	0.956	0.455	0.219	0.236	0.951
Nondurable aggregate	1.123	0.626	0.497	0.915	1.111	0.625	0.486	0.879
Sepincep	1.021	0.581	0.440	0.998	0.997	0.526	0.471	0.998
OBE data—long sales								
Durable aggregate	0.592	0.200	0.392	0.688	0.625	0.138	0.487	0.413
Sepincep	0.633	0.006	0.627	0.965	0.616	−0.079	0.695	0.942
Nondurable aggregate	0.967	0.362	0.605	0.926	0.800	0.268	0.532	0.814
Sepincep	0.943	0.427	0.516	0.997	0.814	0.261	0.553	0.996
Pooled Firm—Short Sales								
Nonferrous metals	0.489	0.266	0.223	0.291	0.651	0.247	0.404	0.389
Electrical machinery	0.756	0.364	0.392	0.619	0.649	0.557	0.092	0.612
Nonelectrical machinery	0.879	0.485	0.394	0.763	0.896	0.533	0.363	0.730
Chemicals	0.902	0.355	0.547	0.788	0.900	0.248	0.652	0.671
Petroleum	0.877	0.594	0.283	0.737	0.975	0.708	0.267	0.771
Pooled Firm—Long Sales								
Nonferrous metals	0.588	0.088	0.500	0.378	0.718	0.072	0.646	0.412
Electrical machinery	0.755	0.142	0.613	0.632	0.553	0.451	0.102	0.454
Nonelectrical machinery	0.725	0.245	0.480	0.716	0.831	0.272	0.569	0.730
Chemicals	0.883	0.282	0.601	0.866	0.877	0.175	0.702	0.708
Petroleum	0.866	0.348	0.518	0.326	0.951	0.300	0.651	0.654

[a] Ferber [1953, pp. 70, 76, and 91].

Ferber investigated the possibility that actual railroad shipments are regressive. Specifically, he reran the equation constituting his law of expectations formation with actual shipments replacing anticipated shipments as the dependent variable. He found that the reversal coefficient, $\beta - \gamma$, was much smaller when equation 2.1 was employed with actual sales than with anticipations as the dependent variable.[11] On the basis of this evidence, reproduced in the top right-hand panel of Table 5.2.5, Ferber [1953, p. 76] concluded:

> This test . . . confirms the absence of any significant tendency on the part of actual shipments to regress towards the past; regression is a property of anticipations and has no counterpart in the actual course of events.

[11] Ferber [1953, pp. 70, 76, and 91] reported the figures reproduced in the upper left panel for anticipations and in the upper right panel for actual sales as the dependent variable.

TABLE 5.2.6. FERBER EXTRAPOLATION—ACTUAL SHORT

$$\text{SALE} = \alpha' + \beta'\text{SALE}_{-4} + \gamma'\text{SALE}_{-4}\left(\frac{\text{SALE}_{-1} - \text{SALE}_{-5}}{\text{SALE}_{-5}}\right) + \epsilon$$

Durable Manufacturing Regressions

Industry	1	2	3	4	5	6	7	Aggregate	Pooled	Pooled With Separate Intercept
df	10	10	10	10	10	10	10	10	88	82
$\bar{R}^2$	−0.1731	−0.0530	0.6956	0.8607	0.3010	0.2299	0.7213	0.3499	0.9285	0.9507
$\bar{S}_{est}$	530.63	85.81	232.44	271.26	1048.02	218.96	156.93	2461.00	633.04	525.64
d	1.110	1.371	0.924	0.515	2.008	1.399	1.788	1.409	1.781	1.736
Variables										
α'	3712.893	1113.560	568.647	−116.830	2618.939	2700.742	1459.935	15617.11	71.259	1951.127
	(576.260)	(454.642)	(1081.279)	1157.966)	(1844.739)	(1146.472)	(803.533)	(8645.906)	(159.662)	(335.856)
β'	0.037	0.293	0.919	1.030	0.626	0.324	0.576	0.554	1.009	0.455
	(0.140)	(0.290)	(0.179)	(0.137)	0.297)	(0.284)	(0.237)	(0.257)	(0.031)	(0.089)
γ'	−0.048	0.154	0.577	0.593	0.305	0.467	0.797	0.418	0.241	0.219
	(0.128)	(0.222)	(0.212)	(0.206)	(0.277)	(0.203)	(0.158)	(0.246)	(0.102)	(0.086)

$F = 4.75$ with 18, 70 degress of freedom if all coefficients identical
$F = 2.49$ with 12, 70 degrees of freedom if all coefficients identical except intercepts

Nondurable Manufacturing Regressions

Industry	1	2	3	4	5	6	7	Aggregate	Pooled	Pooled With Separate Intercept
df	10	10	10	10	10	10	10	10	88	82
$\bar{R}^2$	0.8894	0.5905	0.7734	0.8358	0.3565	0.6315	0.5126	0.8790	0.9976	0.9976
$\bar{S}_{est}$	204.50	192.05	101.43	299.65	128.41	74.23	281.34	754.48	202.50	202.08
d	2.046	1.243	1.739	0.822	1.818	1.370	1.883	0.964	1.771	1.688
Variables										
α'	−4002.710	1633.570	354.306	−180.075	3905.054	426.914	1539.223	−4584.176	17.777	126.567
	(2177.658)	(1023.103)	(480.246)	(1009.206)	(1989.247)	(367.222)	(1650.226)	(6142.520)	(41.412)	(456.536)
β'	1.303	0.572	0.937	1.052	0.596	0.731	0.809	1.111	1.009	0.997
	(0.156)	(0.274)	(0.148)	(0.136)	(0.208)	(0.237)	(0.232)	(0.132)	(0.006)	(0.063)
γ'	0.336	0.717	0.179	0.598	0.270	0.724)	0.277	0.625	0.632	0.526
	(0.235)	(0.185)	(0.295)	(0.214)	(0.249)	(0.185	(0.265)	(0.202)	(0.072)	(0.084)

$F = 1.12$ with 18, 70 degrees of freedom if all coefficients identical
$F = 1.14$ with 12, 70 degrees of freedom if all coefficients identical except intercepts

(continued)

TABLE 5.2.6 (*continued*). FERBER EXTRAPOLATION—ACTUAL SHORT

$$\text{SALE} = \alpha_f' + \beta'\text{SALE}_{-4} + \gamma'\text{SALE}_{-4}\left(\frac{\text{SALE}_{-1} - \text{SALE}_{-5}}{\text{SALE}_{-5}}\right) + \epsilon$$

Pooled Firm Data (Separate Intercepts)

	Nonferrous Metals	Electrical Machinery	Nonelectrical Machinery	Chemicals	Petroleum
Partial $\bar{R}^2$	0.3890	0.6119	0.7304	0.6712	0.7706
$\bar{S}_{est}$	7673.5	8079.5	11314.	13724.	8346.7
df	178	290	282	354	389
F	1.09	3.68	0.41	1.65	1.56
$\bar{d}$	1.38	1.81	1.65	1.82	1.78
Number of firms	10	17	16	20	20
Variables					
β'	0.651	0.649	0.896	0.900	0.975
	(0.068)	(0.040)	(0.034)	(0.037)	(0.032)
γ'	0.247	0.557	0.533	0.248	0.708
	(0.057)	(0.040)	(0.044)	(0.048)	(0.041)

A quite different result is obtained with the new data. Inspection of the lower right-hand panels of Table 5.2.5 reveals that when the Ferber extrapolative equation is used to explain actual sales developments rather than expectations, essentially the same coefficients are obtained as when expected sales is the dependent variable. More detailed results are presented in Tables 5.2.6 and 5.2.7. Note that actual sales are predicted quite closely in those industries, both durable and nondurable, for which the Ferber equation gave a good fit in explaining anticipations. Again, however, the Ferber model is grossly unsatisfactory for explaining actual aggregate sales for iron and steel and for nonferrous metals—these are the two industries for which Ferber's law for the formation of anticipations is unsatisfactory. Thus, we see that regressivity in anticipations is quite consistent with accurate sales forecasting because actual realizations are regressive.

If the regressive characteristic of *actual* sales serves to explain the regressive nature of *anticipations*, it also serves to cast at least some doubt upon Ferber's law of anticipation formation. We have seen that forecasters behave "as though" they use the Ferber model. Of course, only a model that is itself capable of accurate prediction can fit *accurate* forecast data. Conversely, the systematic features of the realizations must be mirrored in any set of *accurate* forecasts, however they are derived. The Ferber model may do well at explaining the forecasts only because it mirrors certain characteristics of the realizations; thus, it has not been shown that it is actually used in deriving the forecasts.

Ferber presented two arguments against the hypothesis that his model fits the anticipations data only because it captures certain systematic tendencies of actual realizations. Ferber [1953, p. 75] argued that the lower $\bar{R}^2$ that he obtained when he used actual rather than anticipated carloadings as the dependent variable suggested that the good fits obtained with his model were not a spurious consequence of the correlation of anticipations with actual realizations. He also pointed out that his reversal coefficients, $\beta - \gamma$, were considerably smaller when actual sales rather than anticipations were used as the dependent variable. With the new data, however, the results with the two tests that Ferber suggested are quite different. For five of the fourteen industries, the benchmark adjusted data yielded higher correlation coefficients when Ferber's law was used to explain actual sales rather than ASSALE. Furthermore, the reversal coefficients are not consistently smaller with the actual sales as opposed to the ASSALE regressions.[12] It is clear that in those industries (for example, iron and steel) for which the Ferber equation would

[12] Indeed, the average of the reversal coefficients obtained over the 14 industries with the benchmark adjusted data are 0.276 when SALE is the dependent variable and 0.281 when ASSALE is the dependent variable. In terms of the six-month horizon, the averages are 0.356 for SALE and 0.457 for ALSALE.

TABLE 5.2.7. FERBER EXTRAPOLATION—ACTUAL LONG

$$\text{SALE} = \alpha' + \beta'\text{SALE}_{-4} + \text{SALE}_{-4}\left(\frac{\text{SALE}_{-2} - \text{SALE}_{-6}}{\text{SALE}_{-6}}\right) + \epsilon$$

Durable Manufacturing Regressions

Industry	1	2	3	4	5	6	7	Aggregate	Pooled	Pooled With Separate Intercept
df	12	12	12	12	12	12	12	12	102	96
$\bar{R}^2$	0.2176	0.1140	0.6951	0.7632	0.3723	0.0382	0.5447	0.4133	0.9244	0.9419
$\bar{S}_{est}$	744.48	83.09	286.84	399.86	1004.26	272.91	202.36	2507.49	640.46	561.26
d	2.385	1.470	0.734	0.786	1.446	1.252	0.849	1.213	1.365	1.604
Variables										
α'	2936.547	1083.106	1973.319	2505.211	2667.008	3166.050	1945.232	13892.08	62.069	1461.196
	(965.645)	(247.175)	(777.520)	(952.021)	(1392.252)	(796.545)	(763.067)	(6385.923)	(149.863)	(305.805)
β'	0.257	0.318	0.702	0.749	0.643	0.209	0.437	0.625	1.054	0.616
	(0.250)	(0.163)	(0.137)	(0.116)	(0.235)	(0.206)	(0.233)	(0.198)	(0.030)	(0.082)
γ'	−0.298	0.001	0.249	0.240	0.172	0.191	0.592	0.138	−0.127	−0.079
	(0.126)	(0.160)	(0.199)	(0.174)	(0.230)	(0.179)	(0.201)	(0.218)	(0.078)	(0.069)

$F = 3.78$ with 18, 84 degrees of freedom if all coefficients identical
$F = 2.15$ with 12, 84 degrees of freedom if all coefficients identical except intercepts

Nondurable Manufacturing Regressions

Industry	1	2	3	4	5	6	7	Aggregate	Pooled	Pooled With Separate Intercept
df	12	12	12	12	12	12	12	12	102	96
$\bar{R}^2$	0.9112	0.3847	0.9039	0.8203	0.4475	0.2922	0.4928	0.8136	0.9953	0.9961
$\bar{S}_{est}$	231.97	230.91	81.84	378.52	122.18	97.75	315.39	1139.95	283.16	258.24
d	1.059	0.631	1.635	0.826	1.587	0.756	1.551	0.511	0.901	0.889
Variables										
α'	483.799	2136.494	557.318	762.917	7079.365	930.392	2933.761	10724.79	88.926	1555.712
	(1406.190)	(750.078)	(248.404)	(846.872)	(695.279)	(336.484)	(1169.369)	(4812.422)	(53.712)	(363.984)
β'	0.986	0.446	0.877	0.964	0.266	0.412	0.621	0.800	1.018	0.814
	(0.104)	(0.207)	(0.079)	(0.124)	(0.074)	(0.225)	(0.168)	(0.106)	(0.007)	(0.052)
γ'	0.509	0.416	0.196	0.074	0.052	0.351	0.159	0.268	0.319	0.261
	(0.253)	(0.192)	(0.215)	(0.261)	(0.084)	(0.203)	(0.190)	(0.205)	(0.082)	(0.081)

$F = 3.68$ with 18, 84 degrees of freedom if all coefficients identical
$F = 2.80$ with 12, 84 degrees of freedom if all coefficients identical except intercepts

(continued)

TABLE 5.2.7 (*continued*). FERBER EXTRAPOLATION—ACTUAL LONG

$$\text{SALE} = \alpha_f' + \beta'\text{SALE}_{-4} + \gamma'\text{SALE}_{-4}\left(\frac{\text{SALE}_{-2} - \text{SALE}_{-6}}{\text{SALE}_{-6}}\right) + \epsilon$$

Pooled Firm Data (Separate Intercepts)

	Nonferrous Metals	Electrical Machinery	Nonelectrical Machinery	Chemicals	Petroleum
Partial $\bar{R}^2$	0.4117	0.4538	0.7299	0.7079	0.6543
$\bar{S}_{est}$	7991.8	10168	13352	13882	10671
df	198	317	308	390	428
F	0.47	7.67	0.44	0.61	1.25
$\bar{d}$	1.20	1.59	1.04	1.43	1.24
Number of firms	10	17	16	20	20
Variables					
β'	0.718	0.553	0.831	0.877	0.951
	(0.064)	(0.051)	(0.031)	(0.030)	(0.035)
γ'	0.072	0.451	0.272	0.175	0.300
	(0.056)	(0.046)	(0.045)	(0.048)	(0.054)

yield poor predictions, expectations must be generated by some alternative process. Clearly, Ferber's law does not generally hold true. It is possible that Ferber's law for anticipations formation is employed only where it will work, and that in other sectors some alternative procedure is used in making forecasts.

5.3 ADAPTIVE EXPECTATIONS

The Nerlove model of adaptive expectations, which stems from J. R. Hicks' [1939] concept of the elasticity of expectations, constitutes an alternative to the Ferber extrapolative model. The basic form of the adaptive expectations model is:

$$\begin{aligned} P &= \lambda P_{-1} + (1 - \lambda)A_{-1} + \epsilon \\ &= (1 - \lambda)\sum_{i=0}^{\infty} \lambda^i A_{-1-i} + \sum_{i=0}^{\infty} \lambda^i \epsilon_{-i}, \qquad 0 \le \lambda < 1 \qquad (3.1) \end{aligned}$$

Here P is anticipated and A the actual realization.[13] Thus, in terms of the first equality, expectations concerning tomorrow's outcome change from expectations about today in proportion to the error we made in anticipating today's outcome. If $\lambda = 0$, we have the naive forecast of same-as-last-period. On the other hand, if $\lambda = 1$, expectations are unrevised as a result of errors made in period t. The second equality, valid for $\lambda < 1$, suggests that expectations are a weighted average of past experience, where the weights decline geometrically. The λ coefficient is nonnegative; otherwise, the knowledge provided by past experience would enter into the formation of expectations with weights of alternating sign, which does not seem to make much sense.

Although Nerlove [1958b] stressed originally that his model is concerned with the derivation of "normal" or long-run expectations, it is nonetheless interesting to test this model against the short horizon sales forecast data provided by the OBE survey. For one thing, Nerlove [1958b, p. 219] pointed out that his model is capable of generating anticipations data with the substantial errors and regressivity characterizing the railroad shippers' forecast data analyzed by Ferber. This meant, Nerlove argued, that the

[13] The second equality may be derived from the first by successive elimination of the lagged expectations term; e.g., since the first equality holds true for all t, including $t - 1$, we have $P = (1 - \lambda)A_{-1} + \lambda(1 - \lambda)A_{-2} + \lambda^2 P_{-1} + \epsilon + \lambda\epsilon_{-1}$. Successive substitution results in the second equality, for the restricted range on the λ coefficient guarantees convergence.

regressivity phenomenon might result from a tendency of respondents to reply with forecasts about the long-run normal situation even when polled concerning immediate prospects.[14] Even if respondents to the OBE survey did misinterpret the questions in the way Nerlove suggests, his model might still constitute a useful framework for explaining reported anticipations.

There is reason to believe, however, that valid short-run rather than "normal" expectations data might behave in accordance with the Nerlove model. The adaptive expectations formulation, sometimes called "exponential smoothing," is advocated by such writers as Brown [1959], Winters [1960], and Holt, Modigliani, Muth, and Simon [1960] as a procedure that should be used by firms in preparing short-run forecasts for purposes of making production and inventory decisions. The conditions under which the exponential forecasting procedure is optimal have been considered by Muth [1960], Theil and Wage [1964], and Nerlove and Wage [1964]. To the extent that this growing literature leads to the adoption of the exponential forecasting procedure, Nerlove's model will serve to explain the data on actual expectations collected by the OBE survey.

The adaptive expectations model has not been subject to intensive direct empirical testing. Rather, the adaptive expectations concept has been frequently incorporated by econometricians as part of the maintained hypothesis. This was one of the approaches used by Ball and Drake [1963] in their study of inventory behavior in the United Kingdom. The same procedure has been utilized in studies of inflation by P. Cagan [1956], of fixed investment by F. Hammer [1964] and R. Schramm [1967], and of consumption by Zellner, Huang, and Chau [1965]. Clearly, the validity of the assumption that anticipations are generated in the way that Nerlove suggests deserves investigation.

Several econometric problems deserve consideration before the Nerlove model is subjected to direct empirical test. First, a slight generalization to allow for trend needs to be mentioned. After all, if sales have a consistent upward trend, equation 3.1 implies that expected sales will consistently fall below the trend line; in particular, no change would be forecast if it happened that $P_{-1} = A_{-1}$. An obvious generalization is:[15]

$$\begin{aligned} P &= \alpha + \lambda' P_{-1} + (1 - \lambda) A_{-1} + \epsilon \\ &= (1 - \lambda) \sum_{i=0}^{\infty} \lambda'^{i} A_{-1-i} + \alpha/(1 - \lambda') + \sum_{i=0}^{\infty} \lambda'^{i} \epsilon_{-i} \end{aligned} \tag{3.2}$$

[14] On the other hand, Theil [1961, p. 182] has argued that "predicted changes will look more precise if we interpret them as referring to a period which is shorter than the one to which they are supposed to refer." As explained at the beginning of 5.3.2 below, there are circumstances in which the long and short forecast should be identical.

[15] This is the form of the Nerlove equation employed by Zellner, Huang, and Chau [1965, p. 575–576] in their study of consumption behavior.

For testing the hypothesis that $\lambda = \lambda'$, it is convenient to rewrite the first equality as

$$P - A_{-1} = \alpha + \lambda'(P_{-1} - A_{-1}) + (\lambda' - \lambda)A_{-1} + \varepsilon, \tag{3.3}$$

where ϵ is a stochastic disturbance with zero expected value. Thus, the trend complication only leads to an additional term in the basic equation.

A second problem concerns the properties that may reasonably be attributed to the stochastic disturbance. If the ϵ in equation 3.3 are assumed to be independently distributed, the resulting disturbance in the distributed lag expression for P will not be free of serial correlation. Conversely, if expectations are regarded as a weighted average of past experience with geometrically declining weights plus an additive random disturbance, the stochastic term of equation 3.3 cannot be independently distributed. Clearly, the first assumption, that ϵ of equation 3.3 is distributed independently, is more convenient. It is a reasonable assumption, for a forecaster who uses the first instead of the second equality of 3.2 in preparing his forecast has to remember only the forecast made last period rather than the firm's entire sales history.[16] But even if we are permitted to invoke this assumption and also to assume that actual sales are exogenous, the presence of P_{-1} on the right-hand side of equation 3.3 means that the disturbance cannot be distributed independently of the explanatory variables. Consequently, application of least squares will be subject to the Hurwicz [1950] bias. Fortunately, a theorem of Mann and Wald [1943] implies that least squares will yield maximum likelihood estimates in the nonexplosive case $(-1 < \lambda < 1)$, provided that the variance of ϵ is constant.[17]

This homoscedasticity assumption is questionable, however, for it can be argued that the variance of the disturbance would be larger the higher the level of sales. It may be more reasonable to assume that the deflated error term ϵ/A_{-1} has constant variance, and we have already assumed that A_{-1} is exogenous. Then equation 3.3 is appropriately transformed to

$$\frac{P - A_{-1}}{A_1} = (\lambda - \lambda') + \lambda \frac{P_{-1} - A_{-1}}{A_{-1}} + \epsilon/A_{-1} \tag{3.4}$$

[16] The advocates of exponential forecasting emphasize that their approach economizes on information storage.

[17] An alternative approach, used by many writers including Cagan [1956], is to search over alternative values of $\hat{\lambda}$, $0 \leq \hat{\lambda} \leq 1$. For each value of $\hat{\lambda}$ a time series of estimated forecasts $P_t(\hat{\lambda})$ is obtained from the last equality of 3.2; i.e., $P(\hat{\lambda}) = \sum \hat{\lambda}^i A_{-i}$. If the disturbance term is normally and independently distributed, the value of $\hat{\lambda}$ yielding the sequence of estimated forecasts that are closest in the root-mean-square-error sense to the measured anticipations constitutes the maximum likelihood estimate of the smoothing parameter.

provided $\alpha = 0$.[18] The hypothesis $\lambda = \lambda'$ implies that the intercept is zero for this equation.

A third and fundamental statistical problem concerns the criteria that can be appropriately invoked in order to choose between the adaptive expectations model and Ferber's law. It is customary, of course, to reject a model that yields parameter estimates of incorrect sign or unreasonable magnitude, particularly if the estimate departs from the anticipated range by several standard deviations. Furthermore, it is also customary to compare $\bar{R}^2$'s in choosing between two alternative models that both yield parameter estimates of reasonable magnitude. Our reasons for using this criterion are explained in Chapter 2.2.3. It should be noted that this criterion may be prejudiced in favor of the adaptive expectations model.[19]

We shall proceed by considering the regressions obtained with short and long OBE *ex ante* data in Sections 5.3.1 and 5.3.2, respectively. Then, in Section 5.3.3, we shall consider whether the process by which initial expectations are revised with the passage of time conforms with the hypotheses of Meiselman and others.

5.3.1 *Short Anticipations*

The results of running equations 3.3 and 3.4 on the short sales anticipations benchmark adjusted data are reported on Table 5.3.1. Clearly, the model appears grossly unsatisfactory. For 9 of the 14 industry aggregates, the estimated value of λ is negative. Inspection of the ratio form of the regressions, reported on Table 5.3.2, reveals that seven estimated values of λ are negative, and the coefficient for iron and steel is slightly larger than unity. Further, where the coefficients are of reasonable magnitude, the equations do not yield a tight fit. The individual firm regressions yield quite small $\bar{R}^2$'s, on the average, and 22 of the 82 estimates of λ lie outside the zero-to-one range. While the pooled regressions, based on many more degrees of freedom, all yield estimated values of λ within the appropriate range, the correlation coefficients are considerably lower than those reported on Table 5.2.2 for the Ferber model.

There is an obvious explanation for these unsatisfactory results. In contrast to the Ferber model of expectations formation, the adaptive theory of

[18] If we had thought the intercept of 3.3 essential, we could have added $1/A_{-1}$ as another regressor.

[19] With a lagged dependent variable, the method of least squares sacrifices the property of unbiasedness in selecting that parameter estimate that maximizes $\bar{R}^2$. This suggests, but by no means establishes, that for purposes of comparison the $\bar{R}^2$ yielded by the adaptive expectations model may be inflated. The problem is more serious still if the error terms are autocorrelated.

expectations, in the simple form we have been considering, does not take problems of seasonality explicitly into account. The adaptive expectations approach is more reasonably applied to seasonally adjusted data, rather than raw time series. Holt, Modigliani, Muth, and Simon [1960, Ch. 14] consider this problem explicitly in explaining how the exponential smoothing approach should be employed by a firm in forecasting sales volume. In essence, they recommend that a multiplicative seasonal correction term be employed, where the seasonal correction factor is also estimated by an adaptive forecasting formula rather than assumed constant. While their procedure is of a form that may be easily employed by the firm in practical business forecasting applications, it does not lend itself easily to the econometric task we have of analyzing the forecasting accomplishments of firms responding to the OBE survey.

The approach that we have employed is to add seasonal dummy variables to the equations. Adding seasonal dummies to equation 3.3 would be equivalent to correcting the data for a constant *additive* seasonal pattern,[20] which does not seem reasonable. Introducing seasonal dummies into the ratio form of the adaptive expectations model, equation 3.4, is equivalent to allowing for a constant multiplicative seasonal pattern. The resulting equation is:

$$\frac{P - A_{-1}}{A_{-1}} = \alpha_0 + \lambda \frac{P_{-1} - A_{-1}}{A_{-1}} + \alpha_1 S_1 + \alpha_2 S_2 + \alpha_3 S_3 + \epsilon / A_{-1} \quad (3.5)$$

$$\text{where the dummy variable } S_i = \begin{cases} 1 \text{ in quarter } i \\ 0 \text{ otherwise} \end{cases}$$

The regressions are reported on Table 5.3.3.

The results obtained with the benchmark aggregate industry data are still unacceptable; after all, six of the industries yield estimates of λ outside the zero to unity range. The pooled industry regressions are much better, for the estimated values of λ are all within the appropriate range. But while the addition of the seasonal dummy variables has served to raise the pooled regression adjusted $\bar{R}^2$'s considerably, they are still uniformly smaller than those reported for the Ferber model on Table 5.2.2. If, for want of a better criterion, we base the comparison on $\bar{R}^2$'s, the two regressions obtained by pooling all durable and all nondurable data suggest that the Ferber model dominates the Nerlove adaptive expectations formulation.

[20] For further discussion, see Lovell [1963]. Of course, it would have been possible to use a standard ratio-to-moving average procedure, such as is employed in the preparation of unemployment data. But since the statistical implications of such an approach have not been worked out, this procedure did not appear to warrant application.

TABLE 5.3.1. ADAPTIVE EXPECTATIONS—SHORT

$$ASSALE - SALE_{-1} = \alpha + \lambda(ASSALE_{-1} - SALE_{-1}) + (\lambda - \lambda')SALE_{-1} + \epsilon$$

Durable Manufacturing Regressions

Industry	1	2	3	4	5	6	7	Aggregate	Pooled	Pooled With Separate Intercept
df	14	14	14	14	14	14	14	14	116	110
$\bar{R}^2$	0.7122	0.5002	0.1125	0.0334	0.4237	0.1423	0.0842	0.2709	0.0122	0.4096
$\bar{S}_{est}$	646.79	64.26	311.89	502.35	1245.85	190.69	265.67	2741.49	792.46	612.67
d	1.173	1.784	2.945	2.640	2.054	2.615	2.426	2.071	2.531	1.873
Variables										
α	4916.381	963.129	1912.442	2154.112	5625.161	1966.947	1275.783	20057.67	287.284	2983.657
	(882.540)	(384.543)	(1077.789)	(1649.170)	(1713.479)	(945.073)	(872.925)	(9018.791)	(173.180)	(345.929)
λ	−1.084	0.330	0.582	0.361	−2.139	−0.023	−0.582	0.398	0.289	−0.585
	(0.673)	(0.337)	(0.835)	(0.703)	(1.636)	(0.333)	(0.443)	(1.107)	(0.411)	(0.335)
$\lambda - \lambda'$	−1.241	−0.613	−0.296	−0.231	−0.875	−0.471	−0.334	−0.575	−0.052	−0.823
	(0.212)	(0.245)	(0.175)	(0.186)	(0.256)	(0.232)	(0.249)	(0.258)	(0.032)	(0.088)

$F = 6.21$ with 18, 98 degrees of freedom if all coefficients identical
$F = 1.74$ with 12, 98 degrees of freedom if all coefficients identical except intercepts

Nondurable Manufacturing Regressions

Industry	1	2	3	4	5	6	7	Aggregate	Pooled	Pooled With Separate Intercept
df	14	14	14	14	14	14	14	14	116	110
$\bar{R}^2$	0.0327	−0.0289	0.1320	−0.1124	0.1718	0.0375	0.0557	0.0365	−0.0039	0.0037
$\bar{S}_{est}$	485.13	162.54	61.50	365.99	225.25	119.12	523.56	966.33	326.01	324.76
d	2.238	2.303	0.965	2.499	2.333	2.056	1.719	1.927	2.344	2.177
Variables										
α	1490.250	650.025	−311.529	603.381	5448.369	432.689	3908.290	−1781.707	31.976	1251.910
	(2690.705)	(612.558)	(211.449)	(861.574)	(2672.335)	(431.194)	(2239.180)	β (4925.194)	(58.012)	(497.445)
λ	0.759	−0.288	0.154	−0.115	−0.150	−0.574	−0.148	−0.671	0.073	0.041
	(0.530)	(0.306)	(0.178)	(0.425)	(0.332)	(0.472)	(0.600)	(0.421)	(0.173)	(0.177)
$\lambda - \lambda'$	−0.092	−0.175	0.114	−0.066	−0.559	−0.239	−0.518	0.051	0.008	−0.153
	(0.185	(0.161)	(0.063)	(0.114)	(0.281)	(0.274)	(0.307)	(0.103)	(0.007)	(0.067)

$F = 1.05$ with 18, 98 degrees of freedom if all coefficients identical
$F = 1.00$ with 12, 98 degrees of freedom if all coefficients identical except intercepts

(*continued*)

TABLE 5.3.1 (*continued*). ADAPTIVE EXPECTATIONS—SHORT

$$\text{ASSALE} - \text{SALE}_{-1} = \alpha_f + \lambda(\text{ASSALE}_{-1} - \text{SALE}_{-1}) + (\lambda - \lambda')\text{SALE}_{-1} + \epsilon$$

Pooled Firm Data (Separate Intercepts)

	Nonferrous Metals	Electrical Machinery	Nonelectrical Machinery	Chemicals	Petroleum
Partial $\bar{R}^2$	0.3075	0.3298	0.2941	0.1361	0.1186
$\bar{S}_{est}$	5948.5	10187	18814	13067	11691
df	179	323	313	394	443
F	1.78	1.23	0.21	1.30	2.10
$\bar{d}$	1.89	1.94	2.15	2.16	2.01
Number of firms	9	17	16	20	20
Variables					
λ	0.522	0.434	0.605	0.518	0.335
	(0.078)	(0.096)	(0.157)	(0.100)	(0.070)
$\lambda - \lambda'$	−0.174	−0.418	−0.432	−0.127	−0.161
	(0.049)	(0.049)	(0.053)	(0.027)	(0.034)

The individual firm regression results may be briefly summarized. They suggest that at the level of the firm it is the adaptive expectations model that is superior. Only 11 of the 82 individual firm regressions yielded estimates of λ outside of the appropriate zero-one range.[21] Furthermore, at the level of the individual firm the adaptive expectations model provided a somewhat tighter fit than Ferber's law. The average firm $\bar{R}^2$ is larger for the Nerlove than for the Ferber model in each of the five industries. Indeed, for only 28 out of 82 firms did Ferber's law yield a tighter fit than that obtained with the Nerlove model. If, in fact, the Ferber model was the correct one, we would be extremely unlikely to have obtained a proportion of $28/82 = 34$ percent. After all, under the null hypothesis that $\pi = 0.5$, the probability of 28 or fewer successes out of 82 independent trials is only 0.0014. Subject to the caveat that Theil's $\bar{R}^2$ criterion for selecting between alternative models may not be strictly valid because of the presence of the predetermined variable in Nerlove's model, the individual firm regression results definitely suggest that the adaptive expectations formulation is superior.

Obviously, the evidence is conflicting, for Ferber's model appears to dominate in explaining both the aggregate and the pooled regressions while the Nerlove model does better at the level of the individual firm. Discrepancies between aggregate and micro results are hardly surprising, of course, for they have been encountered by econometricians studying such behavior as consumption. In this case, we suspect that the discrepancy may arise from seasonality problems in the aggregation of data. It will be remembered that the form of seasonal adjustment recommended by Holt, Modigliani, Muth, and Simon [1960] in advocating adaptive forecasting procedures involved a multiplicative seasonal. For the individual firm regressions, we introduced dummy variables that assumed a constant multiplicative type of seasonal movement. It appears that for firms this approach is reasonably satisfactory. For the pooled regressions, however, the seasonal dummies for all firms were constrained to be of the same magnitude, and this approach is inadequate if the seasonal patterns of sales experienced by different firms in the same industry are markedly different. Furthermore, the multiplicative seasonal can be expected to yield even more serious problems when it is applied to the industry aggregates. Thus, the Nerlove model with multiplicative seasonals might be expected to yield unsatisfactory results at the aggregate level, even if individual firms formulate their expectations in this way. On the other hand, Ferber's law was formulated so as to obviate seasonal problems through the inclusion of the experience of the corresponding quarter of last year in the equation. In effect, this allows for variations in the seasonal pattern facing individual firms even in the pooled regressions. It is for this reason, we

[21] An insufficient number of observations prevented us from obtaining regression results for one of the 83 firms in our sample.

TABLE 5.3.2. ADAPTIVE EXPECTATIONS—SHORT RATIO

$$\frac{\text{ASSALE} - \text{SALE}_{-1}}{\text{SALE}_{-1}} = \lambda - \lambda' + \lambda\left(\frac{\text{ASSALE}_{-1} - \text{SALE}_{-1}}{\text{SALE}_{-1}}\right) + \frac{\epsilon}{\text{SALE}_{-1}}$$

Durable Manufacturing Regressions

Industry	1	2	3	4	5	6	7	Aggregate	Pooled	Pooled With Separate Intercepts
df	15	15	15	15	15	15	15	15	117	111
$\bar{R}^2$	0.1955	0.2861	0.0018	−0.0086	0.0781	−0.0293	0.0342	0.0727	0.0619	0.0131
$\bar{S}_{est}$	0.26	0.05	0.05	0.06	0.26	0.05	0.08	0.09	0.15	0.15
d	1.964	2.329	3.295	3.040	2.942	3.276	2.695	2.955	2.562	2.572
Variables										
$\lambda - \lambda'$	0.004	0.002	0.017	0.014	0.008	0.014	0.032	0.004	0.015	0.020
	(0.065)	(0.012)	(0.014)	(0.014)	(0.064)	(0.013)	(0.019)	(0.023)	(0.014)	(0.037)
λ	1.052	0.832	0.877	0.598	−3.130	0.269	−0.549	1.548	0.689	0.686
	(0.476)	(0.306)	(0.865)	(0.644)	(2.040)	(0.364)	(0.439)	(1.031)	(0.232)	(0.244)

$F = 1.29$ with 12, 105 degrees of freedom if all coefficients identical
$F = 2.54$ with 6, 105 degrees of freedom if all coefficients identical except intercepts

Nondurable Manufacturing Regressions

Industry	1	2	3	4	5	6	7	Aggregate	Pooled	Pooled With Separate Intercepts
df	15	15	15	15	15	15	15	15	117	111
$\bar{R}^2$	0.0806	−0.0418	−0.0006	−0.0657	0.0095	0.0198	−0.0636	0.0797	−0.0056	−0.0208
$\bar{S}_{est}$	0.03	0.04	0.02	0.05	0.03	0.08	0.08	0.02	0.05	0.05
d	2.433	2.311	0.885	2.593	2.210	2.267	2.124	1.861	2.309	2.391
Variables										
$\lambda - \lambda'$	0.011	−0.003	0.021	0.016	0.013	0.036	0.020	0.013	0.015	0.020
	(0.008)	(0.011)	(0.005)	(0.011)	(0.007)	(0.020)	(0.019)	(0.005)	(0.005)	(0.012)
λ	0.781	−0.172	0.174	−0.043	−0.367	−0.550	−0.131	−0.605	−0.087	−0.174
	(0.504)	(0.288)	(0.175)	(0.368)	(0.342)	(0.478)	(0.633)	(0.391)	(0.150)	(0.159)

$F = 0.65$ with 12, 105 degrees of freedom if all coefficients identical
$F = 0.61$ with 6, 105 degrees of freedom if all coefficients identical except intercepts

(continued)

TABLE 5.3.2 (*continued*). ADAPTIVE EXPECTATIONS—SHORT RATIO

$$\frac{\text{ASSALE} - \text{SALE}_{-1}}{\text{SALE}_{-1}} = \lambda - \lambda' + \lambda\left(\frac{\text{ASSALE}_{-1} - \text{SALE}_{-1}}{\text{SALE}_{-1}}\right) + \frac{\epsilon}{\text{SALE}_{-1}}$$

Pooled Firm Data

	Nonferrous Metals	Electrical Machinery	Nonelectrical Machinery	Chemicals	Petroleum
$\bar{R}^2$	0.3997	0.1945	0.2490	0.2025	0.2401
$\bar{S}_{est}$	0.13	0.28	0.12	0.18	0.11
df	188	340	329	414	463
*F	1.24	0.52	1.50	0.88	0.80
$\bar{d}$	2.14	2.35	2.52	2.46	2.24
Number of firms	9	17	16	20	20
Variables					
$\lambda - \lambda'$	0.013	0.037	0.026	0.029	0.015
	(0.009)	(0.015)	(0.007)	(0.009)	(0.005)
λ	0.711	0.782	0.664	0.984	0.587
	(0.063)	(0.086)	(0.063)	(0.095)	(0.048)

believe, that Ferber's law is more satisfactory with data pooled over individual firms as well as for the aggregates.

5.3.2 *Long Anticipations*

Let us now consider the problem of explaining the generation of long sales anticipations within the adaptive expectations framework. A difficulty with this approach must be noted at the outset. Muth [1960] considered the case in which the actual realizations are a linear function of independently distributed random shocks; he showed that if the function is of the particular form that makes exponentially weighted forecasting an optimal procedure for predicting short sales anticipations, then the long sales forecast should be identical to the short.[22] Now in practice, we do not find ALSALE = ASSALE_{-1}. This fact does not imply that forecasters are unaware of Muth's theorem; nor does it imply that forecasters do not utilize exponential forecasting procedures. It is possible, after all, that forecasters regard the actual realization as being generated by a different class of processes from that which Muth considered in deriving his theorem. Further, it is likely that if forecasters do utilize exponential smoothing, it is because it is a relatively simple procedure rather than because it is regarded as optimal.

A modification of the adaptive expectations framework is required for purposes of explaining the long sales anticipations data. Since the long anticipation is formulated before SALE_{-1} is known, it is clear that equation 3.1 cannot be applied directly. One possibility would be to introduce a two-quarter rather than a one-quarter lag on the terms to the right of the first equality; in other words,

$$\text{ALSALE} = \lambda\text{ALSALE}_{-2} + (1-\lambda)\text{SALE}_{-2}, \quad 0 < \lambda < 1 \tag{3.6}$$

But successive substitution yields

$$\begin{aligned}\text{ALSALE} &= (1-\lambda)\text{SALE}_{-2} + (1-\lambda)\lambda\text{SALE}_{-4} + \lambda^2\text{ALSALE}_{-4} \\ &= (1-\lambda)\sum_{i=0}\lambda^i\text{SALE}_{-2(1+i)}\end{aligned} \tag{3.7}$$

This is obviously unsatisfactory, for it implies that only every other quarter

[22] More precisely, suppose that SALE = $\sum_i w_i\epsilon_{-i}$, where the ϵ are independently distributed with zero mean and constant variance σ^2. Then, Muth shows, equation 3.1 constitutes an optimal procedure for predicting SALE only if $w_0 = 1$ and $w_i = \lambda$. Further, precisely these circumstances imply that the long forecast should be $\text{ALSALE}_{+1} = \text{ASSALE}$; the best prediction for the day after tomorrow is identical with our prediction for tomorrow.

TABLE 5.3.3. ADAPTIVE EXPECTATIONS—SHORT RATIO SEASONAL DUMMIES

$$\frac{\text{ASSALE} - \text{SALE}_{-1}}{\text{SALE}_{-1}} = \lambda - \lambda' + \lambda\left(\frac{\text{ASSALE}_{-1} - \text{SALE}_{-1}}{\text{SALE}_{-1}}\right) + \alpha_1 S_1 + \alpha_2 S_2 + \alpha_3 S_3 + \frac{\epsilon}{\text{SALE}_{-1}}$$

Durable Manufacturing Regressions

Industry	1	2	3	4	5	6	7	Aggregate	Pooled	Pooled With Separate Intercepts
df	11	11	11	11	11	11	11	11	107	101
$\bar{R}^2$	0.3618	0.4508	0.9209	0.8833	0.7384	0.4537	0.9179	0.6882	0.2229	0.1867
$\bar{S}_{est}$	0.23	0.04	0.02	0.02	0.14	0.04	0.02	0.05	0.14	0.14
d	1.910	2.717	2.355	1.728	2.565	2.191	1.761	2.238	2.430	2.458
Variables										
$\lambda - \lambda'$	0.085	0.022	0.089	0.038	0.325	0.065	0.050	0.119	0.103	0.100
	(0.129)	(0.022)	(0.008)	(0.013)	(0.070)	(0.022)	(0.012)	(0.030)	(0.027)	(0.043)
λ	1.271	0.374	−0.170	0.073	−2.931	−0.133	0.190	−0.347	0.509	0.497
	(0.665)	(0.300)	(0.290)	(0.354)	(1.268)	(0.309)	(0.158)	(0.680)	(0.275)	(0.283)
α_1	0.121	0.005	−0.146	−0.022	−0.335	−0.088	−0.154	−0.112	−0.093	−0.093
	(0.171)	(0.030)	(0.012)	(0.014)	(0.098)	(0.029)	(0.016)	(0.038)	(0.037)	(0.038)
α_2	−0.098	0.004	−0.045	0.045	−0.214	−0.015	0.061	−0.060	−0.046	−0.047
	(0.166)	(0.029)	(0.012)	(0.018)	(0.102)	(0.029)	(0.018)	(0.039)	(0.037)	(0.038)
α_3	−0.210	−0.071	−0.073	−0.097	−0.603	−0.094	−0.013	−0.224	−0.178	−0.178
	(0.193)	(0.033)	(0.011)	(0.019)	(0.098)	(0.032)	(0.017)	(0.043)	(0.038)	(0.039)

$F = 3.49$ with 30, 77 degrees of freedom if all coefficients identical
$F = 4.27$ with 24, 77 degrees of freedom if all coefficients identical except intercepts

										Nondurable Manufacturing Regressions
Industry	1	2	3	4	5	6	7	Aggregate	Pooled	Pooled With Separate Intercepts
df	11	11	11	11	11	11	11	11	107	101
$\bar{R}^2$	0.9307	0.7634	−0.0614	0.7705	0.8918	0.6789	0.8345	0.7861	0.1155	0.0999
$\bar{S}_{est}$	0.01	0.02	0.02	0.02	0.01	0.04	0.03	0.01	0.05	0.05
d	2.069	2.199	0.891	2.096	2.658	2.392	2.237	2.413	2.124	2.191
Variables										
$\lambda - \lambda'$	−0.008	0.033	0.016	0.012	0.018	−0.002	−0.030	0.002	0.005	0.004
	(0.005)	(0.011)	(0.010)	(0.010)	(0.005)	(0.026)	(0.014)	(0.005)	(0.009)	(0.014)
λ	0.064	0.110	0.180	−0.120	0.344	−0.150	0.206	0.174	0.101	0.027
	(0.206)	(0.196)	(0.222)	(0.236)	(0.158)	(0.340)	(0.331)	(0.226)	(0.154)	(0.162)
α_1	−0.020	−0.096	0.001	0.004	−0.004	0.012	−0.012	−0.016	−0.015	−0.016
	(0.007)	(0.015)	(0.014)	(0.016)	(0.007)	(0.036)	(0.021)	(0.007)	(0.012)	(0.012)
α_2	0.066	−0.031	0.016	0.065	−0.053	0.144	0.031	0.029	0.035	0.034
	(0.007)	(0.017)	(0.013)	(0.015)	(0.006)	(0.033)	(0.024)	(0.007)	(0.013)	(0.013)
α_3	0.029	−0.005	−0.001	−0.043	0.023	−0.019	0.152	0.028	0.019	0.018
	(0.008)	(0.018)	(0.015)	(0.017)	(0.008)	(0.032)	(0.020)	(0.007)	(0.013)	(0.013)

$F = 10.14$ with 30, 77 degrees of freedom if all coefficients identical
$F = 12.05$ with 24, 77 degrees of freedom if all coefficients identical except intercepts

(continued)

TABLE 5.3.3 (*continued*). ADAPTIVE EXPECTATIONS—SHORT RATIO SEASONAL DUMMIES

$$\frac{\text{ASSALE} - \text{SALE}_{-1}}{\text{SALE}_{-1}} = \lambda - \lambda' + \lambda\left(\frac{\text{ASSALE}_{-1} - \text{SALE}_{-1}}{\text{SALE}_{-1}}\right) + \alpha_1 S_1 + \alpha_2 S_2 + \alpha_3 S_3 + \frac{\epsilon}{\text{SALE}_{-1}}$$

Pooled Firm Data

	Nonferrous Metals	Electrical Machinery	Nonelectrical Machinery	Chemicals	Petroleum
$\bar{R}^2$	0.4479	0.2156	0.2867	0.3069	0.2817
$\bar{S}_{est}$	0.12	0.27	0.11	0.17	0.11
df	185	337	326	411	460
F	1.75	5.56	4.74	12.74	3.28
$\bar{d}$	2.00	2.18	2.13	2.33	2.20
Number of firms	9	17	16	20	20
Variables					
$\lambda - \lambda'$	−0.038	−0.014	0.034	−0.044	0.036
	(0.017)	(0.028)	(0.012)	(0.016)	(0.010)
λ	0.708	0.786	0.671	0.918	0.555
	(0.062)	(0.085)	(0.062)	(0.090)	(0.048)
α_1	0.039	0.021	0.028	0.030	−0.058
	(0.025)	(0.040)	(0.017)	(0.022)	(0.014)
α_2	0.082	0.065	−0.051	0.145	−0.034)
	(0.026)	(0.042)	(0.018)	(0.023)	(0.014)
α_3	0.101	0.134	−0.019	0.147	0.011
	(0.025)	(0.041)	(0.018)	(0.023)	(0.014)

is considered in formulating the forecast. We shall consider an alternative procedure that appears to be more appropriate.[23]

The long expectation, ALSALE, is formulated shortly after the end of period $t - 2$, when both ALSALE_{-1} and SALE_{-2} are obviously known. If we utilize SALE_{-2} rather than last period's realization in equation 3.1, we obtain:

$$\begin{aligned}\text{ALSALE} &= \text{ALSALE}_{-1} + (1 - \lambda)(\text{SALE}_{-2} - \text{ALSALE}_{-1}) + \epsilon \\ &= (1 - \lambda) \sum_{i=0} \lambda^i \text{SALE}_{-i-2} + \sum_{i=0} \lambda^i \epsilon_{-i}, \qquad 0 < \lambda < 1 \end{aligned} \tag{3.8}$$

The second inequality reveals that this approach makes expectations a geometrically declined weighted average of all past sales experience, rather than that of every other quarter. In order to allow for trend, the approach used in developing equation 3.3 suggests the generalization:

$$\begin{aligned}&\text{ALSALE} - \text{SALE}_{-2} \\ &\quad = \alpha + \lambda(\text{ALSALE}_{-1} - \text{SALE}_{-2}) + (\lambda - \lambda')\text{SALE}_{-2} + \epsilon \end{aligned} \tag{3.9}$$

The ratio adjustment for heteroscedasticity yields, if $\alpha = 0$:

$$\frac{\text{ALSALE} - \text{SALE}_{-2}}{\text{SALE}_{-2}} = (\lambda - \lambda') + \lambda \frac{\text{ALSALE}_{-1} - \text{SALE}_{-2}}{\text{SALE}_{-2}} + \frac{\epsilon}{\text{SALE}_{-2}} \tag{3.10}$$

The regressions obtained with equation 3.10, excluding seasonal dummies, are reported on Table 5.3.4. They are more satisfactory than those obtained when the adaptive expectations equation without seasonal dummies was utilized to explain the shorter anticipations. All of the regressions obtained with the aggregated industry data yield reasonable values of λ. Furthermore, the adaptive expectations model does quite well at explaining the generation of expectations in both the iron and steel industry and the primary nonferrous metals industry, which is precisely where the Ferber model is grossly unsatisfactory. With the added exception of transportation equipment, however, Ferber's law dominates the adaptive expectations equation without seasonal

[23] Another alternative, in addition to that reported here, was tested empirically and rejected. This approach involved the hypothesis that the forecaster prepared a six-month forecast adaptively; this forecast is simply $\text{ALSALE}_{+2} + \text{ASSALE}_{+1}$. The forecast ALSALE_{+2} reported to the OBE was then assumed to result by subtracting the three-month forecast from this six-month forecast. But we found that this alternative adaptive expectations model was completely inadequate as a description of the process generating the six-month forecast.

TABLE 5.3.4. ADAPTIVE EXPECTATIONS—LONG RATIO

$$\frac{\text{ALSALE} - \text{SALE}_{-2}}{\text{SALE}_{-2}} = \lambda - \lambda' + \lambda\left(\frac{\text{ALSALE}_{-1} - \text{SALE}_{-2}}{\text{SALE}_{-2}}\right) + \frac{\epsilon}{\text{SALE}_{-2}}$$

Durable Manufacturing Regressions

Industry	1	2	3	4	5	6	7	Aggregate	Pooled	Pooled With Separate Intercepts
df	15	15	15	15	15	15	15	15	117	111
$\bar{R}^2$	0.8782	0.4358	0.3099	0.5170	0.4214	0.2525	0.0204	0.5412	0.7276	0.7154
$\bar{S}_{est}$	0.15	0.04	0.04	0.04	0.20	0.05	0.10	0.05	0.10	0.11
d	2.695	2.423	1.697	2.399	2.000	1.530	2.136	2.038	2.270	2.272
Variables										
$\lambda - \lambda'$	0.016	0.016	0.034	0.022	0.051	0.023	0.039	0.032	0.024	0.024
	(0.039)	(0.010)	(0.011)	(0.010)	(0.049)	(0.013)	(0.028)	(0.013)	(0.010)	(0.026)
λ	0.824	0.510	0.501	0.701	0.636	0.491	0.376	0.528	0.765	0.762
	(0.076)	(0.139)	(0.175)	(0.165)	(0.179)	(0.194)	(0.326)	(0.119)	(0.043)	(0.045)

$F = 0.54$ with 12, 105 degrees of freedom if all coefficients identical
$F = 0.91$ with 6, 105 degrees of freedom if all coefficients identical except intercepts

Nondurable Manufacturing Regressions

Industry	1	2	3	4	5	6	7	Aggregate	Pooled	Pooled With Separate Intercepts
df	15	15	15	15	15	15	15	15	117	111
$\bar{R}^2$	0.1873	−0.0525	0.3189	0.4413	0.0032	0.0638	0.1239	0.0787	0.1733	0.1479
$\bar{S}_{est}$	0.04	0.05	0.02	0.03	0.04	0.08	0.07	0.02	0.05	0.05
d	1.944	1.828	1.940	2.215	1.877	1.930	2.178	1.972	2.081	2.148
Variables										
$\lambda - \lambda'$	0.140	0.014	0.025	0.026	0.016	0.035	0.023	0.016	0.022	0.025
	(0.010)	(0.013)	(0.007)	(0.008)	(0.012)	(0.025)	(0.020)	(0.008)	(0.005)	(0.013)
λ	0.513	0.119	0.567	0.713	0.315	0.453	0.519	0.680	0.489	0.451
	(0.237)	(0.266)	(0.195)	(0.193)	(0.307)	(0.314)	(0.287)	(0.442)	(0.096)	(0.103)

$F = 0.41$ with 12, 105 degrees of freedom if all coefficients identical
$F = 0.42$ with 6, 105 degrees of freedom if all coefficients identical except intercepts

(continued)

TABLE 5.3.4 (*continued*). ADAPTIVE EXPECTATIONS—LONG RATIO

$$\frac{\text{ALSALE} - \text{SALE}_{-2}}{\text{SALE}_{-2}} = \lambda - \lambda' + \lambda\left(\frac{\text{ALSALE}_{-1} - \text{SALE}_{-2}}{\text{SALE}_{-2}}\right) + \frac{\epsilon}{\text{SALE}_{-2}}$$

Pooled Firm Data

	Nonferrous Metals	Electrical Machinery	Nonelectrical Machinery	Chemicals	Petroleum
$\bar{R}^2$	0.7258	0.4618	0.4169	0.4484	0.2225
$\bar{S}_{est}$	0.09	0.23	0.12	0.18	0.13
df	177	316	313	381	433
F	0.80	0.90	1.06	1.24	0.72
$\bar{d}$	2.06	2.22	2.11	2.11	2.13
Number of firms	9	17	16	20	20
Variables					
$\lambda - \lambda'$	0.021	0.037	0.028	0.026	0.017
	(0.007)	(0.013)	(0.007)	(0.010)	(0.006)
λ	0.716	0.743	0.722	0.826	0.474
	(0.033)	(0.045)	(0.048)	(0.047)	(0.042)

adjustment in all the other industries and for the aggregate and pooled regressions at the durable and nondurable level. When we turn to the individual firm regressions, we find that with the exception of one non-electrical and two chemical firms, all the estimated values of λ are of reasonable magnitude.

The effects of adding seasonal dummy variables to equation 3.10 are revealed on Table 5.3.5. The adaptive expectations model yields reasonable estimates of λ for all but two industries, food and beverage and chemicals. Now that adjustment has been made for seasonality, the adaptive expectations model generally provides a tighter fit than Ferber's law. Transportation equipment constitutes the only exception at the aggregate level. Furthermore, the pooled firm data regression for the petroleum industry, while yielding a reasonable estimate of λ, does not fit as well as Ferber's law. We shall briefly summarize the individual firm regressions rather than report them on detailed tables. We found that only eight of the individual firm regressions yielded a λ estimate outside the hypothesized zero to one range. Of 72 individual firm regressions, the adaptive expectations model was preferable in terms of the highest $\bar{R}^2$ criterion for 45 firms. Since the probability of obtaining 45 or more successes out of 72 tosses of a fair coin is 0.0222, the evidence again suggests that it is reasonable to accept the Nerlove rather than the Ferber model for explaining the formation of expectations at the firm level. With the exception of the petroleum industry, where precisely one half of the firms gave a higher $\bar{R}^2$ to the Ferber model, more than two thirds of the firms in each industry yielded a higher fit to the adaptive expectations hypothesis of expectations formation.

5.3.3 *Expectation Revision*

A generalization of the exponential forecasting procedure is embodied in the concept of expectations revision that David Meiselman exploited in his empirical study of *The Term Structure of Interest Rates* [1962]. Now it will be remembered that ALSALE, a preliminary forecast of SALE, is formulated at the beginning of period $t - 1$, while ASSALE constitutes a revised forecast of the same variable formulated at the beginning of period t. A reasonable conjecture is that the magnitude of the revision depends, in part, upon the extent to which developments in period $t - 1$ departed from expectation.[24] After all, if the forecaster is not surprised during period $t - 1$, why should he revise his initial forecast? If we hypothesize that the major source of

[24] This concept of expectation revision is closely related to the realization concept of investment behavior; see Modigliani and Cohen [1961].

TABLE 5.3.5. ADAPTIVE EXPECTATIONS—LONG RATIO SEASONAL DUMMIES

$$\frac{\text{ALSALE} - \text{SALE}_{-2}}{\text{SALE}_{-2}} = \lambda - \lambda' + \lambda\left(\frac{\text{ALSALE}_{-1} - \text{SALE}_{-2}}{\text{SALE}_{-2}}\right) + \alpha_1 S_1 + \alpha_2 S_2 + \alpha_3 S_3 + \frac{\epsilon}{\text{SALE}_{-2}}$$

Durable Manufacturing Regressions

Industry	1	2	3	4	5	6	7	Aggregate	Pooled	Pooled With Separate Intercepts
df	12	12	12	12	12	12	12	12	114	108
$\bar{R}^2$	0.9483	0.4340	0.8414	0.9148	0.9253	0.2264	0.9035	0.8678	0.7583	0.7472
$\bar{S}_{est}$	0.0990	0.0405	0.0189	0.0166	0.0717	0.0496	0.0314	0.0260	0.0983	0.1006
d	1.852	2.336	0.952	1.304	1.678	1.766	2.176	0.899		
Variables										
$\lambda - \lambda'$	0.056	0.008	0.078	−0.009	0.294	0.050	0.068	0.087	0.071	0.071
	(0.045)	(0.022)	(0.012)	(0.013)	(0.056)	(0.023)	(0.020)	(0.016)	(0.017)	(0.028)
λ	0.846	0.444	0.422	0.435	0.924	0.627	0.235	0.887	0.818	0.818
	(0.060)	(0.207)	(0.200)	(0.173)	(0.176)	(0.261)	(0.160)	(0.145)	(0.045)	(0.048)
α_1	−0.073	0.021	−0.079	0.050	−0.233	−0.042	−0.125	−0.097	−0.074	−0.074
	(0.080)	(0.039)	(0.016)	(0.022)	(0.132)	(0.044)	(0.021)	(0.040)	(0.028)	(0.028)
α_2	0.108	0.031	−0.073	0.096	−0.343	−0.053	−0.089	−0.055	−0.033	−0.033
	(0.069)	(0.032)	(0.022)	(0.021)	(0.077)	(0.034)	(0.031)	(0.023)	(0.025)	(0.026)
α_3	−0.221	−0.014	−0.025	0.010	−0.520	−0.034	0.117	−0.141	−0.103	−0.103
	(0.068)	(0.033)	(0.013)	(0.026)	(0.071)	(0.036)	(0.022)	(0.026)	(0.025)	(0.026)

$F = 9.65$ with 30, 84 degrees of freedom if all coefficients identical
$F = 11.92$ with 24, 84 degrees of freedom if all coefficients identical except intercepts

Nondurable Manufacturing Regressions

Industry	1	2	3	4	5	6	7	Aggregate	Pooled	Pooled With Separate Intercepts
df	12	12	12	12	12	12	12	12	114	108
$\bar{R}^2$	0.8556	0.9602	0.3487	0.7542	0.8169	0.6681	0.8593	0.9117	0.3053	0.2868
$\bar{S}_{est}$	0.0162	0.0101	0.0220	0.0217	0.0191	0.0488	0.0300	0.0077	0.0475	0.0482
d	1.802	2.865	1.599	2.070	1.755	2.196	1.773	1.998		
Variables										
$\lambda - \lambda'$	0.021	0.078	0.015	−0.019	0.065	−0.028	0.091	0.030	0.024	0.027
	(0.011)	(0.005)	(0.010)	(0.013)	(0.009)	(0.022)	(0.033)	(0.006)	(0.008)	(0.014)
λ	−0.198	0.449	0.384	−0.045	0.005	0.224	0.150	0.265	0.485	0.446
	(0.217)	(0.079)	(0.216)	(0.218)	(0.246)	(0.255)	(0.266)	(0.182)	(0.089)	(0.095)
α_1	−0.060	−0.116	0.010	0.045	−0.020	0.028	−0.139	−0.037	−0.033	−0.033
	(0.016)	(0.009)	(0.015)	(0.019)	(0.015)	(0.033)	(0.037)	(0.006)	(0.012)	(0.012)
α_1	−0.013	−0.112	0.024	0.100	−0.102	0.154	−0.125	−0.022	−0.004	−0.005
	(0.019)	(0.007)	(0.016)	(0.022)	(0.013)	(0.033)	(0.035)	(0.007)	(0.012)	(0.012)
α_3	0.066	−0.038	0.028	0.085	−0.067	0.133	0.015	0.026	0.031	0.031
	(0.011)	(0.007)	(0.016)	(0.023)	(0.018)	(0.042)	(0.043)	(0.005)	(0.012)	(0.012)

$F = 9.30$ with 30, 84 degrees of freedom if all coefficients identical

$F = 11.21$ with 24, 84 degrees of freedom if all coefficients identical except intercepts

(continued)

TABLE 5.3.5 (*continued*). ADAPTIVE EXPECTATIONS—LONG RATIO SEASONAL DUMMIES

$$\frac{\text{ALSALE} - \text{SALE}_{-2}}{\text{SALE}_{-2}} = \lambda - \lambda' + \lambda\left(\frac{\text{ALSALE}_{-1} - \text{SALE}_{-2}}{\text{SALE}_{-2}}\right) + \alpha_1 S_1 + \alpha_1 S_1 + \alpha_3 S_3 + \frac{\epsilon}{\text{SALE}_{-2}}$$

Pooled Firm Data

	Nonferrous Metals	Electrical Machinery	Nonelectrical Machinery	Chemicals	Petroleum
$\bar{R}^2$	0.7351	0.4824	0.4499	0.5315	0.2780
$\bar{S}_{est}$	0.08	0.23	0.11	0.17	0.12
df	174	313	310	378	430
F	1.33	5.27	2.78		3.56
$\bar{d}$	2.01	2.16	2.14	2.03	2.05
Number of firms	9	17	16	20	20
Variables:					
$\lambda - \lambda'$	0.012	0.030	0.081	−0.034	−0.007
	(0.012)	(0.024)	(0.012)	(0.016)	(0.012)
λ	0.716	0.746	0.741	0.768	0.456
	(0.034)	(0.045)	(0.048)	(0.047)	(0.043)
α_1	0.006	−0.029	−0.083	0.115	−0.012
	(0.018)	(0.036)	(0.018)	(0.024)	(0.017)
α_2	0.043	0.095	−0.037	0.166	0.035
	(0.018)	(0.036)	(0.018)	(0.026)	(0.017)
α_3	−0.009	−0.034	−0.022	−0.009	0.084
	(0.018)	(0.036)	(0.018)	(0.025)	(0.017)

surprise concerns the sales forecast error, we have:[25]

$$\text{ASSALE} - \text{ALSALE} = \beta(\text{SALE}_{-1} - \text{ASSALE}_{-1}) + \epsilon \qquad (3.11)$$

While intuition may suggest that β should be positive, Eisner [1958] has pointed out that β might conceivably be negative. For example, if sales in period $t - 1$ exceed the anticipated level because favorable production conditions have enabled the firm to fill an outstanding order sooner than planned, it may be reasonable for the firm to revise its sales forecast for period t in a downward direction.

The relationship between revision equation 3.11 and the adaptive expectations concept deserves consideration.[26] Suppose that the short anticipation is determined by the following equation:

$$\text{ASSALE} = \sum_{i=1}^{\infty} \lambda_i \text{SALE}_{-i} + \epsilon' \qquad (3.12)$$

where the weights do not necessarily decline geometrically. When the earlier expectation concerning sales in period t was formulated, SALE_{-1} had not been observed. Suppose that the forecaster replaces this variable with its anticipated value, ASSALE_{-1}, when he formulates his long horizon forecast. We would then have:

$$\text{ALSALE} = \lambda_1 \text{ASSALE}_{-1} + \sum_{i=2}^{\infty} \lambda_i \text{SALE}_{-i} + \epsilon'' \qquad (3.13)$$

Subtracting this equation from 3.12 yields revision equation 3.11. Note that $\beta = \lambda_1$.[27] Furthermore, since $\epsilon = \epsilon' - \epsilon''$, it will have zero expected value if ϵ' and ϵ'' have the same expected value; thus, an additive seasonal would conveniently cancel out. It must be noted, however, that a more complicated revision equation than 3.12 is implied by Ferber's law.

The regression results obtained by fitting equation 3.11 to benchmark adjusted industry data are reported on Table 5.3.6; all variables are divided by SALE_{-1} in an attempt to achieve homoscedasticity. These estimates must be interpreted with caution, for the method of least squares is applicable only under quite restrictive conditions; specifically, it is necessary for ϵ to be distributed independently of $\text{SALE}_{-1} - \text{ASSALE}_{-1}$ if the method of least

[25] In terms of the "prescript" type of notation customarily utilized in studies of the term structure of interest rate, this equation might be written as ${}_{t+1}S_t - {}_{t+1}S_{t-1} = \beta(S_t - {}_tS_{t-1})$, where S_t is actual sales in period t, ${}_{t+1}S_t$ is the short anticipation of sales for period $t + 1$ held at the end of period t, and ${}_{t+1}S_{t-1}$ is the long anticipation about period $t + 1$, as formulated at the end of period $t - 1$.

[26] For a more detailed discussion, see Jacob Mincer [1966].

[27] In the special case of adaptive forecasting, in which the weights λ_i decline geometrically, $\lambda_i = (1 - \lambda)\lambda^i$ in terms of equation 3.1, and it is easily shown that $\text{ALSALE}_{+1} = \text{ASSALE}$.

TABLE 5.3.6. EXPECTATION REVISION

$$\frac{\text{SALE} - \text{ALSALE}}{\text{SALE}_{-1}} = \alpha + \beta\left(\frac{\text{SALE}_{-1} - \text{ASSALE}_{-1}}{\text{SALE}_{-1}}\right) + \epsilon$$

Durable Manufacturing Regressions

Industry	1	2	3	4	5	6	7	Aggregate	Pooled	Pooled With Separate Intercept
df	15	15	15	15	15	15	15	15	117	111
$\bar{R}^2$	0.8485	0.4968	0.5199	0.2554	−0.0286	0.4878	0.6171	0.3546	0.6804	0.7010
$\bar{S}_{est}$	0.13	0.03	0.02	0.03	0.11	0.04	0.04	0.04	0.08	0.08
d	1.108	1.994	1.725	0.835	2.031	1.795	1.856	0.864	1.266	1.450
Variables										
α	−0.058	−0.016	−0.004	−0.002	−0.035	−0.003	−0.002	−0.018	−0.017	0.006
	(0.032)	(0.007)	(0.005)	(0.006)	(0.028)	(0.009)	(0.010)	(0.009)	(0.007)	(0.019)
β	2.247	0.757	1.343	0.755	0.659	0.968	1.176	1.346	1.950	1.897
	(0.236)	(0.185)	(0.314)	(0.296)	(0.885)	(0.240)	(0.227)	(0.430)	(0.123)	(0.121)

$F = 3.80$ with 12, 105 degrees of freedom if all coefficients identical

$F = 4.78$ with 6, 105 degrees of freedom if all coefficients identical except intercepts

Nondurable Manufacturing Regressions

Industry	1	2	3	4	5	6	7	Aggregate	Pooled	Pooled With Separate Intercept
df	15	15	15	15	15	15	15	15	117	111
$\bar{R}^2$	0.6857	0.7504	0.5441	0.6024	0.2641	0.6721	0.4174	0.5160	0.5927	0.5962
$\bar{S}_{est}$	0.01	0.02	0.02	0.02	0.02	0.04	0.03	0.01	0.02	0.02
d	1.596	1.293	1.489	2.370	2.232	1.494	2.287	1.553	1.864	1.949
Variables										
α	0.004	−0.013	0.004	−0.001	0.001	0.004	−0.007	−0.001	−0.002	−0.007
	(0.003)	(0.005)	(0.004)	(0.006)	(0.005)	(0.010)	(0.007)	(0.003)	(0.002)	(0.006)
β	1.160	0.997	0.730	0.956	0.721	1.370	0.852	0.945	0.988	1.024
	(0.194)	(0.142)	(0.163)	(0.190)	(0.278)	(0.236)	(0.241)	(0.222)	(0.075)	(0.079)

$F = 1.32$ with 12, 105 degrees of freedom if all coefficients identical
$F = 1.44$ with 6, 105 degrees of freedom if all coefficients identical except intercepts

(continued)

TABLE 5.3.6 (*continued*). EXPECTATION REVISION

$$\frac{\text{SALE} - \text{ALSALE}}{\text{SALE}_{-1}} = \alpha + \beta\left(\frac{\text{SALE}_{-1} - \text{ASSALE}_{-1}}{\text{SALE}_{-1}}\right) + \epsilon$$

Pooled Firm Data

	Nonferrous Metals	Electrical Machinery	Nonelectrical Machinery	Chemicals	Petroleum
$\bar{R}^2$	0.1875	0.0016	0.0591	0.0048	0.1492
$\bar{S}_{est}$	0.10	0.17	0.09	0.09	0.10
df	187	334	329	407	455
F	1.92	2.65	4.50	2.13	1.10
$\bar{d}$	1.84	1.78	1.76	1.85	2.11
Number of firms	9	17	16	20	20
Variables					
α	−0.008	−0.004	−0.006	0.007	0.007
	(0.007)	(0.010)	(0.005)	(0.004)	(0.005)
β	0.318	0.067	0.229	0.084	0.394
	(0.048)	(0.054)	(0.049)	(0.049)	(0.044)

squares is to yield maximum likelihood parameter estimates.[28] In terms of the $\bar{R}^2$ criterion, the fits are not unreasonable, except for the motor vehicles and equipment industry. In contrast to Meiselman's term-structure results, however, we find that a number of the estimated revision coefficients, the β's, are greater than unity. The large coefficient for iron and steel implies that if this quarter's sales exceeded the anticipated level by 5 percent, the typical forecaster revises his anticipations for next period upwards by more than 10 percent! This is an extreme case, and the iron and steel industry may be subject to distortions from strikes. For none of the other industries does the revision coefficient exceed unity by more than twice its standard error. Notice, however, that the pooled durable regressions provide estimates of the revision coefficient that exceed unity by several standard errors.

To summarize, we find that there is at least some evidence that expectations are subject to quite volatile revisions as the forecaster moves closer to the horizon of his prediction. Certainly, we do not find any indication that an unexpectedly large volume of sales in the current quarter is interpreted by entrepreneurs as simply an intertemporial shift in demand toward the present at the expense of a reduction in sales volume for the subsequent quarter. But we also find that the revision hypothesis does not explain too substantial a portion of the change in the sales prediction. We suspect that there may be other surprises, in addition to the error made in predicting the current quarter's sales volume, that cause the firm to revise its sales expectation for the coming period. If this is indeed so, and if we are permitted to generalize from these results, we must conclude that in order to explain revisions in such phenomenon as interest rate futures, it may well be necessary to include errors made in predicting a variety of variables.

5.4 "RATIONAL" OR "IMPLICIT" EXPECTATIONS

In contrast to the behavioral models of Ferber and Nerlove, the rational expectations hypothesis advanced by Muth [1961] is a normative proposition rather than a theory of how expectations are actually formed. Muth reserved the term "rational" for expectations possessing certain desirable attributes. One aspect of Muth's rational expectations concept concerns the statistical properties of the forecast error. He hypothesized that the discrepancy between the forecast, P, and the actual realization, A, *should* be a random variable with zero expected value. In addition, he argued that the forecast error *should* be uncorrelated with P. Thus,

$$A = P + \epsilon \qquad E(\epsilon) = 0,\ E(P\epsilon) = 0 \tag{4.1}$$

[28] Because of the presence of the lagged dependent variable the method of least squares may be expected to yield a biased if consistent estimate of β.

While it may seem strange to regard A as a random variable, Muth noted that the forecast is obviously known at the time the prediction is made, while A is not only unknown but can also be regarded as yet to be determined by a process that may well be stochastic.

Is it reasonable to expect that respondents will report anticipations that are rational in the sense in which Muth defines the term? A brief review of three types of forecasts considered in Chapter 4.2.2 will remind us that this is an empirical question that cannot be resolved solely on the basis of theoretical considerations. In that chapter, we considered forecasts derived directly from a customer survey, forecasts obtained by subjecting the raw customer survey data to optimal linear correlation, and forecasts derived with an econometric model. We found that the raw customer survey forecasts will yield prediction errors correlated with the forecasts—hence they cannot be "rational." On the other hand, rational forecasts uncorrelated with the prediction error will be obtained by the other two procedures. That is, the assumption that $E(P\epsilon) = 0$ is intuitively appealing, for if it were violated it would be possible to improve on the accuracy of the forecasts with a simple corrective adjustment. Still, an ambiguity does remain, for the answer to the question of whether forecasts are rational or not may hinge in part upon whether respondents transform their customer survey data in advance of reporting the information to the OBE.

The respondent will report anticipations satisfying Muth's rationality postulate if they are being used as "certainty equivalents" in determining the firm's optimal output level within the context of the Holt, Modigliani, Muth, and Simon [1960] model of production smoothing and inventory control. The certainty equivalence theorem of Simon [1956] and Theil [1957]—applicable when the loss function is quadratic, the parameters of the system are known precisely, and the variance of the disturbance is unaffected by the actions of the decision maker—states that when the magnitude of the state variables are not known precisely, the optimal decision may still be made by substituting a "certainty equivalent" forecast into the same linear decision rule that would be applicable if one actually knew the magnitudes of the variables that must be forecast. For more complicated problems, a point forecast will not suffice and higher moments of the decision maker's prior distribution may be involved in making an optimal decision. Under these circumstances, a certainty equivalence forecast may not exist, and the concept of "rational" expectations loses much of its force.

We shall first consider the empirical question of whether observed anticipations satisfy certain restrictions that Muth imposed in formulating his concept of rational expectations. Then, in Section 5.4.2 we shall examine empirical evidence concerning Mills' [1957, 1962] conjecture that the actual realization can be fruitfully employed as an implicit proxy for *ex ante* variables in econometric applications whenever anticipations are not directly observable.

5.4.1 *On the "Sufficiency" of Anticipations*

Muth [1960] also argues that a "rational" forecaster will incorporate all the information available to him at the time he makes his forecast. In a rough sense, then, Muth's rationality concept is related to the statistician's concept of *sufficiency*. Muth argues, for example, that it should be impossible to predict actual developments more precisely by incorporating, in addition to the forecast, information concerning prior sales volume. Consider, for illustrative purposes, the following model:

$$A = \beta_0 + \beta_1 P + \beta_2 A_{-1} + \epsilon \tag{4.2}$$

If the forecast P has been made by a forecaster who is rational in the sense in which the term is defined by Muth, we must have $\beta_0 = \beta_2 = 0$ and $\beta_1 = 1$. Otherwise, the forecaster could have achieved a smaller root-mean-square error[29] by adjusting his forecast with the information readily available at the time the forecast is made.

This sufficiency aspect of Muth's rational expectations concept has important implications with regard to the problem of analyzing such phenomena as inventory behavior when actual anticipations cannot be directly observed. In a study of inventory investment, Lovell [1961] invoked the more general hypothesis that actual sales are a weighted average of the two extremes of static and perfect forecasting.[30] Specifically, it was assumed:

$$P = \rho A_{-1} + (1 - \rho)A, \qquad 0 \leq \rho \leq 1 \tag{4.3}$$

This assumption was motivated by John Maynard Keynes' [1936, p. 51] remark that:

> . . . it is sensible for producers to base their expectations on the assumption that the most recently realized results will continue except insofar as there are definite reasons for expecting a change.

It is consistent with the empirical claim of Theil [1958] that forecasters typically underestimate change. Note that if ρ is unity, we have the extreme of static expectations; $\rho = 0$ corresponds to the opposite case in which there is no systematic tendency either to over- or underestimate the actual change in sales; if ρ were negative, it would imply that the actual change in sales is generally overestimated. Lovell [1964, pp. 205–206] tested 4.3 with sales

[29] This measure of forecasting precision is defined in Chapter 3.2.

[30] Ball and Drake [1963] compared the usefulness of this hypothesis with the Nerlove model in analyzing inventory movements in the United Kingdom.

anticipations data available for the cement industry.[31] It was found that the alternative model,

$$P = \rho A_{-4} + (1 - \rho)A, \qquad 0 \leq \rho \leq 1 \tag{4.4}$$

was more satisfactory for this industry, which is subject to marked seasonal fluctuations; ρ was found to be approximately 0.7, rather than zero. It should be noted, however, that while these results suggested that ρ, the anticipations coefficient, was significantly different from zero, this does not constitute a valid test of Muth's hypothesis. Under Muth's hypothesis that ϵ in 4.1 or 4.2 is distributed independently of P, the dependent variable must be A if consistent estimates of ρ are to be obtained.

In examining the validity of the sufficiency aspect of Muth's rational expectations assumption for short sales anticipations, we considered the following equation:

$$\text{SALE} = \beta_1 + \beta_2\text{ASSALE} + \beta_3\text{SALE}_{-1} + \beta_4\text{SALE}_{-4} + \epsilon \tag{4.5}$$

Under Muth's hypothesis, $\beta_2 = 1$ and $\beta_1 = \beta_3 = \beta_4 = 0$; in addition, ϵ and ASSALE are independently distributed. While the presence of lagged values of actual sales means that the parameter estimates are subject to Hurwicz bias, they are maximum likelihood estimates if ϵ is distributed normally and is free of serial correlation. The regressions obtained in fitting this model to the benchmarked aggregate data and to the individual firm data are reported on Table 5.4.1. For durable manufacturing industry aggregates, the results are on the whole reassuring for the Muth hypothesis. All the β_2 coefficients are reasonably close to unity. The negative t value of β_3 for iron and steel is inconsistent with Lovell's conjecture, equation 4.3, as well as Muth's hypothesis. Only the value of $\beta_3 = 0.318$ for the other durables industry constitutes a significant violation of Muth's model. For the nondurable aggregates on the other hand, β_2 is substantially less than unity for a number of industries. Furthermore, too many of the estimated values of β_3 and β_4 have large t values. The individual firm data results are also a source of disappointment, even in durable industries. Inspection of the pooled regressions reveals that β_2 is generally too small for Muth, while β_3 and β_4 are both positive and significant in practically every case. Since these pooled regressions are based on a substantial number of degrees of freedom, the consistency property of the parameter estimates suggest that these departures from Muth's sufficiency hypothesis cannot be attributed to Hurwicz bias.

Because it is conceivable that these results might be the consequence of heteroscedasticity, equation 4.5 was transformed by dividing through by

[31] Lovell [1961] had tested the equation indirectly within the context of a regression model explaining inventory investment. But in that study, for which observations on anticipated sales were not employed, the parameter ρ was not identified.

SALE_{-1} under the assumption that $\beta_1 = 0$:

$$\left(\frac{\text{SALE} - \text{SALE}_{-1}}{\text{SALE}_{-1}}\right) = \beta_1' + \beta_2'\left(\frac{\text{ASSALE} - \text{SALE}_{-1}}{\text{SALE}_{-1}}\right) + \beta_3'\left(\frac{\text{SALE}_{-1} - \text{SALE}_{-4}}{\text{SALE}_{-1}}\right) + \frac{\epsilon}{\text{SALE}_{-1}} \quad (4.6)$$

where

$$\beta_1' = \beta_3 + \beta_2 + \beta_4 - 1$$
$$\beta_2' = \beta_2$$
$$\beta_3' = \beta_4$$

Under Muth's hypothesis we should have $\beta_2' = 1$ and $\beta_1' = \beta_3' = 0$. Inspection of the regressions reported on Table 5.4.2 again suggests that at the aggregate industry level, the rationality hypothesis is quite satisfactory in durables; for nondurables, Muth's hypothesis again runs into some difficulty. Furthermore, in the pooled regressions, β_2 is generally less than the value of unity hypothesized by Muth. The fact that with the exception of nonferrous metals β_3' is significantly less than zero suggests that nondurable firms do not rationally employ the information provided by recent sales experience in formulating their short sales forecasts.

Essentially the same results were achieved in the analysis of the sufficiency aspect of long sales anticipations. On Table 5.4.3 we report regressions of the form

$$\text{SALE} = \beta_1 + \beta_2\text{ALSALE} + \beta_3\text{SALE}_{-2} + \beta_4\text{SALE}_{-4} + \epsilon \quad (4.7)$$

Because SALE_{-1} is not observed by the forecaster at the time his long prediction is formulated, SALE_{-2} is substituted for that variable. Dividing this equation by SALE_{-2} yields the regression form utilized in obtaining the alternative set of results reported on Table 5.4.4; again it turns out that the results are not sensitive to this adjustment for homoscedasticity. Examination of the tables reveals that for long anticipations the sufficiency aspect of Muth's rational expectations hypothesis is not entirely consistent with the evidence, although it fares rather better with the durable than with the nondurable industries. The pooled regressions based on individual firm data are particularly disappointing, for only the nonratio pooled regression for electrical machinery is satisfactory. With this one exception, the pooled firm estimates of β_2 are substantially below unity and both β_3 and β_4 are more than twice their standard errors in magnitude.

In summary, it appears that firms do not rationally employ the information provided by past sales experience in preparing either their short or their long sales forecasts. It is not difficult, however, to explain why there may be a systematic departure from the sufficiency aspect of Muth's rationality

TABLE 5.4.1. RATIONAL EXPECTATIONS—SHORT

$$SALE = \beta_1 + \beta_2 ASSALE + \beta_3 SALE_{-1} + \beta_4 SALE_{-4} + \epsilon$$

Durable Manufacturing Regressions

Industry	1	2	3	4	5	6	7	Aggregate	Pooled	Pooled With Separate Intercept
df	11	11	11	11	11	11	11	11	101	95
$\bar{R}^2$	0.9429	0.5641	0.9429	0.9460	0.9799	0.5335	0.8626	0.9816	0.9956	0.9957
$\bar{S}_{est}$	190.67	55.43	104.80	171.69	179.71	159.85	105.49	434.28	155.11	153.63
d	1.687	1.222	1.594	1.790	1.649	1.576	1.638	2.215	1.469	1.566
Variables										
β_1	283.382	−102.265	−198.725	−364.534	−146.280	420.503	248.618	−4484.414	−48.060	−0.420
	(461.847)	(495.149)	(442.451)	(721.651)	(394.490)	(1006.154)	(561.952)	(1980.689)	(36.878)	(125.200)
β_2	1.066	1.071	0.979	1.029	0.969	0.837	0.756	1.099	1.027	1.011
	(0.081)	(0.270)	(0.126)	(0.154)	(0.050)	(0.240)	(0.130)	(0.057)	(0.027)	(0.030)
β_3	−0.199	−0.114	0.036	−0.082	0.013	0.013	0.318	−0.011	−0.051	−0.057
	(0.061)	(0.210)	(0.089)	(0.111)	(0.044)	(0.224)	(0.123)	(0.049)	(0.020)	(0.026)
β_4	0.031	0.105	0.011	0.092	0.043	0.037	−0.159	0.032	0.025	0.034
	(0.050)	(0.148)	(0.091)	(0.101)	(0.053)	(0.131)	(0.182)	(0.047)	(0.025)	(0.026)

$F = 1.55$ with 24, 77 degrees of freedom if all coefficients identical
$F = 1.58$ with 18, 77 degrees of freedom if all coefficients identical except intercepts

Nondurable Manufacturing Regressions

Industry	1	2	3	4	5	6	7	Aggregate	Pooled	Pooled With Separate Intercept
df	11	11	11	11	11	11	11	11	101	95
$\bar{R}^2$	0.9158	0.7845	0.9064	0.9214	0.3728	0.7568	0.7399	0.9406	0.9984	0.9985
$\bar{S}_{est}$	189.17	131.92	72.23	213.74	125.82	56.55	197.51	548.00	163.46	162.06
d	2.247	1.698	2.671	1.559	1.924	2.042	2.424	1.530	1.993	1.980
Variables										
β_1	−1536.417	−108.441	250.851	260.587	4646.946	164.771	1635.630	653.086	10.496	251.551
	(1374.575)	(633.272)	(295.498)	(662.865)	(2108.979)	(365.856)	(1062.136)	(3276.819)	(31.261)	(310.009)
β_2	0.481	0.561	0.541	0.947	0.378	0.660	0.862	0.855	0.784	0.741
	(0.166)	(0.224)	(0.319)	(0.231)	(0.231)	(0.162)	(0.191)	(0.178)	(0.067)	(0.070)
β_3	0.202	0.533	−0.006	−0.161	0.095	0.172	0.048	0.244	0.155	0.126
	(0.117)	(0.224)	(0.382)	(0.192)	(0.211)	(0.199)	(0.134)	(0.159)	(0.053)	(0.057)
β_4	0.439	−0.057	0.410	0.193	0.040	0.052	−0.135	−0.116	0.062	0.107
	(0.199)	(0.166)	(0.184)	(0.169)	(0.186)	(0.201)	(0.206)	(0.150)	(0.063)	(0.069)

$F = 1.58$ with 24, 77 degrees of freedom if all coefficients identical
$F = 1.63$ with 18, 77 degrees of freedom if all coefficients identical except intercepts

(continued)

TABLE 5.4.1 (*continued*). RATIONAL EXPECTATIONS—SHORT

$$\text{SALE} = \beta_f + \beta_3\text{ASSALE} + \beta_2\text{SALE}_{-1} + \beta_4\text{SALE}_{-4} + \epsilon$$

Pooled Firm Data (Separate Intercepts)

	Nonferrous Metals	Electrical Machinery	Nonelectrical Machinery	Chemicals	Petroleum
Partial $\bar{R}^2$	0.6930	0.7167	0.9003	0.9052	0.8268
$\bar{S}_{est}$	5316.6	7052.0	7446.5	7730.9	7284.1
df	175	310	305	384	424
F	0.42	2.01	0.60	2.41	3.11
$\bar{d}$	1.77	1.78	1.84	1.77	1.81
Number of firms	9	17	16	20	20
Variables					
β_2	0.521	0.704	0.878	0.899	0.652
	(0.065)	(0.052)	(0.037)	(0.040)	(0.037)
β_3	0.266	0.097	0.074	0.078	0.205
	(0.061)	(0.036)	(0.023)	(0.029)	(0.032)
β_4	0.234	0.236	0.085	0.031	0.215
	(0.055)	(0.056)	(0.032)	(0.036)	(0.039)

concept. Suppose that in each quarter a prediction procedure provides a decision maker with a three-month sales forecast. Then if he knew the parameters of equation 4.5, he could obviously achieve better results by simply revising the original forecast in the light of prior sales history. The revised forecasts would be more accurate in terms of the RMSE criterion, and they would satisfy Muth's rationality criterion. But, in practice, the decision maker cannot revise the original forecasts that he receives in this way, for we benefited from hindsight in obtaining our estimates of the parameters of equation 4.5; we used data from our entire sample period. Unless the decision maker has a long history of experience with the nature of the forecasts that are being provided to him, he is unable to achieve the degree of forecasting precision suggested by Muth's definition of rational expectations. He may nonetheless be rationally revising his estimates of the parameters of 4.5 as each quarter provides new information concerning the systematic errors that are present in the forecasts that are being provided to him.

5.4.2 *Actual Realizations as a Proxy for Anticipations*

Equation 4.1 suggests that actual realizations may be employed as a proxy for anticipations in econometric work when observations on expected sales are not available. This is the "implicit expectations" approach utilized by Edwin Mills [1957, 1962] in his pathbreaking investigations of the production decision; the procedure was implicit in a pioneering econometric model by Klein [1950] based on data on the U.S. economy for the interwar period.[32] It constitutes an intriguing alternative to the more complicated procedure, utilized by such writers as Johnston [1961], of invoking Ferber's law as part of the maintained hypothesis in order to circumvent the problem created when *ex ante* data are not available.[33] The fruitfulness of the "implicit" expectations concept depends, in part, upon how precise firms are at predicting sales volume. While it is clear that the implicit expectations hypothesis

[32] Mills' concept of "implicit expectations" involves an alternative specification from Muth's of the stochastic properties of the disturbance of equation 4.1, for Mills requires that ϵ be distributed independently of A rather than P. If the forecast is derived from a survey of the firm's customers, the disturbance will have the desired property; "implicit" as opposed to "rational" expectations will be obtained. As Mills [1962, pp. 37–38] explains, this alternative specification permits one to obtain appropriate parameter estimates when A is used to replace P as an explanatory variable; for example, if the model explains production in terms of expected sales and predetermined variables, maximum likelihood parameter estimates may be obtained under Mill's specification if the error terms are normally distributed. To obtain maximum likelihood estimates with Muth's specification, it would be necessary to transform the equation by making the sales proxy the dependent variable.

[33] See also Moriguchi [1967].

TABLE 5.4.2. RATIONAL EXPECTATIONS—SHORT RATIO

$$\frac{\text{SALE} - \text{SALE}_{-1}}{\text{SALE}_{-1}} = \beta_1' + \beta_2'\left(\frac{\text{ASSALE} - \text{SALE}_{-1}}{\text{SALE}_{-1}}\right) + \beta\left(\frac{\text{SALE}_{-1} - \text{SALE}_{-4}}{\text{SALE}_{-1}}\right) + \frac{\epsilon}{\text{SALE}_{-1}}$$

Durable Manufacturing Regressions

Industry	1	2	3	4	5	6	7	Aggregate	Pooled	Pooled With Separate Intercept
df	12	12	12	12	12	12	12	12	102	96
$\bar{R}^2$	0.9738	0.7805	0.9140	0.9209	0.9893	0.6489	0.7759	0.9781	0.9543	0.9553
S_{est}	0.0437	0.0342	0.0166	0.0191	0.0289	0.0369	0.0304	0.0151	0.0327	0.0323
d	1.475	1.180	1.563	1.776	1.479	1.577	1.674	1.720		
Variables										
β_1'	−0.030	−0.004	−0.007	−0.003	0.003	−0.009	−0.011	−0.011	−0.010	−0.013
	(0.011)	(0.010)	(0.007)	(0.009)	(0.008)	(0.011)	(0.010)	(0.005)	(0.003)	(0.008)
β_2'	1.064	1.067	0.988	1.029	0.950	0.875	0.762	1.074	1.004	0.993
	(0.057)	(0.227)	(0.115)	(0.149)	(0.049)	(0.208)	(0.132)	(0.066)	(0.029)	(0.029)
β_3'	−0.025	−0.086	−0.004	−0.081	−0.052	−0.048	0.106	0.007	−0.020	−0.033
	(0.043)	(0.131)	(0.086)	(0.096)	(0.052)	(0.109)	(0.131)	(0.053)	(0.025)	(0.025)

$F = 1.51$ with 18, 84 degrees of freedom if all coefficients identical
$F = 1.54$ with 12, 84 degrees of freedom if all coefficients identical except intercepts

Nondurable Manufacturing Regressions

Industry	1	2	3	4	5	6	7	Aggregate	Pooled	Pooled With Separate Intercept
df	12	12	12	12	12	12	12	12	102	96
$\bar{S}^2$	0.7992	0.2593	0.3108	0.7408	0.5585	0.7215	0.8323	0.6823	0.6534	0.6682
$\bar{R}_{est}$	0.0134	0.0344	0.0217	0.0295	0.0153	0.0346	0.0288	0.0111	0.0278	0.0272
d	2.043	1.714	2.708	1.486	2.651	2.212	2.603	1.600		
Variables										
β_1'	0.014	0.009	0.021	0.015	−0.008	−0.009	−0.001	−0.004	0.004	0.009
	(0.007)	(0.010)	(0.012)	(0.014)	(0.006)	(0.011)	(0.011)	(0.007)	(0.004)	(0.007)
β_2'	0.471	0.576	0.487	0.933	0.762	0.657	1.004	0.883	0.719	0.737
	(0.169)	(0.225)	(0.320)	(0.235)	(0.181)	(0.148)	(0.182)	(0.173)	(0.067)	(0.068)
β_3'	−0.378	0.059	−0.416	−0.204	0.219	−0.106	0.160	0.134	−0.071	−0.082
	(0.192)	(0.140)	(0.181)	(0.163)	(0.168)	(0.131)	(0.210)	(0.140)	(0.058)	(0.059)

$F = 1.51$ with 18, 84 degrees of freedom if all coefficients identical
$F = 1.35$ with 12, 84 degrees of freedom if all coefficients identical except intercepts

(continued)

TABLE 5.4.2 (*continued*). RATIONAL EXPECTATIONS—SHORT RATIO

$$\frac{\text{SALE} - \text{SALE}_{-1}}{\text{SALE}_{-1}} = \beta_1' + \beta_2'\left(\frac{\text{ASSALE} - \text{SALE}_{-1}}{\text{SALE}_{-1}}\right) + \beta_3'\left(\frac{\text{SALE}_{-1} - \text{SALE}_{-4}}{\text{SALE}_{-1}}\right) + \frac{\epsilon}{\text{SALE}_{-1}}$$

	Nonferrous Metals	Electrical Machinery	Nonelectrical Machinery	Chemicals	Petroleum
			Pooled Firm Data		
$\bar{R}^2$	0.7947	0.6821	0.5558	0.7751	0.3933
$\bar{S}_{est}$	0.10	0.15	0.10	0.10	0.10
df	184	327	321	404	444
F	1.91	2.41	1.69	1.74	1.55
$\bar{d}$	1.74	1.77	1.81	1.62	1.76
Number of firms	9	17	16	20	20
Variables					
β_1'	0.006	0.021	−0.003	0.023	0.015
	(0.008)	(0.009)	(0.006)	(0.006)	(0.005)
β_2'	0.804	0.517	0.736	0.799	0.486
	(0.053)	(0.038)	(0.049)	(0.045)	(0.041)
β_3'	−0.054	−0.275	−0.105	−0.138	−0.179
	(0.041)	(0.041)	(0.040)	(0.044)	(0.036)

would be unsatisfactory if expectations were as imprecise as Ferber's [1953] analysis of the railroad shippers' carloading anticipations data had suggested, the evidence concerning the accuracy of anticipations data presented in Chapter 3 implies that the approaches of Mills and Muth deserve careful consideration.

In addition, the rational expectations hypothesis suggests another test of the validity of the Ferber and adaptive expectations hypotheses. Serious doubt will be cast upon the validity of Ferber's law of expectations formation to the extent that we find the actual realization providing a closer estimate of anticipations than can be obtained with his extrapolative equation. Such evidence would suggest that the regression results obtained with the Ferber model may be spurious and that his equation appears reasonably successful at predicting anticipations because actual sales developments move in conformity with his equation rather than because his model captures the essence of the process by which expectations are generated. Now the root-mean-square-error (RMSE) provides a measure of how accurately anticipations can be approximated with the rational expectations approach. If the RMSE's are generally smaller than the standard errors of the estimate obtained with regressions based on Ferber's hypothesis, the validity of his law of expectations formation will be open to serious question. Similarly, if the RMSE's of sales anticipations are generally smaller than the standard errors obtained with Nerlove's model, the validity of the adaptive expectations approach will be in doubt. In practice, how the RMSE's compare with the standard errors generated by the Ferber and Nerlove hypotheses hinges, in part, upon the level of aggregation.

At the aggregate level, the analysis of the benchmark adjusted industry data is not too encouraging for the structural hypothesis. Specifically, we find that for short sales anticipations the standard errors of estimate obtained with ratio regressions based on Ferber's law are larger than the RMSE's for nine of fourteen industries and for both the durable and non-durable aggregates. The adaptive expectations hypothesis, with seasonal dummies, does only slightly better at explaining short anticipations; for eight industries and the nondurable aggregates its predictions are closer than actual sales to anticipations. For long sales anticipations, which are not as accurate, Ferber's law is more satisfactory, for it dominates the use of actual sales as a proxy for long anticipations in all the industries except iron and steel. The adaptive expectations hypothesis dominates the actual realization proxy for seven industries and the durable aggregates.

Examination of the pooled firm data tells much the same story. Because of the accuracy of sales anticipations, the sales proxy does quite well. Indeed, actual sales provide a better approximation to the short anticipations in the majority of the five industries for which pooled regression results are available.

TABLE 5.4.3. RATIONAL EXPECTATIONS—LONG

$$SALE = \beta_1 + \beta_2 ALSALE + \beta_3 SALE_{-2} + \beta_4 SALE_{-4} + \epsilon$$

Durable Manufacturing Regressions

Industry	1	2	3	4	5	6	7	Aggregate	Pooled	Pooled With Separate Intercept
df	13	13	13	13	13	13	13	13	115	109
$\bar{R}^2$	0.5930	0.3189	0.8360	0.8861	0.8859	0.4852	0.5966	0.8274	0.9704	0.9713
$\bar{S}_{est}$	506.89	91.35	238.58	329.07	473.67	244.40	186.16	1545.15	395.57	389.32
d	2.033	1.272	0.986	1.076	1.542	1.499	1.192	1.078	1.956	2.149
Variables										
β_1	5562.550	511.981	−141.883	−100.979	−1150.530	1307.686	383.831	−3320.614	−114.349	7.519
	(1549.732)	(329.235)	(715.364)	(804.703)	(818.440)	(792.116)	(689.399)	(4434.109)	(88.404)	(245.010)
β_2	0.673	0.347	0.738	1.210	1.018	0.524	0.502	1.217	0.937	0.945
	(0.251)	(0.398)	(0.304)	(0.257)	(0.123)	(0.270)	(0.196)	(0.218)	(0.071)	(0.074)
β_3	−0.841	0.207	0.232	−0.251	0.196	0.254	0.458	−0.160	0.030	0.002
	(0.201)	(0.334)	(0.239)	(0.182)	(0.095)	(0.342)	(0.184)	(0.164)	(0.049)	(0.055)
β_4	−0.346	0.117	0.048	0.034	−0.034	−0.120	−0.073	0.008	0.037	0.034
	(0.159)	(0.204)	(0.198)	(0.185)	(0.137)	(0.243)	(0.277)	(0.155)	(0.064)	(0.066)

$F = 3.21$ with 24, 91 degrees of freedom if all coefficients identical
$F = 3.52$ with 18, 91 degrees of freedom if all coefficients identical except intercepts

Nondurable Manufacturing Regressions

Industry	1	2	3	4	5	6	7	Aggregate	Pooled	Pooled With Separate Intercept
df	13	13	13	13	13	13	13	13	115	109
$\bar{R}^2$	0.9230	0.6892	0.9381	0.8750	0.7409	0.3941	0.7153	0.8831	0.9967	0.9968
$\bar{S}_{est}$	218.26	180.58	72.52	322.73	176.96	94.71	268.12	1011.83	235.93	232.86
d	1.078	0.974	2.140	1.298	1.744	0.810	2.568	1.225	1.408	1.484
Variables										
β_1	−1297.977	977.168	197.346	−368.132	4044.949	328.380	1607.164	3818.206	33.603	451.850
	(1196.065)	(553.746)	(202.567)	(755.324)	(956.971)	(365.091)	(1034.565)	(4025.722)	(42.125)	(319.806)
β_2	0.306	0.348	0.536	0.915	0.515	0.342	0.657	0.494	0.538	0.480
	(0.154)	(0.300)	(0.233)	(0.438)	(0.131)	(0.255)	(0.181)	(0.273)	(0.077)	(0.081)
β_3	0.181	0.844	0.015	−0.361	0.208	0.303	0.168	0.342	0.191	0.170
	(0.093)	(0.275)	(0.251)	(0.304)	(0.151)	(0.264)	(0.145)	(0.209)	(0.061)	(0.062)
β_4	0.628	−0.443	0.409	0.519	−0.152	0.148	−0.048	0.094	0.282	0.300
	(0.205)	(0.291)	(0.178)	(0.236)	(0.166)	(0.250)	(0.210)	(0.237)	(0.079)	(0.087)

$F = 2.39$ with 24, 91 degrees of freedom if all coefficients identical
$F = 2.56$ with 18, 91 degrees of freedom if all coefficients identical except intercepts

(continued)

TABLE 5.4.3 (*continued*). RATIONAL EXPECTATIONS—LONG

$$\text{SALE} = \beta_f + \beta_2\text{ALSALE} + \beta_3\text{SALE}_{-2} + \beta_4\text{SALE}_{-4} + \epsilon$$

Pooled Firm Data (Separate Intercepts)

	Nonferrous Metals	Electrical Machinery	Nonelectrical Machinery	Chemicals	Petroleum
Partial $\bar{R}^2$	0.6133	0.5487	0.8612	0.8469	0.6988
$\bar{S}_{est}$	6283.2	9311.9	10361	10429	10358
df	190	336	331	407	454
F	0.69	1.55	0.66	1.10	6.43
d	1.44	1.66	1.42	1.43	1.60
Number of firms	9	17	16	20	20
Variables					
β_2	0.388	1.053	0.753	0.695	0.061
	(0.068)	(0.080)	(0.043)	(0.058)	(0.025)
β_3	0.343	0.036	0.201	0.207	0.249
	(0.061)	(0.042)	(0.031)	(0.037)	(0.038)
β_4	0.263	−0.171	0.161	0.101	0.807
	(0.063)	(0.075)	(0.043)	(0.053)	(0.041)

One exception is petroleum, where both the Ferber and the Nerlove models dominate; the other is nonferrous metals where the Ferber model proves superior to the naive proxy.

It was only when we turned to the individual firm regressions that we found clear evidence that Ferber's law and the adaptive expectations model are superior to the implicit proxy. For only about one fourth of the firms did either the Ferber or the Nerlove models do worse than the actual realization as a predictor of short sales anticipations. And the evidence is even more decisive for long anticipations. The actual realization provides a better fit than Ferber's law, equation 2.3′, in explaining long anticipations for only 12 percent of the firms. The adaptive expectations approach, equation 3.10 with seasonal dummies added, was dominated by the actual realization for only 9 percent of the firms.

In sum, then, the use of the actual realization as an implicit proxy fails only at the individual firm level, where both the Nerlove and Ferber models prove superior. Both structural models lose out in the process of aggregating and data pooling, the errors of aggregation and the homogeneity assumption involved in pooling data serving to restrict the force with which the Ferber and Nerlove models operate relative to the effectiveness of the proxy procedure.

Even at the firm level, however, both Ferber's law and the adaptive expectations model are in trouble when compared with Lovell's [1961] slightly more complicated proxy procedure for approximating anticipated sales. This procedure, embodied in equation 4.3, becomes in ratio form:[34]

$$\frac{P - A_{-1}}{A_{-1}} = (1 - \rho)\frac{A - A_{-1}}{A_{-1}} + (\rho' - \rho) + \epsilon. \tag{4.8}$$

This constitutes a relaxation of the sufficiency aspect of Muth's rational expectations hypothesis (i.e., the restriction that $\rho = \rho' = 0$). With sufficient data for estimating the parameters of 4.8, this proxy can hardly do worse than the implicit proxy procedure, which did well except at the individual firm level. Comparison of the ability of equation 4.8 to predict expectations with that of the Nerlove and Ferber model was discouraging for the structural models. For short anticipations, Lovell's proxy dominated Ferber's equation for 56 of 82 firms; it dominated the adaptive expectations equation for just over half of the firms. For long anticipations, both structural models are only

[34] The intercept is nonzero only if the expectation is regarded as a weighted average of last period's actual figure and the realization with weights *not* summing to unity; i.e., $P = \rho A_{-1} + (1 - \rho')A$.

TABLE 5.4.4. RATIONAL EXPECTATIONS—LONG RATIO

$$\frac{\text{SALE} - \text{SALE}_{-2}}{\text{SALE}_{-2}} = \beta_1' + \beta_2'\left(\frac{\text{ALSALE} - \text{SALE}_{-2}}{\text{SALE}_{-2}}\right) + \beta_3'\left(\frac{\text{SALE}_{-2} - \text{SALE}_{-4}}{\text{SALE}_{-2}}\right) + \frac{\epsilon}{\text{SALE}_{-2}}$$

Durable Manufacturing Regressions

Industry	1	2	3	4	5	6	7	Aggregate	Pooled	Pooled With Separate Intercept
df	14	14	14	14	14	14	14	14	116	110
$\bar{R}^2$	0.8918	0.2333	0.3675	0.7657	0.9181	0.2353	0.4511	0.8041	0.8531	0.8572
$\bar{S}_{est}$	0.1704	0.0632	0.0402	0.0388	0.0914	0.0684	0.0544	0.0460	0.0899	0.0886
d	2.199	1.163	1.045	1.099	1.952	1.281	0.992	1.196		
Variables										
β_1'	−0.116	−0.002	−0.010	−0.022	−0.013	−0.010	0.002	−0.037	−0.026	−0.022
	(0.047)	(0.022)	(0.018)	(0.016)	(0.024)	(0.019)	(0.018)	(0.016)	(0.009)	(0.022)
β_2'	1.234	0.733	0.767	1.295	1.016	0.719	0.525	1.219	1.008	1.024
	(0.211)	(0.374)	(0.263)	(0.232)	(0.115)	(0.274)	(0.197)	(0.182)	(0.069)	(0.068)
β_3'	0.067	−0.132	0.021	−0.005	0.148	−0.064	−0.036	0.053	−0.014	−0.026
	(0.173)	(0.193)	(0.183)	(0.162)	(0.141)	(0.230)	(0.231)	(0.138)	(0.063)	(0.063)

$F = 1.54$ with 18, 98 degrees of freedom if all coefficients identical

$F = 1.49$ with 12, 98 degrees of freedom if all coefficients identical except intercepts

Nondurable Manufacturing Regressions

Industry	1	2	3	4	5	6	7	Aggregate	Pooled	Pooled With Separate Intercept
df	14	14	14	14	14	14	14	14	116	110
$\bar{R}^2$	0.8554	−0.0459	0.4458	0.6554	0.3151	0.2221	0.6264	0.3459	0.3946	0.3972
$\bar{S}_{est}$	0.0155	0.0550	0.0233	0.0441	0.0300	0.0612	0.0408	0.0222	0.0431	0.0430
d	1.049	0.923	2.025	1.131	1.132	0.860	2.288	1.135		
Variable										
β_1'	0.021	0.020	0.022	0.026	0.005	0.010	0.005	0.013	0.017	0.013
	(0.006)	(0.015)	(0.014)	(0.026)	(0.009)	(0.022)	(0.012)	(0.011)	(0.005)	(0.011)
β_2'	0.337	0.390	0.550	0.795	0.517	0.357	0.682	0.540	0.479	0.483
	(0.152)	(0.346)	(0.257)	(0.424)	(0.204)	(0.252)	(0.187)	(0.278)	(0.088)	(0.097)
β_3'	−0.521	0.242	−0.422	−0.522	−0.005	−0.219	−0.050	−0.122	−0.209	−0.228
	(0.180)	(0.304)	(0.183)	(0.233)	(0.247)	(0.201)	(0.186)	(0.218)	(0.081)	(0.084)

$F = 1.50$ with 18, 98 degrees of freedom if all coefficients identical
$F = 1.67$ with 12, 98 degrees of freedom if all coefficients identical except intercepts

(*Continued*)

TABLE 5.4.4 (*continued*). RATIONAL EXPECTATIONS—LONG RATIO

$$\frac{\text{SALE} - \text{SALE}_{-2}}{\text{SALE}_{-2}} = \beta_1' + \beta_3'\left(\frac{\text{ALSALE} - \text{SALE}_{-2}}{\text{SALE}_{-2}}\right) + \beta_3'\left(\frac{\text{SALE}_{-2} - \text{SALE}_{-4}}{\text{SALE}_{-2}}\right) + \frac{\epsilon}{\text{SALE}_{-2}}$$

Pooled Firm Data

	Nonferrous Metals	Electrical Machinery	Nonelectrical Machinery	Chemicals	Petroleum
$\bar{R}^2$	0.6309	0.6017	0.4539	0.7537	0.5166
$\bar{S}_{est}$	0.15	0.18	0.13	0.13	0.13
df	199	353	347	427	474
F	1.53	2.27	1.48	2.61	1.74
$\bar{d}$	1.45	1.68	1.42	1.38	1.50
Number of firms	9	17	16	20	20
Variables					
β_1'	0.017	0.018	0.003	0.051	0.029
	(0.012)	(0.010)	(0.008)	(0.007)	(0.006)
β_2'	0.726	0.551	0.686	0.563	0.470
	(0.069)	(0.042)	(0.055)	(0.058)	(0.049)
β_3'	−0.179	−0.266	−0.123	−0.389	−0.336
	(0.071)	(0.050)	(0.054)	(0.059)	(0.049)

marginally superior, the Ferber equation yielding a tighter fit for 44 out of the 82 firms and Nerlove's model dominating for 55 out of 81.[35]

The strength of the proxy procedures, in addition to casting doubt upon the validity of Ferber's law and the adaptive expectations model, also has implications for the econometrician concerned with parameter estimation but unable to directly observe anticipations.[36] Specifically, it appears that the best approach is to assume that the anticipated change is proportional to the actual change rather than to incorporate either Ferber's law or the adaptive expectations model as part of the maintained hypothesis in order to substitute out for the unobserved anticipations variable. With the proxy procedure, the behavioral parameters of the model may be estimated in this way, although in some applications the identification of certain of the parameters may hinge upon Muth's sufficiency conjecture that ρ of equation 4.3 is unity. Thus, it was impossible for Lovell [1962, p. 307] to segregate empirically the effects of production plan flexibility from ρ in a study of inventory investment.[37] Since the evidence we have been considering suggests that it is unreasonable to presume that ρ is always unity, it does not seem possible to resolve identification problems of this type when observations on *ex ante* variables are not available.

5.5 SUMMARY AND CONCLUSIONS

In rectrospect, the most surprising outcome of our empirical investigation of expectations formation is the fact that each of the models we considered proved rather more successful, when confronted with the new data, than we had any right to anticipate. Although the problem of aggregation presented some difficulties, it did not prove as critical a factor as we had anticipated on the basis of econometric experience in other areas.[38] Indeed, if we had looked in isolation at any one of the models that we have been considering, the

[35] In making the long comparisons, Lovell's proxy was utilized with a two-quarter lag rather than the one-quarter lag of equation 4.8. For the Nerlove model more than half of the firms in each of the five industries yielded a tighter fit; eight of nine firms in nonferrous metals yielded a closer fit with the adaptive expectations equation. Ferber's law on the other hand, dominated for only 4 of 17 firms in electrical machinery and achieved its highest proportion of success in petroleum with 11 of 20 firms.

[36] The proxy procedure may also be worth invoking if expectations are observed with substantial measurement error. Lovell [1964, p. 205] reports that the use of transformed railroad shippers' forecast *ex ante* data proved only marginally superior to the surrogate procedure in explaining finished goods inventory behavior over the period 1948–1955; also, Edwin Mills [1962, p. 213] found the implicit proxy procedure more satisfactory in predicting cement production than the railroad shippers' anticipations.

[37] This procedure is discussed in Chapter 6.3.3.

[38] Ferber [1958] emphasized the importance of the aggregation problem in his comparison of firm and industry employment anticipations data.

results would have been quite reassuring for the most part. Obviously, more decisive conclusions could be presented if it had proved possible to reject one or two of the models because the regression coefficients were consistently of the wrong sign or the $\bar{R}$'s extremely low.

Quite frankly, we were rather surprised at finding that Ferber's model performed reasonably well at both the firm and the industry level. His original analysis was based on aggregative *ex ante* data. Since the railroad shippers' anticipations data had erroneously suggested that entrepreneurs are extremely inaccurate forecasters, it did not seem reasonable for us, *ex ante*, to be optimistic concerning the validity of Ferber's law of expectations formation. We found that while Ferber's law does not work well for certain industries, notably iron and steel, it performs quite satisfactorily in the majority of applications at both the firm and aggregate level.

The adaptive expectations model, utilized as part of the maintained hypothesis by Nerlove and others in econometric work, is quite successful at explaining both the short and longer horizon sales anticipations at the firm level once the complication of seasonality is acknowledged through the introduction of seasonal dummy variables. But it proves difficult to establish whether Ferber's law or the adaptive expectations model should be utilized by the economic theorist interested in constructing dynamic models involving sales anticipations. Ferber's law does prove superior to the adaptive expectations hypothesis in explaining short anticipations with both industry aggregates and pooled firm data. But the adaptive expectations model provides a better fit at explaining anticipations at the level of the firm, and we argued tentatively in Section 3.1 that the difficulty the adaptive model encounters with aggregative data may arise from problems involved in eliminating a multiplicative seasonal in summing across firms. For long sales anticipations the evidence in favor of the adaptive expectations approach is somewhat more decisive. The adaptive model performed better than Ferber's at the aggregate as well as the firm level. Nonetheless, the evidence is not quite conclusive, for the Ferber model was stronger in the transportation equipment industry aggregate and in the pooled firm regressions for chemicals and petroleum. Tentatively, we believe the evidence suggests that the builder of dynamic business cycle models should utilize the adaptive expectations approach rather than Ferber's law to explain the generation of sales expectations.

Both Ferber's law and the adaptive expectations hypothesis provided, for the most part, reasonably tight structural explanations of how sales anticipations are generated. But we found that a closer approximation is provided by a naive proxy procedure, equation 4.3, which was utilized by Lovell [1961] in an empirical study of inventory behavior. As explained in Section 4.2, expectations are so accurate that the anticipated change in sales is more closely approximated by the actual change than by either of the two structural hypotheses. While Lovell's hypothesis that the anticipated change is proportional to the actual change tells nothing about the way in which anticipations are generated, this result does serve to raise serious doubts concerning the validity of Ferber's law and the adaptive expectations model. For one thing, it casts doubt upon their common assumption that expectations are formed by a technical extrapolation of past sales experience without recourse to information about demand conditions provided by such other variables as unfilled orders, delivery lags, and so forth. Furthermore, it sheds some light on the question of how the econometrician should proceed to handle the problems involved in estimating the parameters of behavioral equations when observations on sales anticipations are not available. Neither Ferber's law nor the adaptive expectations equation should be substituted into the inventory behavior equation in order to obtain an expression for inventories in terms of observable variables. Rather, it should be assumed that the anticipated change is proportional to the actual change; that is, equation 4.1, or equivalently 4.8, should be employed. This procedure will be illustrated in Chapter 6.3.3. While this approach can be employed to estimate certain parameters of inventory investment models, it obviously cannot be used to predict future inventory investment without solving simultaneously for sales volume within the context of a simultaneous equation model.[39]

The data provided by the OBE survey on two successive forecasts of sales volume for the same quarter enabled us to investigate in Section 3.6 the way in which surprises lead to the revision of initial forecasts. It may well seem reasonable to hypothesize that if the short-term forecast for the current quarter turns out to be exceeded by the actual realization, the forecaster will revise his initial forecast for the following quarter in an upward direction; this is the revision hypothesis utilized by Meiselman [1962] in his study of the term structure of interest rates. But at least for sales, the opposite response cannot be rejected as unreasonable. As Eisner [1958] suggested, it is conceivable that the forecaster may regard the error that he made in forecasting the current quarter's sales ($SALE - ASSALE_{-1}$) as a mistake he made in predicting the distribution of sales between quarter t and quarter $t + 1$. If the forecaster regards the error as arising from such an intertemporal substitution of delivery dates he might well respond by revising his long-run forecast in the opposite direction from the short-run forecast error. Our evidence, however, reveals that this does not occur. Instead, the forecaster who is surprised this quarter is likely to revise his forecast about tomorrow's sales in the same direction and by a sizable amount.

[39] Lovell [1962b] considered the dynamic implications of perfect forecasts within the context of a multisector model recognizing the simultaneous prediction problem, and found the system unstable.

Rather more startling is the regressive characteristic displayed by our anticipations data. It had been suggested that Ferber's railroad shippers data provided inaccurate forecasts because of the regressivity property, the apparent tendency for entrepreneurs to forecast a return to the corresponding quarter of the preceding year rather than a projection of recently observed trend. If this conjecture were correct, it would mean that the accurate forecasting record of the new OBE data reported in Chapter 3 could not have been generated by regressive forecasts. In fact, however, the new OBE forecasts are *both* accurate and regressive. Far from being mutually exclusive concepts, it may well be that anticipations are simultaneously regressive, accurate, and adaptive.

CHAPTER 6

Inventories and Production

6.1 INTRODUCTION

We have studied both the structure explaining how expectations are generated and the magnitude of prediction errors. Now we shall look at the way in which expectations about future market conditions influence the production decision and planned inventory behavior. We shall also study how firms revise their plans when surprised by forecast errors. Obviously, these are not new topics; a glance at the bibliography will reveal a substantial number of empirical studies of inventory behavior. But econometricians have not allocated to inventories the same attention that has been lavished upon consumption and fixed investment spending. The relative neglect of the inventory sector may be explained, at least in part, by the difficulties involved in measuring *ex ante* concepts. The new OBE data provide an opportunity to test in depth certain propositions concerning the determinants of inventory behavior that earlier investigators had to accept as part of the maintained hypothesis.

Planned production is not observed directly. But the firm's planned level of output can be inferred from observations on planned finished goods inventory and anticipated sales. This approach is feasible only for our sample of individual firms, for we do not have benchmark adjusted industry aggregates partitioned by stage-of-fabrication. In Section 6.2, we discuss the way in which sales expectations influence the firm's production decision; we then proceed to study the way departures from plan are induced by forecast errors. We shall argue that the customary realization function approach is not optimal for this task. Rather, we shall work in terms of a two equation recursive model. Also, we shall examine reduced form estimates of finished goods inventory investment in an attempt to determine the extent to which observations on planned inventory investment assist in predicting actual realizations. Furthermore, we shall test a proxy procedure often employed in studies of inventory investment when observations on sales anticipations are not available. A similar strategy will be followed in studying purchased materials and goods in process stocks in Section 6.4.

The distinction between finished goods and other stocks must be abandoned when we study industry aggregates in Section 6.5. As a result, we are not able to measure production. But it is still interesting to inquire as to the determinants of planned total inventory holdings and to investigate the way in which expectational errors lead to a departure of realized from planned inventory. One advantage we are able to exploit in processing the aggregate data is the opportunity to use a more sophisticated but involved nonlinear estimation procedure that could not be conveniently applied in analyzing the more extensive data on individual firms.[1]

6.2 PLANNED PRODUCTION AND FINISHED GOODS INVENTORY BEHAVIOR

Decisions concerning production and the planned level of finished goods inventory are intimately related. Indeed, production may be defined as the sum of sales plus the change in finished inventories.[2] With this definition, consistent planning implies that the planned level of production must equal the sum of anticipated sales volume plus the planned change in finished goods inventory. We shall consider models of the production decision that have been advanced by such writers as Johnston [1961] and Mills [1957, 1962] in analyzing the determinants of anticipated finished goods inventory. First, however, we shall develop in a quite *ad hoc* fashion, a simple accelerator model; then we shall elaborate by introducing various modifications suggested by the more sophisticated theories of the production decision.

6.2.1 *The Model*

Let us begin, as has been customary in many studies of inventory behavior, by postulating that the equilibrium level of end-of-quarter finished goods

[1] We did not find it feasible to employ nonlinear estimation procedures on the individual firm data.

[2] Defined in this way, production may not be too closely correlated with fluctuations in employment or the rate at which value-added accumulates. That is, a good share of the labor input may be involved in the processing of goods in process rather than the conversion of goods in process into finished goods. This caveat is particularly important when dealing with highly aggregated data. Quite apart from this difficulty, we shall have to be careful in subsequent discussion to take into account the complications created by the fact that both inventories and sales are measured in dollars rather than physical units.

inventory, FIN^e, is a linear function of current and next period's sales:

$$FIN^e = \beta_1 + \beta_2 SALE + \beta_3 SALE_{+1} + \epsilon_1 \tag{2.1}$$

The unobserved variable, FIN^e, denotes the level of inventories that the firm would attempt to obtain if it knew future demand and had no costs of adjustment. Of course, firms are not clairvoyant. A more useful concept is anticipated equilibrium or "desired" inventory, $\widehat{FIN^e}$:

$$\widehat{FIN^e} = \beta_1 + \beta_2 ASSALE + \beta_3 ALSALE_{+1} + \epsilon_2 \tag{2.2}$$

FIN^e and $\widehat{FIN^e}$ are unobservable variables; it is impossible to calculate directly the magnitude of the gap between equilibrium and actual inventories. Of course, equilibrium concepts can be approximated once estimates of the parameters of equation 2.1 have been obtained.[3] Also, the sign, if not the magnitude of the gap between equilibrium and desired inventories, is revealed by the COND dummy variable, which indicates whether the firm regards its inventories as high, low, or about right relative to current sales volume and the order backlog.[4] One way to proceed in the absence of direct observations on equilibrium stocks is to adopt an assumption made by Lloyd Metzler [1941] in the construction of his inventory cycle models. He assumed that firms always plan on a prompt elimination of any imbalance between inherited and equilibrium stocks, which implies that $FINAS = \widehat{FIN^e}$. We shall work with a somewhat more general hypothesis involving delayed adjustment behavior.

Business firms may not attempt an immediate adjustment of inventory to $\widehat{FIN^e}$. The costs of abruptly adjusting inventory may exceed the penalties arising from continued inventory imbalance, $\widehat{FIN^e} - FIN_{-1}$. If, as is customary, we assume that firms attempt to eliminate a fraction δ of the discrepancy between the equilibrium inventory and the stock inherited from

[3] Time series constructed in this way by Lovell [1961, 1964] suggested that firms tolerated a substantial inventory deficiency throughout most of the Korean War period.

[4] As an aid for business analysts, the *Survey of Current Business* reports for durables and for nondurables the *proportion* of firms in its sample that regard inventories as high, low, or about right. Lovell [1967, p. 559–560] discussed an attempt to explain this proportion in terms of current and anticipated future sales, the unfilled order backlog, and actual inventory. The results were reasonable only for durables; the unfilled orders term was insignificant in both regressions. We included the COND variable in most of the regression models reported on in this chapter, but it invariably had an insignificant coefficient; since the other statistics of the regressions were virtually unaffected, we shall be reporting the results with this variable excluded.

the past, we have for planned inventory investment:

$$\text{FINAS} - \text{FIN}_{-1} = \delta(\widehat{\text{FIN}^e} - \text{FIN}_{-1}) + \epsilon_3 \qquad 0 < \delta \leq 1 \tag{2.3}$$

$$= \delta\beta_1 + \delta\beta_2\text{ASSALE} + \delta\beta_3\text{ALSALE}_{+1} - \delta\text{FIN}_{-1} + \epsilon_4 \tag{2.4}$$

where

$$\epsilon_4 = \delta\epsilon_2 + \epsilon_3$$

All the variables in equation 2.4 are now observable, thanks to the OBE Survey of Inventory and Sales Anticipations.[5] To obtain an expression for the planned inventory stock from 2.4, it is only necessary to add FIN_{-1} to both sides, which yields:

$$\text{FINAS} = \delta\beta_1 + \delta\beta_2\text{ASSALE} + \delta\beta_3\text{ALSALE}_{+1} + (1 - \delta)\text{FIN}_{-1} + \epsilon_4 \tag{2.4'}$$

The implications of this accelerator approach for the production decision may be derived from this last expression, once an accounting evaluation problem is recognized. Our data concern a variety of concepts measured in terms of dollars rather than physical units. Furthermore, a unit of finished goods inventory is customarily evaluated on a lower-of-cost-or-market basis rather than at final sales price. If our data were measured in physical units, we could define production as the sum of sales plus the change in finished goods inventory. Again, if we had data recorded on a cost-of-goods-sold basis, we could define production evaluated at cost as the sum of cost-of-goods-sold plus the change in the dollar value of inventory; that is, if SALE′ denotes sales evaluated net of the profit markup on a cost-of-goods-sold basis, we would have as production:

$$Q = \text{SALE}' + \text{FIN} - \text{FIN}_{-1} \tag{2.5}$$

One way to proceed, in the absence of data on SALE′, is to assume that the customary markup on merchandise, denoted by m, is a constant; we then have price $= (1 + m)$cost, and SALE′ $= 1/(1 + m)$SALE. Substituting into equation 2.5 then yields an estimate of quantity. Precisely the same procedure can be used to define planned production:

$$\text{QAS} = \frac{1}{1 + m}\text{ASSALE} + \text{FINAS} - \text{FIN}_{-1} \tag{2.6}$$

With this in mind, we observe that adding $1/(1 + m)$ASSALE to both sides of

[5] Procedures that have been invoked when FINAS was not observable will be discussed later.

2.4 yields as the equation for planned production:

$$\text{QAS} = \delta\beta_1 + [\delta\beta_2 + 1/(1+m)]\text{ASSALE} + \delta\beta_3\text{ALSALE}_{+1} - \delta\text{FIN}_{-1} + \epsilon_4 \quad (2.7)$$

While we do not directly observe QAS, estimates of the parameters of equation 2.7, other than the markup factor m, are provided by reverting to regressions 2.4 or 2.4′. Indeed, precisely the same parameter estimates will be obtained from any one of these regressions, although the anticipated inventory investment regression may be expected to yield the smallest correlation coefficient.[6]

Admittedly, we have advanced this accelerator model on an intuitive basis. Is it unreasonable to hope that the vast operations research literature would dictate the appropriate form of the model to be used for our statistical investigation? If the assumption that firms schedule production to minimize costs sufficed to determine a particular behavioral equation for planned output, it would be possible to invoke 2.6 to obtain a corresponding equation for planned finished goods inventory. Unfortunately, no categorical imperative is dictated by the assumption that firms optimize. Quite the contrary, Holt and Modigliani [1961, p. 13] have shown that depending on the way in which the theoretician happens to specify the cost structure, any of a variety of behavioral rules may be shown to be compatible with the assumption that firms schedule production so as to minimize costs. Holt and Modigliani specified a cost structure that serves to generate a simplified version of equation 2.7. Thus, our model is compatible with the assumption that firms maximize profits.

Beyond this, the normative literature suggests two important complications deserving careful evaluation. One problem is how to handle appropriately the firm's attempt to smooth the impact of sales fluctuations upon production and employment. The second issue concerns the appropriate length of the planning horizon. Both of these interrelated problems deserve our consideration.

Edwin Mills [1962] argues that the effects of production smoothing can be adequately approximated for empirical purposes by

$$\text{QAS} = b_{10} + b_{11}\text{ASSALE} + b_{12}Q_{-1} - b_{13}\text{FIN}_{-1} \quad (2.8)$$

In effect, his approach involves adding the Q_{-1} term to equation 2.7 and setting $\beta_3 = 0$.[7] This is intuitively reasonable, for it means that if production was large in the preceding period, the firm will produce more than would otherwise be the case in order to avoid abruptly curtailing output. The

[6] The proof of these observations is presented in the statistical appendix to this chapter.
[7] This is his equation 9, page 132, in our notation.

planned output equation is easily translated into an equation for planned finished goods inventory investment; in terms of our earlier notation we may add lagged output to 2.4.

$$\text{FINAS} - \text{FIN}_{-1} = \delta\beta_1 + \delta\beta_2\text{ASSALE} + \delta\beta_3\text{ALSALE}_{+1} - \delta\text{FIN}_{-1}$$
$$+ \beta_4\left[\left(\frac{1}{1+m}\right)\text{SALE}_{-1} + \text{FIN}_{-1} - \text{FIN}_{-2}\right] + \epsilon_4 \tag{2.9}$$

For the myopic firm looking only at immediate prospects, we may have $\beta_2 > 0$ and $\beta_3 = 0$. For the forward-looking firm, on the other hand, we might find the opposite extreme of $\beta_2 = 0$ and $\beta_3 > 0$. Indeed, a firm may well look further than just one or two quarters into the future in deciding upon the appropriate level of stocks. In the long-run, interest centers on the determinants of the equilibrium inventory stock, FIN^e. While this variable is not observable, we can see from equation 2.9 that when stocks have adjusted to a steady-state solution characterized by $\text{ALSALE}_{+1} = \text{ASSALE} = \text{SALE}_{-1}$ and $\text{FINAS} = \text{FIN}_{-1} = \text{FIN}_{-2}$ we will have:

$$\text{FIN}^e = \beta_0{}^e + \beta^e\text{SALE} \tag{2.10}$$

where

$$\beta_0{}^e = \beta_1$$
$$\beta^e = \beta_2 + \beta_3 + \frac{\beta_4}{\delta + m\delta}$$

Maximum likelihood estimates of β^e can be calculated from the least squares regression coefficients of equation 2.9, provided that the stochastic disturbance satisfies the customary restrictions. Although we shall present estimates of the β^e, they will not be precise; considerable sampling error arises because the computation of β^e involves the ratios of random variables whose distributions are approximately normal.

How far *should* firms look toward the future in making their current production decision? If average variable cost fluctuates with output in accordance with the law of diminishing returns, it will obviously pay to look to the future in scheduling production. Furthermore, changes in the level of operations are costly, and it may pay the firm that expects an abrupt increase in demand to start expanding production now, accumulating part of the additional output in inventory. The Holt, Modigliani, Muth, and Simon [1960] applications of linear decision rules derived from quadratic cost functions confirm that sizable savings can be realized by the firm that looks toward the future. They also argue, however, that prediction errors *per se* may not be critical, for the adoption of appropriate production scheduling procedures may lead to substantial gains even if quite imprecise forecasts are used; the gain from more precise predictions may well be marginal.

A long planning horizon creates serious econometric problems, even when the decision rule is linear, as is the case with the Holt, Modigliani, Muth, and Simon approach. One procedure, employed by Modigliani and Sauerlander [1955], is to recognize that rather than planning to carry inventories over into the next sales year, the firm may truncate its horizon at the point of the current year in which sales customarily reach their seasonal trough. A disadvantage of this approach, which Modigliani and Sauerlander used in their empirical study of the cement industry, is that it implies that certain coefficients of the model will change quite decidedly from one season to the next. Their plan was to fit a separate regression equation for each quarter, which requires a large number of observations. Jack Johnston [1961] initially employed this procedure, and then resorted to the use of seasonal dummy variables.

A quite different argument for truncating the horizon has been invoked by Edwin Mills [1962, p. 114]. Mills argues that the computations required of the entrepreneur in determining the optimal plan may be so involved that he will elect to neglect all except the immediate future. Alternatively, it can be assumed that it is the problem of predicting the distant future, rather than the burden of computations, that serves to truncate the horizon effectively; that is, the firm may use as its forecast for the more distant future the same prediction it makes for the next quarter, modified only for customary seasonal change.[8]

Throughout our analysis, we shall continue to treat the sales volume of the firm as exogenous, an approach with obvious limitations. As Childs [1967] has emphasized, the firm producing primarily to order may determine the level of shipments by balancing convenience with regard to production scheduling against the loss of customer goodwill involved in delayed shipment; in these circumstances, new orders may be predetermined while sales volume is endogenous. Because we do not observe orders at the firm level, this condition cannot be treated in this study with the care that it deserves. Of course, there is no problem in industries which produce only to stock. Two of the five industries for which we have individual firm data are classified by OBE as producing only to stock; these are chemical and petroleum.

Even for the firm that does not produce to order, it may be appropriate only as a first approximation to treat sales volume as exogeneous. It might be more reasonable to regard price as planned along with production on the basis of the entrepreneur's judgement as to the position of its demand schedule. In addition to 2.7, the simultaneous equation model would then

[8] Indeed, there are circumstances in which this is the optimal way to predict; see Chapter 5.3.2.

include an equation explaining the price-setting policy of the firm, which would presumably be influenced in part by the magnitude of the inventory stock. The demand schedule for the product, as preconceived by the firm, would constitute a third equation of the simultaneous system.[9] It would also be necessary to include additional equations explaining how planned price and production decisions are modified in the light of surprises. While it is to be hoped that in future studies this more involved approach can be pursued, it is precluded here by the very limitations of our data, particularly with respect to prices, as explained in Chapter 2.2. However, the shortcomings of the single equation approach may not be too great. As we argued in Chapter 2, the short-run pricing and production decisions may be made by quite different departments within the firm rather than simultaneously. Indeed, this form of division of labor may explain why most of the operations research literature regards price and sales volume as exogeneous in deriving optimal inventory policy. Furthermore, Mills' [1962, Ch. 8] simulation study suggests that even when the price and output decisions are made simultaneously, the direct application of least squares to equation 2.8 may still yield reasonable results.[10]

Prior to the appearance of the item on the OBE Inventory and Sales Anticipations Survey in 1960, no information was available on either planned finished goods inventory or planned production. As a result, it had not been possible to subject equations explaining the determination of these variables to direct empirical test. One procedure, which may be appropriate when data is collected at frequent intervals, has been to assume that production plans are not subject to revision so that observed production constitutes a valid proxy for planned output. A second approach, to be discussed in the next section, involves the use of equation 2.9 to eliminate planned finished goods inventories from a model purporting to explain how firms adjust production schedules in response to forecasting errors. Because of the obvious difficulties inherent in these approaches, the results obtained with the new OBE data are

[9] Mills [1962, pp. 132–133] suggests that in addition to 2.8 the profit maximizing firm's behavior also involves a price decision rule and a demand equation:

$$p = b_{20} + b_{21}\text{ASSALE} + b_{22}\text{QAS} + b_{23}\text{FIN}_{-1}$$

and

$$\text{ASSALE} = b_{30} + b_{31}p + G(t)$$

Here p is the price of the product and $G(t)$ summarizes the effects of other variables upon demand.

[10] He generated a number of samples with a complicated nonlinear model in which the pricing and production decisions are made simultaneously. He then found that satisfactory results could be obtained when equation 2.8 and the first equation of footnote 9 are used as linear approximations without regard to problems of simultaneous equation estimation.

of particular interest, although we, unfortunately, do not have data on the FINAS variable at the industry level of aggregation.

6.2.2 *Empirical Evidence*

Evidence concerning the behavior of planned finished goods inventory investment is presented in Table 6.2.1, where regressions obtained by fitting equation 2.4 on pooled individual firm data are reported. Furthermore, we present statistics from a second pooled regression based on observations from all small firms with assets below $10 million and from a third pooled regression based on data for the larger firms.[11] We have calculated the values

TABLE 6.2.1a. PLANNED FINISHED GOODS INVENTORY INVESTMENT

$$\text{FINAS} - \text{FIN}_{-1} = \delta\beta_1 + \delta\beta_2\text{ASSALE} + \delta\beta_3\text{ALSALE}_{t+1} - \delta\text{FIN}_{t-1} + \epsilon$$

	Nonferrous Metals	Electrical Machinery	Nonelectrical Machinery	Chemicals	Petroleum
Partial $\bar{R}^2$	0.0004	0.1952	0.1813	0.3966	0.1965
$\bar{S}_{\text{est}}$	1752.3	3353.7	3675.6	2560.2	6037.8
df	100	178	231	248	338
F	0.81	2.28	4.51	1.03	2.15
$\bar{d}$	1.73	1.99	1.51	1.89	1.58
Number of firms	6	14	14	16	19
Variables					
$\delta\beta_2$	−0.014	−0.001	0.054	0.017	−0.056
	(0.026)	(0.025)	(0.015)	(0.016)	(0.027)
$\delta\beta_3$	0.044	0.132	−0.108	0.164	0.014
	(0.029)	(0.024)	(0.017)	(0.016)	(0.015)
$-\delta$	−0.087	−0.238	−0.061	−0.366	−0.236
	(0.081)	(0.062)	(0.030)	(0.039)	(0.029)
β_2	−0.16	0	0.89	0.05	−0.24
β_3	0.51	0.55	−1.77	0.45	0.06
β^e	0.34	0.55	−0.89	0.49	−0.18

[11] Because the form of the equations makes it doubtful that large and small firms would have the same standard error of estimate, the *F* statistics for the all-firm pooled regressions do not constitute a reliable guide on the question of whether the parameters are the same for all firms in the industry.

TABLE 6.2.1b

	Nonferrous Metals	Electrical Machinery	Nonelectrical Machinery	Chemicals	Petroleum
Large Firms					
Partial $\bar{R}^2$	−0.0436	0.1735	0.1646	0.3951	0.1884
$\bar{S}_{est}$	2434.3	5763.8	6106.9	4182.3	8451.9
df	45	59	82	90	171
F	0.63	2.48	5.22	1.03	2.16
Number of firms	3	5	5	6	10
Variables					
$\delta\beta_2$	−0.016	−0.002	0.054	0.019	−0.056
	(0.036)	(0.044)	(0.026)	(0.026)	(0.038)
$\delta\beta_3$	0.039	0.134	−0.109	0.167	0.014
	(0.040)	(0.042)	(0.029)	(0.027)	(0.022)
$-\delta$	−0.044	−0.240	−0.057	−0.369	−0.235
	(0.119)	(0.108)	(0.050)	(0.065)	(0.041)
β_2	−0.36	−0.01	0.95	0.05	−0.24
β_3	0.89	0.56	−1.91	0.45	0.06
Small Firms					
Partial $\bar{R}^2$	0.1987	0.0993	0.2887	0.2584	0.5881
$\bar{S}_{est}$	799.21	533.19	563.87	417.63	622.71
df	52	116	146	155	164
F	2.71	1.98	0.30	2.59	1.15
Number of firms	3	9	9	10	9
Variables					
$\delta\beta_2$	−0.076	0.120	0.068	−0.032	−0.265
	(0.095)	(0.030)	(0.034)	(0.016)	(0.041)
$\delta\beta_3$	0.051	−0.049	0.001	0.090	0.295
	(0.127)	(0.037)	(0.036)	(0.016)	(0.039)
$-\delta$	−0.437	−0.058	−0.369	−0.360	−0.591
	(0.120)	(0.057)	(0.049)	(0.066)	(0.046)
β_2	−0.17	2.07	0.18	−0.09	−0.45
β_3	0.12	−0.84	0	0.25	0.50

of the marginal desired inventory coefficients, β_2 and β_3. The partial $\bar{R}^2$ are quite small, particularly in the three industries producing primarily to order rather than to stock, and no solace should be derived from the thought that much larger coefficients of multiple determination could have been obtained by adding ASSALE to both sides of the equation in order to have planned production as the dependent variable.[12] Fortunately, all the δ coefficients are between zero and unity. But many of the marginal desired inventory coefficients take on inappropriate negative values. Of course, for a myopic firm, β_3 may in fact be zero; β_2 might be zero or negative if the firm's production schedule is so rigid that it plans on sufficing with a lower end-of-quarter inventory when current sales are expected to be higher. The all-firm pooled regressions yield negative β^e for nonelectrical machinery and petroleum, implying that low inventories are planned when high sales are expected to persist; comparison of the small and large pooled regressions suggests that the anomaly arises only among the large firms in these two industries.[13]

Are the difficulties we experience with equation 2.4 due to its neglect of production smoothing complications? Apparently not. We first investigated the question with equation 2.9, which adds last period's production as an additional determinant of the planned finished goods inventory change. Because *m*, the markup coefficient, is not observed directly, this approach required the introduction of *two* new explanatory terms, both $\beta_4/(1 + m) \times [\text{SALE}_{-1}]$ and $\beta_4[\text{FIN}_{-1} - \text{FIN}_{-2}]$. We were disappointed to find that introducing these two variables quite generally led to very wild estimates of both the markup factor *m* and of β_4; furthermore, the other regression coefficients and the standard error of the estimate were virtually unaffected. As an alternative strategy for handling the effects of production smoothing we introduced seasonal dummies, a procedure employed by Johnston [1961], but again the resulting statistics were virtually unaffected.[14] Apparently, any seasonal pattern in planned inventory charge is directly generated by seasonal movements in sales volume. Tentatively, we must conclude that production

[12] It also will be remembered from Chapter 2 that $\bar{R}^2$ is calculated by comparing the standard error of estimate with the second moment of the dependent variable about individual firm means; it would obviously be larger if computed about the grand mean.

[13] The "*t*" statistics for the second and third regression coefficients can be employed for testing the hypothesis that β_1 or β_2 is zero, under the maintained hypothesis that $\delta > 0$. Unfortunately, we did not obtain computer output appropriate for testing whether the sum of the two regression coefficients, $\beta_2 + \beta_3$, differs significantly from zero; it would have been better to have replaced $\delta\beta_2\text{ASSALE} + \delta\beta_3\text{ALSALE}_{+1}$ with $\delta\beta_2[\text{ASSALE} - \text{ALSALE}_{+1}] + (\delta\beta_2 + \delta\beta_3)[\text{ALSALE}_{+1}]$, for then the standard error of the ALSALE_{+1} regression coefficient would have been useful in testing hypothesis about the total influence of anticipated future sales on planned end-of-quarter inventory. Of course, it might be of interest to observe the effects of deleting the ASSALE and/or the ALSALE variables when their regression coefficients are negative.

[14] Since introducing seasonal dummies into pooled regressions amounts to presupposing that all of the firms in each industry are subjected to precisely the same additive seasonal influences, we also ran the regressions with the data subject to prior seasonal adjustment by a simple program that serves to equalize monthly means for each firm; this procedure allowed, in effect, for each firm to have its own set of seasonal dummy variables. But the effect of this alternative procedure was negligible.

smoothing considerations are neglected in the planning of output and finished goods inventory.[15]

Note that in petroleum, nonelectrical machinery, and nonferrous metals, the estimates of δ for the small firms are considerably larger than those provided by the large firms in the same industry. The differences appear to be significant,[16] and we are tempted to conclude that in these three industries the small firms attempt a more rapid adjustment of inventories toward their equilibrium level. However, in electrical machinery, a larger point estimate of δ is provided by the large pool regression, although the difference does not appear to be significant. In chemicals, the estimates are almost identical. We conclude that in some industries large firms are more cumbersome than small at adjusting to change, but the tendency is by no means universal. Costs of adjusting finished goods inventories do not appear to introduce diseconomies of scale in either electrical machinery or chemicals.

6.3 FINISHED GOODS INVENTORY BEHAVIOR

Theoretical models of the inventory cycle customarily involve the assumption that the firm does not revise the level of production it has planned for the current period in response to errors in forecasting sales volume. The entire burden of surprise is borne by adjusting the finished inventory stock rather than by revising the production schedule. While this assumption might be reasonable in empirical studies when firms are observed at weekly or monthly intervals, it seems obvious that some allowance must be made for plan revision when analyzing quarterly data. After all, the production period for the typical firm in most industries may be presumed to be less than one month.[17] The possibility that firms will be able to revise their plans at least

[15] This does not mean that production fluctuates as much as actual sales, for sales anticipations have a smaller variance than the realizations. Furthermore, the way in which the firm adjusts its inventories may have the effect of softening the burden upon output of sales fluctuations.

[16] An approximate test of the difference between large and small firm δ, (which we denote as $\delta_l - \delta_s$) is possible, provided the disturbances of the large and the small firm pooled regressions are distributed independently. Then, δ_l and δ_s will be independently distributed and so $\sigma^2_{\delta_l - \delta_s} = \sigma_{\delta_l}{}^2 + \sigma_{\delta_s}{}^2$. When the two variances constituting this sum are unknown, we are confronted with the Behrens-Fisher problem, but a reasonable approximation is to substitute the estimated standard errors. For electrical machinery we have $\sigma_{\delta_l - \delta_s} = 0.1208$, while $\delta_l - \delta_s = 0.182$, and the observed difference is clearly insignificant. For petroleum, nonelectrical machinery, and chemicals the industry t coefficients, in that order, are -5.775, -4.457, and -2.345.

[17] Calculations made by John A. Carlson with Survey of Manufacturing data suggest that the production period in electrical machinery may be 1.37 months, but only 0.71 for primary metals, 0.53 for furniture and fixtures, 0.26 for petroleum and coal products, and 0.09 for food and kindred products.

partially within a three-month observation period has been recognized in many empirical studies of inventory behavior.

Plan revision is most easily introduced by first considering the extreme case in which complete adjustment can be made to surprise. Equations for realized inventory under this hypothesis may be easily derived by retracing the argument of Section 6.2. Specifically, with complete plan revision, the relevant equilibrium inventory concept would involve end rather than beginning-of-period information; we must consider

$$\widehat{\text{FIN}^{e*}} = \beta_1 + \beta_2\text{SALE} + \beta_3\text{ASSALE}_{+1} + \epsilon_2^* \tag{2.2*}$$

where the asterisk indicates that we are referring to the magnitude the variable would assume *if* complete flexibility were obtainable. The firm's inventory behavior with complete flexibility would involve a slight modification of equation 2.3:

$$\text{FIN}_t^* - \text{FIN}_{t-1} = \delta(\widehat{\text{FIN}^{e*}} - \text{FIN}_{-1}) + \epsilon_3^* \tag{2.3*}$$

and substituting 2.2* into this last expression yields

$$\text{FIN}^* - \text{FIN}_{-1} = \delta\beta_1 + \delta\beta_2\text{SALE} + \delta\beta_3\text{ASSALE}_{+1} - \delta\text{FIN}_{-1} + \epsilon_4^*$$

where (2.4*)

$$\epsilon_4^* = \delta\epsilon_2^* + \epsilon_3^*.$$

This is the level of inventory investment that would be realized if production plans were completely flexible.

If, in practice, plans are only partially revised in the three-month period, actual inventory may be a weighted average of the planned level, FINAS, and the level FIN* that would prevail with complete flexibility; that is, if λ is a coefficient measuring the degree of plan rigidity, we may assume:

$$\text{FIN} = \lambda\text{FINAS} + (1 - \lambda)\text{FIN}^* + \lambda'(\text{ASSALE} - \text{SALE}) + \epsilon_5 \tag{3.1}$$

The last term reflects the immediate impact of forecast errors upon inventory; thus, if $\lambda = \lambda' = 1$, stocks depart from FINAS by the magnitude of the forecast error in accordance with the standard inventory cycle assumption, as invoked by such writers as Metzler [1941].[18] Although it makes sense in many applications to presume $\lambda = \lambda'$, there are circumstances pointed out to us in correspondence by John A. Carlson in which this equality may not hold true. In particular, it may not be easy to revise available warehouse space in order to accommodate stocks larger than FINAS, even though an excess of realized over anticipated sales would make a larger inventory desirable. Furthermore, a manager who has an emotional commitment to the

[18] See also the discussion of Lloyd D. Orr [1967].

achievement of plans may stick to his originally planned level of inventory, FINAS, when market conditions prevent anticipated sales from being realized.[19] This rather extreme mode of behavior would involve $\lambda = 1$ and $\lambda' = 0$. While Lovell [1967, p. 552] presumed $\lambda = \lambda'$ in earlier research, Pashigian's paper [1965] presupposes that $\lambda = 1$ and $\lambda' = 0$. This latter approach is in conformity with the following Modigliani and Sauerlander [1955, p. 350] observation:

> It would appear that firms manage to revise production sufficiently to take care of unanticipated changes in sales, but not sufficiently to change inventories significantly from the level originally planned.

An equation involving only observable variables is obtained by using equation 2.4* to eliminate FIN* from 3.1:

$$\begin{aligned}\mathrm{FIN} - \mathrm{FIN}_{-1} = {} & (1-\lambda)\delta\beta_1 + (1-\lambda)\delta\beta_2\mathrm{SALE} \\ & + (1-\lambda)\delta\beta_3\mathrm{ASSALE}_{+1} + (\lambda\delta - \lambda - \delta)\mathrm{FIN}_{-1} \\ & + \lambda\mathrm{FINAS} + \lambda'(\mathrm{ASSALE} - \mathrm{SALE}) + \epsilon_6 \qquad (3.2)\end{aligned}$$

where

$$\epsilon_6 = (1-\lambda)\epsilon_4{}^* + \epsilon_5.$$

The model may be further elaborated upon by introducing the production smoothing concept. This may be done explicitly, as in Section 6.2, by adding last period's production into the behavioral equations. We then have:

$$\begin{aligned}\mathrm{FIN} - \mathrm{FIN}_{-1} = {} & (1-\lambda)\delta\beta_1 + (1-\lambda)\delta\beta_2\mathrm{SALE} \\ & + (1-\lambda)\beta_4(\mathrm{FIN}_{-1} - \mathrm{FIN}_{-2}) + \beta_4\left(\frac{1-\lambda}{1-m}\right)\mathrm{SALE}_{-1} \\ & + (\lambda\delta - \lambda - \delta)\mathrm{FIN}_{-1} + (1-\lambda)\delta\beta_3\mathrm{ASSALE}_{+1} \\ & + \lambda\mathrm{FINAS} + \lambda'(\mathrm{ASSALE} - \mathrm{SALE}) + \epsilon_6 \qquad (3.3)\end{aligned}$$

Let us now consider certain econometric problems involved in estimating the parameters of this model. We shall regard realized and anticipated sales as predetermined. Furthermore, we must note that equation 3.3 is part of a simultaneous equation system, for it involves the planned end-of-period inventory stock, which is determined by equation 2.9. Fortunately, the two equation system is recursive. That is, the current value of FINAS, planned finished goods inventory, appears in both of these structural equations; however, FIN, the current level of finished goods stocks, does not appear in equation 2.9. Provided that ϵ_4 and ϵ_6 are independently distributed and free of serial correlation, the direct application of least squares to the structural equations will yield consistent parameter estimates, although they will be

[19] Note that either one of these two factors might generate quite rapid correction of the effects of forecast errors even for a firm with a low value of δ.

subject to Hurwicz bias.[20] The independence hypothesis is not unreasonable, for the two equations can be regarded as describing two quite distinct processes that take place sequentially rather than concurrently. That is, the first has to do with the formation of planned inventory accumulation while the second explains why these plans may not materialize; thus, the effect of the random error term ϵ_4 manifests itself upon FINAS before ϵ_6, the disturbance term in the reaction equation, enters into the picture.[21]

An alternative to the direct application of least squares to this recursive model is to work in terms of a *realization function.* That is, the mistake made by the firm in predicting future inventory is explained in terms of both the error the firm makes in predicting current sales and the revision of its anticipations with regard to the future. This approach has been frequently employed in studies of fixed investment as well as inventory behavior.[22] The realization function may be derived from equation 3.3 with the aid of the expression for FINAS provided by 2.9.[23] One eventually obtains:

$$\text{FINAS} - \text{FIN} = [\lambda' - (1 - \lambda)\delta\beta_2](\text{SALE} - \text{ASSALE}) + (1 - \lambda)\delta\beta_3(\text{ALSALE}_{+1} - \text{ASSALE}_{+1}) + \epsilon_6 + (1 - \lambda)\epsilon_4 \quad (3.4)$$

An advantage of this procedure is that less stringent assumptions need to be imposed upon the stochastic disturbances, for only the exogeneous sales realization and expectation terms appear as explanatory variables. But this procedure's limitations are obvious too. For one thing, the term relating to production smoothing has dropped completely out of the equation, and so the parameter β_4 cannot be estimated from the realization function. Furthermore, it is impossible to identify the five parameters with only two regression coefficients. If it were known *a priori* that $\lambda' = 0$, we could estimate β_2/β_3 by taking the ratio of the two regression coefficients; only under the extremely implausible assumption that $\lambda' = \lambda = 0$ and $\delta = 1$ would it be possible to estimate β_2 and β_3 with the realization function regression.

Another approach, to be considered in a later section, is to use the reduced form rather than the structural equation for FIN. We shall see that this is a reasonable way to proceed when FINAS is unobservable. In a later section we shall also consider the effects of constraining $\lambda = \lambda'$ under the presumption

[20] A more efficient estimation procedure will be considered in Section 6.5.

[21] Of course, it is not difficult to think of circumstances in which the stochastic disturbances would not have the desired properties. It is conceivable, for example, that an omitted variable, say liquid assets, influences both the planned inventory stock and the speed of adjustment toward it; further, the liquid asset variable might be autocorrelated.

[22] See Modigliani and Weingartner [1958] and Eisner and Strotz [1963] for discussions of the application of the realization function to fixed investment behavior. For inventories, see Lovell [1967], where realization functions are estimated at the industry level.

[23] From 3.3 we obtained 3.4 by adding and subtracting $(1 - \lambda)$FINAS, using the expressions for FINAS provided by 2.9.

that firms revise their planned inventory levels with the same degree of alacrity with which they move to offset the direct impact of erroneous sales forecasts upon finished goods inventory. For the present, we shall consider an alternative special case in which $\lambda' = 0$, which has also been discussed in the literature.[24]

6.3.1 *The Structural Equation*

The limited degree of success that our model achieves in explaining realized inventory investment is revealed by Table 6.3.1. We again report for each industry three pooled regressions, one for large firms, one for small, and a third pooling observations over all firms. Since these regressions are obtained with equation 3.3, but with $\lambda' = 0$, there are six parameters, and they can be calculated from the regression coefficients. For each industry we report β^e, the marginal equilibrium sales coefficient, on the last line of the table.[25] Unfortunately, two of these coefficients are negative, an incongruous result that we would like to attribute to sampling error.[26]

An important role for production smoothing in all industries except nonelectrical machinery is suggested by the evidence in Table 6.3.1. With that one exception, the coefficients $(1 - \lambda)\beta_4$ of lagged finished goods inventory investment are of expected sign; they are often large relative to their standard errors. However, the implied values of m, the markup coefficient, are not reasonable. For comparison purposes, we also ran regressions with seasonal dummy variables for each firm in place of the lagged production concept; it will be remembered from Section 6.2 that Johnston argued that this was an appropriate way to introduce production smoothing considerations. Furthermore, we ran the same model without any allowance for production smoothing. A comparison of the three alternatives for each industry revealed that with but two exceptions the explicit introduction of lagged production is preferable. One exception was nonelectrical machinery, where a larger $\bar{R}^2$ was obtained for the nonproduction smoothing case; however, the regression coefficients for this industry were almost identical to those reported on Table 6.3.1. The second exception concerned the petroleum regression with seasonal dummies added in accordance with Johnston's suggestion. Only for this one industry was the standard error of estimate smaller than that reported on Table 6.3.1.[27] Here is the pooled seasonal dummies regression

[24] See Pashigian [1965], and the interesting interpretation of Lloyd Orr [1967].

[25] Equation 2.10 explains how β^e is calculated.

[26] Obviously, this difficulty largely results from the negative values of certain of the coefficients through which sales enter into the inventory regressions.

[27] An industry-by-industry check of the all-small and all-large firm pooled regressions revealed that only for the large petroleum pooled regression did the dummy variables lead to a tighter fit than that provided by the inclusion of lagged output.

TABLE 6.3.1a. FINISHED GOODS INVENTORY REALIZATIONS

$$\text{FIN} - \text{FIN}_{-1} = (1-\lambda)\,\delta\beta_1 + (1-\lambda)\,\delta\beta_2\text{SALE} + (1-\lambda)\beta_4[\text{FIN}_{-1} - \text{FIN}_{-2}]$$
$$+ \beta_4\left(\frac{1-\lambda}{1+m}\right)\text{SALE}_{-1} + (\lambda\delta - \lambda - \delta)\text{FIN}_{-1}$$
$$+ (1-\lambda)\,\delta\beta_3\text{ASSALE}_{+1} + \lambda\text{FINAS} + \epsilon_6$$

	Nonferrous Metals	Electrical Machinery	Nonelectrical Machinery	Chemicals	Petroleum
Partial $\bar{R}^2$	0.2728	0.5406	0.4011	0.4754	0.4865
$\bar{S}_{est}$	1657.4	2670.7	3900.9	2719.0	6988.3
df	95	170	221	240	338
F	0.93	1.14	0.46	0.60	4.90
$\bar{d}$	1.94	2.26	1.91	1.92	2.01
Number of firms	6	11	14	16	18
Variables					
$(1-\lambda)\,\delta\beta_2$	−0.076	−0.068	0.032	−0.089	−0.312
	(0.035)	(0.021)	(0.017)	(0.017)	(0.042)
$(1-\lambda)\beta_4$	0.122	0.198	−0.018	0.146	0.340
	(0.095)	(0.064)	(0.060)	(0.057)	(0.054)
$\beta_4\left(\frac{1-\lambda}{1+m}\right)$	0.145	0.053	−0.008	0.076	0.082
	(0.030)	(0.019)	(0.017)	(0.018)	(0.041)
$\lambda\delta - \lambda - \delta$	−0.268	−0.696	−0.693	−0.659	−1.121
	(0.123)	(0.079)	(0.078)	(0.060)	(0.074)
$(1-\lambda)\,\delta\beta_3$	0.014	0.171	−0.040	−0.036	0.268
	(0.028)	(0.018)	(0.020)	(0.020)	(0.034)
λ	−0.132	0.303	0.573	0.478	0.872
	(0.097)	(0.067)	(0.072)	(0.061)	(0.074)
δ	0.353	0.564	0.281	0.347	1.945
β_2	−0.190	−0.173	0.267	−0.492	−1.253
β_3	0.035	0.435	−0.333	−0.199	1.076
β_4	0.108	0.284	−0.042	0.280	2.656
m	−0.159	2.736	1.250	0.921	3.146
β^e	0.208	0.397	−0.133	−0.271	0.153

for petroleum

$$\underset{}{\text{FIN} - \text{FIN}_{-1}} = \beta_0 - \underset{(0.047)}{0.289\text{SALE}} - \underset{(0.060)}{0.952\text{FIN}_{-1}} + \underset{(0.047)}{0.322\text{ASSALE}_{+1}}$$

$$+ \underset{(0.064)}{0.827\text{FINAS}} + \text{seasonal dummies} + \epsilon_t$$

$$\text{Partial } \bar{R}^2 = 0.4944,\ \bar{S}_{\text{est}} = 6086.3,\ df = 286 \qquad (3.5)$$

How is this role of production smoothing in the determination of realized inventory investment in all but the nonelectrical machinery industry to be reconciled with the evidence of Section 6.2? There we reported that evidence was lacking of any decisive influence of production smoothing considerations upon FINAS, the planned finished goods stock; neither last period's production nor the seasonal dummy variables influenced FINAS. Perhaps this

TABLE 6.3.1b

	Nonferrous Metals	Electrical Machinery	Nonelectrical Machinery	Chemicals	Petroleum
Large Firms					
Partial $\bar{R}^2$	0.2919	0.5231	0.3805	0.4598	0.4818
$\bar{S}_{\text{est}}$	2205.1	4534.0	6512.4	4455.1	9713.1
df	42	55	76	87	173
F	0.68	1.83	0.46	0.63	5.35
Number of firms	3	3	5	6	9
Variables					
$(1 - \lambda)\,\delta\beta_2$	−0.079	−0.067	0.033	−0.091	−0.314
	(0.047)	(0.037)	(0.028)	(0.029)	(0.058)
$(1 - \lambda)\beta_4$	0.130	0.194	−0.014	0.144	0.346
	(0.134)	(0.110)	(0.102)	(0.094)	(0.076)
$\beta_4\left(\dfrac{1 - \lambda}{1 + m}\right)$	0.157	0.050	−0.011	0.078	0.083
	(0.040)	(0.034)	(0.029)	(0.030)	(0.057)
$\lambda\delta - \lambda - \delta$	−0.189	−0.684	−0.699	−0.658	−1.132
	(0.175)	(0.136)	(0.131)	(0.099)	(0.103)
$(1 - \lambda)\,\delta\beta_3$	0.013	0.174	−0.039	−0.043	0.269
	(0.037)	(0.031)	(0.034)	(0.033)	(0.048)
λ	−0.214	0.302	0.580	0.489	0.883
	(0.138)	(0.115)	(0.120)	(0.101)	(0.103)
δ	0.332	0.547	0.283	0.331	2.128
β^e	0.226	0.411	−0.143	−0.331	0.153

TABLE 6.3.1b (*continued*)

	Nonferrous Metals	Electrical Machinery	Nonelectrical Machinery	Chemicals	Petroleum
Small Firms					
Partial $\bar{R}^2$	0.4381	0.4653	0.4522	0.5305	0.2948
$\bar{S}_{est}$	742.12	691.22	761.67	391.41	737.86
df	47	109	139	147	159
F	0.86	3.92	1.72	2.21	2.00
Number of firms	3	8	9	10	9
Variables					
$(1 - \lambda)\, \delta\beta_2$	−0.112	−0.087	−0.226	−0.066	−0.201
	(0.091)	(0.036)	(0.045)	(0.015)	(0.045)
$(1 - \lambda)\beta_4$	0.245	0.532	−0.016	0.254	0.014
	(0.148)	(0.113)	(0.083)	(0.073)	(0.076)
$\beta_4\left(\frac{1 - \lambda}{1 + m}\right)$	−0.112	0.225	0.213	0.047	0.201
	(0.085)	(0.037)	(0.041)	(0.014)	(0.046)
$\lambda\delta - \lambda - \delta$	−0.919	−0.826	−0.526	−0.733	−0.338
	(0.170)	(0.172)	(0.132)	(0.086)	(0.070)
$(1 - \lambda)\, \delta\beta_3$	−0.083	−0.011	0.017	0.107	0.054
	(0.103)	(0.038)	(0.059)	(0.014)	(0.046)
λ	0.559	0.189	0.055	0.242	0.157
	(0.145)	(0.129)	(0.127)	(0.077)	(0.086)
δ	0.816	0.785	0.498	0.648	0.215
β^e	−0.853	0.199	0.008	0.179	0.298

discrepancy reflects an actual inconsistency within the firm, rather than a statistical anomaly. It is quite conceivable that even if production smoothing considerations are neglected by the members of the firm in formulating their target end-of-quarter stock, this factor may in practice still have a critical influence on plant operations in a way that affects actual realizations. Departures from plan are induced when the neglected production smoothing considerations impinge upon actual firm operations. Or, to put it another way, if managers neglect the production smoothing complication of equation 2.9 in formulating their planned finished goods investment, FINAS − FIN_{-1}, then the realities of actual plant operations may cause this factor to manifest itself in adjustment equation 3.1.[28] To the extent that the realities of factory operation cause production smoothing considerations to influence the actual outcome, the manager's aspirations for finished goods inventories will not be

[28] Direct verification of 3.1, with or without the production smoothing complication, is impossible because FIN* is unobserved.

satisfied. This phenomenon may help to explain why finished goods inventory anticipations are not very accurate predictors of actual developments. It may well be related to the "controller effect" of Murray Foss, which was discussed in Chapter 4.2.1.

A reasonable degree of plan rigidity is indicated by four of the five λ coefficients obtained by pooling the data for all firms in each industry. The coefficient for nonferrous metals, while negative, is not large in magnitude relative to its standard error. We note that when the regression is run for the large nonferrous firms, the same problem is encountered; for small nonferrous firms, on the other hand, λ is of correct sign and several times its standard error. That the FINAS coefficient results for nonferrous metals are not entirely satisfactory is consistent with our earlier results, for we found in Chapter 3 that firms in this industry are quite unsuccessful in forecasting short-run movements in finished goods inventory.[29] The largest value of λ is for the large pooled petroleum firm regression, although we had expected that electrical machinery would show greater plan rigidity, because of that industry's longer production period.

The unreasonable value of λ for the all pooled nonferrous metals regression provides the only exception to a rather interesting rule. We observe that small firms in the other four industries have a lower value of λ than the larger firms in the same industry.[30] This is consistent with the hypothesis that an advantage of being a small rather than a large firm is greater flexibility; smallness permits more rapid correction for errors made in forecasting sales volume. As already noted, small firms tend to have a larger δ, which implies that they attempt a more rapid correction of inventory imbalances when changing economic conditions generate a gap between equilibrium and actual inventories.

6.3.2 *Reduced Form Estimates*

How valuable is information on planned inventory investment as an aid in predicting actual realizations? This is an important question, for the durable and nondurable *planned* inventory data published in the *Survey of Current Business* are not partitioned by stage of fabrication. Consequently, it is necessary to modify the procedure we have been discussing if it is to be fruitfully employed in analyzing aggregate finished goods inventory realizations.

Our approach will be to work with the reduced form equation for inventories. Using equation 2.9 to eliminate FINAS from 3.3 yields as the finished

[29] See Table 3.4.2b.

[30] The same procedure used at the end of Section 6.2 with the δ's can be applied here to test the significance of the differences between large and small firm λ's. In order, the resulting t ratios are 1.725, 0.65, 3.01, 1.94, and 5.4. A one-tailed test is appropriate, and we are inclined to reject the null hypothesis for three of the five industries.

goods inventory investment reduced form equation:[31]

$$\text{FIN} - \text{FIN}_{-1} = \delta\beta_1 + (\lambda\delta\beta_2 + \lambda')\text{ASSALE} + \lambda\delta\beta_3\text{ALSALE}_{+1} + (1-\lambda)\delta\beta_3\text{ASSALE}_{+1} + [(1-\lambda)\delta\beta_2 - \lambda']\text{SALE} + \beta_4\left(\frac{1}{1+m}\right)\text{SALE}_{-1} + \beta_4(\text{FIN}_{-1} - \text{FIN}_{-2}) - \delta\text{FIN}_{-1} + \epsilon_7 \quad (3.6)$$

where $\epsilon_7 = \epsilon_6 + \lambda\epsilon_4.$

The pooled reduced form regression estimates are reported on Table 6.3.2.

TABLE 6.3.2a. REDUCED FORM FINISHED GOODS INVENTORY INVESTMENT

$$\Delta\text{FIN} = \delta\beta_1 + \lambda\delta\beta_2 + \lambda'\text{ASSALE} + \lambda\delta\beta_3\text{ALSALE}_{t+1} + (1-\lambda)\,\delta\beta_3\text{ASSALE}_{t+1} + [(1-\lambda)\,\delta\beta_2 - \lambda']\text{SALE} - \delta\text{FIN}_{-1} + \epsilon$$

	Nonferrous Metals	Electrical Machinery	Nonelectrical Machinery	Chemicals	Petroleum
Partial $\bar{R}^2$	0.1256	0.4843	0.1958	0.2650	0.2712
$\bar{S}_{est}$	1598.3	2944.9	4308.4	3258.4	8066.4
df	155	201	240	341	365
F	1.33	1.55	0.82	1.07	1.24
$\bar{d}$	1.89	2.23	1.84	1.97	1.90
Number of firms	9	13	14	20	19
$\bar{S}_{est}$,[a] sea dummies	1567.4	2441.5	4200.4	3211.3	8013.3
Variables					
$\lambda\delta\beta_2 + \lambda'$	0.024	−0.030	0.010	−0.116	−0.169
	(0.031)	(0.047)	(0.047)	(0.031)	(0.058)
$\lambda\delta\beta_3$	0.080	−0.022	0.042	0.099	−0.065
	(0.035)	(0.034)	(0.032)	(0.026)	(0.022)
$(1-\lambda)\,\delta\beta_3$	−0.048	0.185	−0.120	0.014	0.296
	(0.034)	(0.030)	(0.029)	(0.025)	(0.038)
$[(1-\lambda)\,\delta\beta_2 - \lambda']$	−0.041	0.013	0.056	0.059	−0.058
	(0.032)	(0.040)	(0.041)	(0.029)	(0.057)
$-\delta$	−0.227	−0.473	−0.117	−0.327	−0.321
	(0.054)	(0.052)	(0.036)	(0.044)	(0.038)
β_2	−0.075	−0.036	0.564	−0.174	−0.707
β_3	0.141	0.345	−0.667	0.346	0.720
λ	2.50	−0.135	−0.538	0.876	−0.281
λ'	0.067	−0.028	0.045	−0.066	−0.233
$\beta_2{}^e$	0.066	0.309	−0.102	0.517	0.012

[a] The statistics in the "$\bar{S}_{est,\ sea\ dummies}$" row are standard errors of estimate, adjusted for degrees of freedom, obtained with seasonal dummy variables included in the regression.

[31] Because the model is recursive, structural equation 2.9 constitutes the other reduced form equation of the model.

TABLE 6.3.2b

	Nonferrous Metals	Electrical Machinery	Nonelectrical Machinery	Chemicals	Petroleum
Large Firms					
Partial $\bar{R}^2$	0.0924	0.4703	0.1695	0.2527	0.2628
$\bar{S}_{\text{est}}$	2243	5183.7	7123.1	4621.1	11181
df	69	61	85	168	189
F	1.65	1.90	0.88	1.12	1.30
Number of firms	4	4	5	10	10
Variables					
$\lambda\delta\beta_2 + \lambda'$	0.018	−0.043	−0.000	−0.118	−0.171
	(0.044)	(0.088)	(0.079)	(0.045)	(0.081)
$\lambda\delta\beta_3$	0.085	−0.026	0.043	0.100	−0.065
	(0.050)	(0.060)	(0.054)	(0.038)	(0.030)
$(1 - \lambda)\,\delta\beta_3$	−0.053	0.190	−0.121	0.012	0.296
	(0.049)	(0.054)	(0.049)	(0.035)	(0.052)
$[(1 - \lambda)\,\delta\beta_2 - \lambda]$	−0.032	0.025	0.065	0.061	−0.056
	(0.046)	(0.075)	(0.069)	(0.041)	(0.080)
$-\delta$	−0.216	−0.465	−0.115	−0.326	−0.321
	(0.078)	(0.095)	(0.060)	(0.063)	(0.053)
λ	2.656	−0.159	−0.551	0.893	−0.281
β^e	0.083	0.314	−0.113	0.169	0.012
Small Firms					
Partial $\bar{R}^2$	0.2264	0.2215	0.5297	0.4744	0.2313
$\bar{S}_{\text{est}}$	717.34	802.35	690.54	408.55	765.70
df	81	135	150	168	171
F	0.82	0.97	1.66	1.53	1.49
Number of firms	5	9	9	10	9
Variables					
$\lambda\delta\beta_2 + \lambda'$	0.129	0.029	0.263	−0.047	−0.051
	(0.110)	(0.046)	(0.048)	(0.029)	(0.059)
$\lambda\delta\beta_3$	−0.067	−0.044	0.199	0.081	0.200
	(0.109)	(0.058)	(0.067)	(0.022)	(0.064)
$(1 - \lambda)\,\delta\beta_3$	−0.013	0.081	−0.111	0.077	0.002
	(0.076)	(0.042)	(0.070)	(0.021)	(0.069)
$[(1 - \lambda)\,\delta\beta_2 - \lambda]$	−0.216	−0.106	−0.303	−0.026	−0.106
	(0.083)	(0.040)	(0.041)	(0.025)	(0.048)
$-\delta$	−0.394	−0.410	−0.667	−0.458	−0.320
	(0.103)	(0.079)	(0.062)	(0.061)	(0.057)
λ	0.838	−1.189	2.261	0.513	0.990
β^e	−0.424	−0.098	0.072	0.186	0.141

These regressions are subject to the restriction that production smoothing is absent; that is, lagged production is excluded by restricting $\beta_4 = 0$, and there are no adjustments for seasonality. We have also considered the same model supplemented with seasonal dummy variables, which was Johnston's procedure for introducing production smoothing. There is no need to report the coefficients obtained with the seasonal dummy pooled regressions, for they are remarkably similar to those reported on Table 6.3.2. However, it is important to note that the effect of introducing production smoothing in this way was to achieve an improvement in fit, after correction for degrees of freedom, in each industry. Since the improvement is significant at the 5 percent level for each industry, this evidence suggests that production smoothing is important. Unfortunately, no regressions were run with last period's output included as an alternative test of the production smoothing concept.

Estimates of the basic model's parameters, derived from the reduced form equation, are presented at the bottom of Table 6.3.2. All the δ coefficients are of reasonable magnitude. However, two of the marginal desired inventory coefficients are of incorrect sign. Furthermore, the calculated estimates of the λ and λ' coefficients are almost all of unreasonable magnitude. One of the five β^e coefficients is of incorrect sign, indicating that the long-run marginal response of stocks to changes in sales volume is negative.

A number of discrepancies are revealed when these reduced form derived estimates are compared with those of Table 6.3.1, which were based on the direct application of least squares to the recursive structural equation. Such discrepancies can arise for several reasons. First, of course, there is the fact that additional noise is introduced by eliminating FINAS_t, the predetermined variable, in obtaining the reduced form equation. Second, a larger number of degrees of freedom are available for the reduced form regressions, in part because a number of observations, indeed entire firms, could not be used for the structural regression because many respondents failed to report planned finished goods inventory stock. Third, there is a difference in specification with regard to the parameter λ', which was constrained to zero in the structural regressions, and also in the treatment of production smoothing. Furthermore, substantial sampling error is unavoidable when parameter estimates are calculated by transforming regression coefficients. Since the λ' parameter is small in magnitude and frequently has the wrong sign in the reduced form equation, it may not have been inappropriate to constrain it to zero in estimating the structural equations on Table 6.3.1. We also note that the reduced form regressions generally yield lower estimates of both δ and β^e. As expected, the reduced form equations usually have larger standard errors of estimate, after adjustment for degrees of freedom, than the structural equations. The nonferrous metal pooled regression is one exception to this rule; also, when the data are partitioned by size of firm two additional exceptions are provided by small nonferrous metals and small nonelectrical machinery. But in spite of these exceptions, it is clear that much is to be gained when observations on anticipated inventory investment make it unnecessary for the investigator to resort to reduced form estimation.

Aggregate inventory behavior can also be studied with the reduced form, even in the absence of observations on aggregate planned finished goods inventory, for that equation does not involve observations on FINAS. We must content ourselves, however, with an examination of the durable and nondurable benchmark aggregates, for it has not proved convenient to work with stage-of-fabrication data by individual industries.[32] The equations were estimated in the following form:

$$\begin{aligned} \text{FIN} - \text{FIN}_{-1} = {} & \delta\beta_1 + \lambda(\text{ASSALE} - \text{SALE}) \\ & + \delta\beta_2[\lambda\text{ASSALE} + (1 - \lambda)\text{SALE}] \\ & + \delta\beta_3[\lambda\text{ALSALE}_{+1} + (1 - \lambda)\text{ASSALE}_{+1}] \\ & - \delta\text{FIN}_{-1} + \epsilon \end{aligned} \tag{3.7}$$

This equation is obtained from 3.6 under the restriction that $\beta_4 = 0$ and $\lambda = \lambda'$; that is, it is presumed that the effects of production smoothing are negligible and that the extent of error correction stemming from erroneous forecasting is uniform.[33] Although the equation is nonlinear, a slight modification of the standard least squares approach yields maximum likelihood estimates of the five parameters of the model, provided that the stochastic disturbance is normally and independently distributed.[34] For durable manufacturing we have:

$$\begin{aligned} \text{FIN} - \text{FIN}_{-1} = {} & \underset{(1083.4)}{-465.6} + 0.055(\text{ASSALE} - \text{SALE}) \\ & + \underset{(0.0246)}{0.0727}[0.055\text{ASSALE} + 0.945\text{SALE}] \\ & + \underset{(0.0273)}{0.0376}[0.055\text{ALSALE}_{+1} + 0.945\text{ASSALE}_{+1}] \\ & - \underset{(0.1338)}{0.3929}\text{FIN}_{-1} + e \end{aligned} \tag{3.8a}$$

$\bar{R}^2 = 0.3802$, $d = 1.31$, $\bar{S}^2 = 262.47$,

$\lambda = 0.055$, $\delta = 0.3929$, $\beta_1 = -1172.8$, $\beta_2 = 0.183$, and $\beta_3 = 0.095$.

[32] Although OBE now publishes stage-of-fabrication data by individual industry, the industry classification is not compatible with that of the inventory anticipation survey.
[33] The distinction between λ and λ' was discussed at the beginning of Section 6.3.
[34] The estimation procedure is described in Appendix B of this chapter.

For nondurable manufacturing we can report:

$$\begin{aligned}\text{FIN} - \text{FIN}_{-1} = {} & \underset{(482.6)}{543.7} + 0.13(\text{ASSALE} - \text{SALE}) \\ & + \underset{(0.0311)}{0.0476}[0.13\text{ASSALE} + 0.87\text{SALE}] \\ & + \underset{(0.0255)}{0.0459}[0.13\text{ALSALE}_{+1} + 0.87\text{ASSALE}_{+1}] \\ & + \underset{(0.085)}{0.493}\text{FIN}_{-1} + e \end{aligned} \tag{3.8b}$$

$\bar{R}^2 = 0.6268$, $\bar{S}^2_{\text{est}} = 95.5$, $d = 1.60$,

$\lambda = 0.13$, $\delta = 0.493$, $\beta_1 = 1102.8$, $\beta_2 = 0.0996$, and $\beta_3 = 0.0931$.

For both sectors, the parameter estimates are of reasonable magnitude. The estimates of δ suggest that within each calendar quarter, firms attempt to adjust their inventories between one third and one half of the way toward their equilibrium level. The value of λ is small, particularly in durables; this implies that firms are quite adept at correcting when surprised by sales developments. Judging by the standard errors, which are only approximate, we see that in durables β_3 but not β_2 is significant at the 5 percent level, provided we have as part of the maintained hypothesis that $\delta \neq 0$; precisely the reverse conclusion holds true for nondurables. While the results are encouraging, it must be conceded that they are based on a very small number of observations; there are only 12 degrees of freedom for these aggregate regressions.

6.3.3 *Sales Proxies in Predicting Inventory Behavior*

In the majority of applications, investigators of inventory behavior have not been blessed with data on anticipated sales volume. A number of economists developed models of expectational behavior in response to this problem. In Chapter 5, a partial evaluation of these proxy procedures was provided by comparing the effectiveness of the alternatives in predicting observed sales anticipations. A proxy approach can be subjected to a further check by comparing the parameter estimates it generates with those obtained with the *ex ante* data.

The particular proxy procedure that we shall evaluate is one employed by Lovell [1961] in an investigation of finished goods inventory behavior. This procedure has also been employed by a number of other investigators, including Ball and Drake [1963] and Ando, Brown, Kareken, and Solow

[1963]. Lovell's proxy procedure, already reviewed in some detail in Chapter 5.4.1, involves the use of the equation

$$\text{ASSALE}_t = \rho\text{SALE}_{t-1} + (1 - \rho)\text{SALE}, \qquad 0 \leq \rho \leq 1 \qquad (3.9)$$

Substituting this expression into reduced form equation 3.6 will yield the model employed by Lovell only if certain additional restrictions are imposed. Specifically, if we assume that $\beta_3 = \beta_4 = 0$ and $\lambda = \lambda'$ the reduced form equation simplifies, when equation 3.9 is used to eliminate SAS_t, to:

$$\Delta\text{FIN} = \delta\beta_1 + \delta\beta_2\text{SALE} - \lambda(\delta\beta_2 + 1)\rho\,\Delta\text{SALE} - \delta\text{FIN}_{-1} + \epsilon \quad (3.10)$$

It will be observed that in the absence of further restrictions the parameters λ and ρ are not identified; this is not too surprising, for ρ is a measure of a type of systematic error firms may make in predicting sales, while λ is an index of the extent to which firms manage to revise production plans in response to error.

Evidence on the efficiency of the proxy procedure is provided by Table 6.3.3. Comparison of the standard errors of the estimate obtained with the

TABLE 6.3.3. SALES PROXIES IN PREDICTING INVENTORY BAHAVIOR WITH SEASONAL DUMMIES

$$\Delta\text{FIN} = \delta\beta_{1f} + \delta\beta_2\text{SALE} - \lambda(\delta\beta_2 + 1)\rho\,\Delta\text{SALE} - \delta\text{FIN}_{-1} + \text{Seasonal Dummies} + \epsilon$$

	Nonferrous Metals	Electrical Machinery	Nonelectrical Machinery	Chemicals	Petroleum
Partial $\bar{R}^2$	0.1525	0.2171	0.1702	0.2613	0.1476
$\bar{S}_{\text{est}}$	1687.1	3620.3	4395.5	3245.7	8451.8
df	191	231	265	383	393
F	1.78	5.51	2.68	4.07	0.74
$\bar{d}$	1.81	1.95	1.68	1.79	1.74
Number of firms	10	14	14	20	19
Variables[a]					
$\delta\beta_2$	−0.004	0.031	0.037	0.047	0.009
	(0.014)	(0.021)	(0.018)	(0.012)	(0.028)
$-\lambda(\delta\beta_2 + 1)\rho$	−0.034	−0.022	0.021	−0.089	−0.069
	(0.019)	(0.020)	(0.016)	(0.013)	(0.042)
$-\delta$	−0.198	−0.336	−0.163	−0.277	−0.266
	(0.046)	(0.049)	(0.035)	(0.036)	(0.038)
β_2	−0.020	0.092	0.227	0.170	0.034
$\lambda\rho$	0.034	0.021	−0.020	0.085	0.068

[a] Regression coefficients for the seasonal dummies are omitted.

proxy procedure with the corresponding statistics from the reduced form regressions utilizing actual sales anticipations is informative, for it is clear that an even looser fit is generated with the proxy approach. Observe, however, that most of the parameter estimates obtained by the proxy procedure are of reasonable magnitude; one exception is the coefficient of SALE in the nonferrous metals regression and another is the coefficient of the change in sales for nonelectrical machinery. It must be conceded, however, that most of the proxy procedure regression coefficients have large standard errors. One further point: the proxy procedure yields in four out of five cases a substantially lower estimate of δ, the adjustment speed, than was obtained with the sales anticipation regressions. All in all, we must conclude that while the proxy approach may constitute a reasonable way to proceed when *ex ante* data are unavailable, it clearly leads to a considerable loss of precision.

When this same proxy procedure was used in examining the behavior of the durable finished goods inventory benchmark aggregate, we obtained:

$$\begin{aligned}\Delta\text{FIN} = {} & \underset{(1133.6)}{180.7} + \underset{(0.0394)}{0.0616}\text{SALE} + \underset{(0.0314)}{0.0106}(\text{SALE} - \text{SALE}_{-1}) \\ & - \underset{(0.1612)}{0.2683}\text{FIN}_{-1} + e \end{aligned} \tag{3.11a}$$

$$\bar{R}^2 = 0.2901, \quad d = 1.58, \quad \bar{S}^2_{\text{est}} = 280.89, \quad df = 13$$

For nondurables we have:

$$\begin{aligned}\Delta\text{FIN} = {} & \underset{(567.9)}{306.9} + \underset{(0.0300)}{0.0471}\text{SALE} + \underset{(0.0412)}{0.0639}(\text{SALE} - \text{SALE}_{-1}) \\ & - \underset{(0.1318)}{0.2477}\text{FIN}_{-1} + e \end{aligned} \tag{3.11b}$$

$$\bar{R}^2 = 0.4878, \quad d = 1.604, \quad \bar{S}^2_{\text{est}} = 111.3, \quad df = 13.$$

In both sectors we find that the change-in-sale term has a positive coefficient that is small relative to the standard error; the negative sign for $\lambda\rho$ is contrary to intuition and inconsistent with the results obtained with four of the five pooled industry regressions of Table 6.3.3; it is also inconsistent with results obtained with regressions run on industry data for an earlier time period.[35] The fit provided by the proxy procedure is considerably weaker than that obtained with observations on sales anticipations in the reduced form, equations 3.8a and 3.8b. It must be reported, however, that when β_3 was constrained to zero in equation 3.9, so that only ASSALE was involved, we found that $\bar{R}^2 = 0.2903$ for durables and 0.5508 for nondurables; thus the

[35] Lovell [1961] obtained negative coefficients for sales changes in a study of aggregate data over the period 1948–1955.

gain becomes substantial for durables only when data on ALSALE as well as ASSALE are available.

6.4 STOCKS OF PURCHASED MATERIALS AND GOODS IN PROCESS

The same accelerator model customarily used in studies of finished goods inventory is often employed, with only minor modification, for purchased materials and goods in process. The principal modification has been to replace sales with production. In addition, new and unfilled orders have been successfully exploited in studies of this category of inventory investment.[36] The new OBE data now make it possible to attempt to analyze the behavior of planned accumulation of stocks in terms of anticipated sales and production levels—these variables had not been observable in prior studies. We are, however, seriously handicapped by the specification error arising from the fact that observations are lacking on the critical order variables.

Stocks of purchased materials and work in process will be examined in much the same way as finished goods inventory. Specifically, we shall consider the following equation for planned accumulation of stocks:

$$\begin{aligned} \text{PMAS} - \text{PM}_{-1} &= \delta\beta_1 + \delta\beta_2 \frac{1}{1+m}\,\text{ASSALE} \\ &\quad + \delta\beta_2(\text{FINAS} - \text{FIN}_{-1}) + \delta\beta_3\text{ALSALE}_{+1} - \delta\text{PM}_{-1} + \epsilon \qquad (4.1) \end{aligned}$$

This is analogous to 2.4, the equation used to explain planned finished goods accumulation, with the important exception that $\text{FINAS} - \text{FIN}_{-1}$ is included as an additional variable; in this way, the desired level of stocks is made to depend upon planned production as well as anticipated sales. Furthermore, we attempt to explain actual investment in goods in process and purchased material stocks in a manner similar to that used in deriving equation 3.3 for finished goods realizations. Specifically, by taking a weighted average of the level of stocks that would occur with the opposite extremes of complete plan rigidity and complete flexibility, we have the following analogue of equation 3.3:

$$\begin{aligned} \text{PM} - \text{PM}_{-1} &= (1-\lambda)\delta\beta_1 + (1-\lambda)\frac{\delta\beta_2}{1+m}\,\text{SALE} \\ &\quad + (1-\lambda)\delta\beta_2(\text{FIN} - \text{FIN}_{-1}) + (1-\lambda)\delta\beta_3\text{ASSALE}_{+1} \\ &\quad + (\lambda\delta - \lambda - \delta)\text{PM}_{-1} + \lambda\text{PMAS} + \epsilon \qquad (4.2) \end{aligned}$$

[36] This approach, used by Lovell [1961], has been subjected to critical scrutiny by Eisner and Strotz [1963, pp. 212–220]. Courchene [1967] stressed the distinction between production to stock and production to order. The role of orders as a determinant of finished goods inventories, while soft-pedaled in earlier studies, has been emphasized by Childs [1967].

Pooled regressions explaining planned stock behavior are reported in Table 6.4.1. A cursory examination of the coefficients of multiple determination suffices to reveal that the model performs very poorly when observations for all firms in each industry are pooled. Somewhat more encouraging results are obtained when the large and small firms are segregated. The model is still grossly unsatisfactory for large nonferrous metal firms, for $\bar{R}^2$ is only 0.05 and δ is of the wrong sign. Furthermore, we note that while δ is positive for the pooled large firm chemical regression, it is exceedingly small and the fit is again bad. But apart from these two perverse regressions, the results are not entirely unreasonable. It will be noted that small firms generally have a larger value of δ, which implies that they plan to correct a larger proportion of the gap between inherited and equilibrium stocks during the three-month observation period. The tendency for small firms to be more flexible than

TABLE 6.4.1a. PLANNED PURCHASED MATERIAL AND GOODS IN PROCESS INVESTMENT WITH SEASONAL DUMMY VARIABLES

$$\text{PMAS} - \text{PM}_{-1} = \delta\beta_1 + \delta\beta_2 \frac{1}{(1+m)} \text{ASSALE} + \delta\beta_2[\text{FINAS} - \text{FIN}_{-1}] + \delta\beta_3\text{ALSALE}_{+1} - \delta\text{PM} + \text{Seasonal Dummies} + \epsilon$$

	Nonferrous Metals	Electrical Machinery	Nonelectrical Machinery	Chemicals	Petroleum
Partial $\bar{R}^2$	0.0840	0.2205	0.1320	0.0867	0.2455
$\bar{S}_{est}$	6277.1	2376.7	3638.1	2055.2	5279.2
df	96	177	227	243	335
F	0.41	2.86	1.69	1.05	1.93
$\bar{d}$	1.93	1.85	2.17	1.72	1.84
Number of firms	6	11	14	16	18
Variables[a]					
$\delta\beta_2\left(\frac{1}{1+m}\right)$	−0.255 (0.098)	0.009 (0.018)	0.034 (0.017)	−0.006 (0.012)	−0.188 (0.025)
$\delta\beta_2$	0.015 (0.362)	0.010 (0.066)	0.105 (0.068)	0.190 (0.045)	−0.310 (0.053)
$\delta\beta_3$	0.120 (0.110)	0.035 (0.020)	0.086 (0.019)	0.012 (0.017)	0.087 (0.014)
$-\delta$	0.180 (0.085)	−0.309 (0.055)	−0.138 (0.029)	−0.027 (0.058)	−0.119 (0.030)
β_2	−0.083	0.032	0.761	7.037	−2.605
β_3	−0.667	0.113	0.623	0.444	0.731
m	1.059	0.111	2.088	−32.667	0.649
β^e	0.750	0.142	0.870	0.222	−0.849

[a] Regression coefficients for the seasonal dummies are omitted.

TABLE 6.4.1b

	Nonferrous Metals	Electrical Machinery	Nonelectrical Machinery	Chemicals	Petroleum
Large Firms					
Partial $\bar{R}^2$	0.0507	0.3203	0.1084	0.0630	0.2387
$\bar{S}_{est}$	9334.5	3542.9	6067.1	3389.4	7404.3
df	41	57	78	86	168
F	0.35	3.99	1.79	1.08	2.03
Number of firms	3	3	5	6	9
Variables					
$\delta\beta_2\left(\frac{1}{1+m}\right)$	−0.255 (0.156)	0.038 (0.029)	0.043 (0.031)	0.000 (0.021)	−0.185 (0.035)
$\delta\beta_2$	0.200 (0.611)	0.144 (0.117)	0.050 (0.125)	0.197 (0.076)	−0.326 (0.075)
$\delta\beta_3$	0.131 (0.173)	0.003 (0.032)	0.084 (0.033)	0.006 (0.029)	0.084 (0.019)
$-\delta$	0.186 (0.128)	−0.241 (0.087)	−0.140 (0.049)	−0.020 (0.099)	−0.115 (0.043)
β^e	0.667	0.170	0.907	0.300	−0.878
Small Firms					
Partial $\bar{R}^2$	0.3946	0.2962	0.4729	0.3064	0.3752
$\bar{S}_{est}$	521.44	942.56	457.60	265.43	341.86
df	48	113	142	150	160
F	0.87	1.44	1.08	1.67	1.44
Number of firms	3	8	9	10	9
Variables					
$\delta\beta_2\left(\frac{1}{1+m}\right)$	−0.075 (0.073)	0.052 (0.061)	−0.121 (0.033)	0.022 (0.011)	−0.053 (0.027)
$\delta\beta_2$	−0.334 (0.095)	0.326 (0.165)	−0.014 (0.058)	0.069 (0.048)	−0.123 (0.031)
$\delta\beta_3$	0.154 (0.089)	0.051 (0.063)	0.241 (0.031)	0.024 (0.012)	0.055 (0.025)
$-\delta$	−0.181 (0.068)	−0.632 (0.090)	−0.246 (0.033)	−0.301 (0.044)	−0.343 (0.040)
β^e	0.436	0.163	0.488	0.153	0.006

TABLE 6.4.2a. PURCHASED MATERIAL AND GOODS IN PROCESS INVESTMENT WITH SEASONAL DUMMY VARIABLES

$$PM - PM_{-1} = (1 - \lambda)\,\delta\beta_1 + (1 - \lambda)\frac{\delta\beta_2}{1 + m}SALE + (1 - \lambda)\,\delta\beta_2[FIN - FIN_{-1}] + (1 - \lambda)\,\delta\beta_3 ASSALE_{+1} + (\lambda\delta - \lambda - \delta)PM_{-1} + \lambda PMAS + \text{Seasonal Dummies} + \epsilon$$

	Nonferrous Metals	Electrical Machinery	Nonelectrical Machinery	Chemicals	Petroleum
Partial $\bar{R}^2$	0.2496	0.4067	0.2852	0.0975	0.7917
$\bar{S}_{est}$	2690.1	2216.6	4216.2	1822.7	3288.9
df	93	169	219	238	336
F	1.14	1.40	0.97	1.51	3.49
$\bar{d}$	1.79	1.89	1.89	2.06	1.87
Number of firms	6	10	14	16	17
Variables[a]					
$(1 - \lambda)\frac{\delta\beta_2}{1 + m}$	−0.201	−0.045	−0.041	0.033	−0.173
	(0.052)	(0.018)	(0.017)	(0.011)	(0.022)
$(1 - \lambda)\,\delta\beta_2$	−0.216	−0.108	0.112	0.113	−0.699
	(0.147)	(0.060)	(0.065)	(0.036)	(0.024)
$(1 - \lambda)\,\delta\beta_3$	0.111	0.121	0.007	0.014	0.149
	(0.046)	(0.021)	(0.021)	(0.011)	(0.022)
$(\lambda\delta - \lambda - \delta)$	−0.194	−0.392	−0.614	−0.315	−0.410
	(0.061)	(0.080)	(0.074)	(0.071)	(0.033)
λ	0.083	0.103	0.490	0.150	0.296
	(0.042)	(0.080)	(0.077)	(0.054)	(0.032)
δ	0.121	0.322	0.243	0.194	0.162
β_2	−1.946	−0.374	0.903	0.685	−6.132
β_3	1.000	0.419	0.056	0.085	1.307
m	0.075	1.400	−3.732	2.424	3.040
β^e	−0.811	0.263	−0.274	0.285	−0.211

[a] Regression coefficients for the seasonal dummies are omitted.

large firms may explain why such an unsatisfactory picture emerged when the large and small firms were pooled together.[37]

Realized purchased material and goods-in-process behavior is revealed by Table 6.4.2. The fact that the λ coefficients are positive and large relative to their standard errors indicates that the PMAS variable is useful in predicting stock behavior. The sizable values of λ obtained for the large firm nonelectrical machinery and the small chemical and small petroleum regressions

[37] The t coefficients for the difference in δ between large and small firms, calculated as before, are −2.53, −3.11, −1.79, −2.60, and −3.98.

TABLE 6.4.2b

	Nonferrous Metals	Electrical Machinery	Nonelectrical Machinery	Chemicals	Petroleum
Large Firms					
Partial $\bar{R}^2$	0.1976	0.4210	0.2416	0.0957	0.7969
$\bar{S}_{est}$	3962.6	3650.9	7149.6	2911.0	4506.6
df	40	53	74	85	170
F	1.23	1.93	1.06	1.56	3.42
Number of firms	3	3	5	6	9
Variables					
$(1-\lambda)\dfrac{\delta\beta_2}{1+m}$	−0.205	−0.050	−0.039	0.028	−0.164
	(0.084)	(0.032)	(0.031)	(0.019)	(0.031)
$(1-\lambda)\,\delta\beta_2$	−0.264	−0.175	0.132	0.134	−0.702
	(0.248)	(0.114)	(0.117)	(0.061)	(0.033)
$(1-\lambda)\,\delta\beta_3$	0.118	0.122	0.003	0.021	0.144
	(0.074)	(0.039)	(0.038)	(0.018)	(0.031)
$\lambda\delta-\lambda-\delta$	−0.185	−0.332	−0.623	−0.333	−0.406
	(0.091)	(0.153)	(0.128)	(0.117)	(0.045)
λ	0.074	0.065	0.499	0.166	0.292
	(0.064)	(0.153)	(0.132)	(0.088)	(0.044)
δ	0.120	0.286	0.248	0.200	0.161
β^e	−0.784	0.270	−0.290	0.293	−0.175
Small Firms					
Partial $\bar{R}^2$	0.3328	0.3157	0.3837	0.3317	0.3830
$\bar{S}_{est}$	660.83	602.70	709.92	385.97	472.21
df	45	108	137	145	158
F	2.51	3.19	3.51	1.02	1.93
Number of firms	3	7	9	10	8
Variables					
$(1-\lambda)\dfrac{\delta\beta_2}{1+m}$	−0.097	0.161	−0.159	0.025	−0.145
	(0.084)	(0.034)	(0.045)	(0.015)	(0.030)
$(1-\lambda)\,\delta\beta_2$	−0.406	0.006	−0.138	0.165	−0.231
	(0.119)	(0.069)	(0.065)	(0.068)	(0.048)
$(1-\lambda)\,\delta\beta_3$	0.080	0.080	0.310	0.063	0.131
	(0.096)	(0.031)	(0.056)	(0.016)	(0.030)
$\lambda\delta-\lambda-\delta$	−0.240	−0.451	−0.567	−0.797	−0.546
	(0.160)	(0.071)	(0.108)	(0.107)	(0.088)
λ	0.104	0.025	0.308	0.504	0.433
	(0.164)	(0.058)	(0.132)	(0.116)	(0.106)
δ	0.152	0.437	0.374	0.591	0.199
β^e	−0.125	0.566	0.583	0.300	−0.124

suggest that in these sectors it is quite difficult to revise delivery schedules.[38] The marginal desired inventory coefficients are somewhat erratic in sign and as a result $\hat{\beta}^e$, the equilibrium inventory sales coefficient, is often inappropriately negative. Judged in terms of the standard error of the estimate, the accelerator model provides a slightly better explanation of realized rather than planned stocks.

6.5 AGGREGATE INVENTORY BEHAVIOR

The behavior of the individual firm attracts attention primarily as a means of providing insight into what we can expect at the more aggregate level. But when we refocus our attention on inventory aggregates, we lose a substantial number of degrees of freedom. Furthermore, we do not have observations on aggregate inventories partitioned by stage-of-fabrication at the industry level, except in terms of a classification that cannot be easily reconciled with that of our sales anticipation aggregates. There are, however, certain advantages in working with aggregate time series. For one thing, it is possible to use unfilled orders data when dealing with the durable and the nondurable inventory aggregates. Furthermore, it is possible for us to use a somewhat more sophisticated computational technique, rather than relying exclusively upon standard regression procedures.

Turning first to the effect of unfilled orders (UOR) on planned inventory investment for durable manufacturing we obtain:

$$\begin{aligned}\text{INAS} - \text{IN}_{-1} = \underset{(2041.8)}{1639.9} + \underset{(0.0262)}{0.0959}\text{ASSALE} + \underset{(0.0357)}{0.0936}\text{ALSALE}_{+1} \\ - \underset{(0.0349)}{0.0102}\text{UOR} - \underset{(0.0860)}{0.3320}\text{IN}_{-1} + e\end{aligned}$$

$\bar{R}^2 = 0.5161$, $dw = 2.38$, $\bar{S}_{\text{est}} = 215.2$, $df = 13$,

$\beta_1 = 4939$, $\beta_2 = 0.2889$, $\beta_3 = 0.2819$, $\beta_4 = -0.0307$, $\delta = 0.3320$. (5.1a)

For nondurables, we have:

$$\begin{aligned}\text{INAS} - \text{IN}_{-1} = \underset{(1093.1)}{2284.1} + \underset{(0.0364)}{0.0679}\text{ASSALE} + \underset{(0.0494)}{0.0012}\text{ALSALE}_{+1} \\ - \underset{(0.1431)}{0.0980}\text{UOR} - \underset{(0.0983)}{0.2593}\text{IN}_{-1} + e\end{aligned}$$

$\bar{R}^2 = 0.3893$, $dw = 2.24$, $\bar{S}_{\text{est}} = 97.8$, $df = 13$,

$\beta_1 = 8809$, $\beta_2 = 0.2619$, $\beta_3 = 0.0046$, $\beta_4 = -0.3779$, $\delta = 0.2593$. (5.1b)

[38] The standard errors of the difference $\lambda_l - \lambda_s$ are 0.176, 0.164, 0.187, 0.146, and 0.115. Thus the differences between large and small firms are not significant, except in the chemical industry.

Observe that while the sales coefficients and δ are of reasonable magnitude, the unfilled orders coefficients are negative in both sectors. We must reject the hypothesis that unfilled orders influence planned inventory investment. This result is inconsistent with the conclusions of many earlier studies. Of course, in earlier investigations anticipated sales volume was unobserved; it is conceivable that unfilled orders influence inventory investment indirectly by affecting anticipated sales volume.[39] On the other hand, it is conceivable that the orders' influence loses out in the process of aggregation over stages of fabrication.

Now we shall consider an estimation problem that we have neglected heretofore in estimating separately the parameters of the planned and realized inventory investment equations. As total inventory analogues of equations 2.4 and 3.2 for planned and realized inventory investment we shall consider:[40]

$$\text{INAS} = \delta\beta_1 + \delta\beta_2\text{ASSALE} + \delta\beta_3\text{ALSALE}_{+1} + (1 - \delta)\text{IN}_{-1} + \epsilon_1 \quad (5.2)$$

and

$$\text{IN} = (1 - \lambda)\delta\beta_1 + (1 - \lambda)\delta\beta_2\text{ASSALE} + (1 - \lambda)\delta\beta_3\text{ASSALE}_{+1} + (1 - \lambda)(1 - \delta)\text{IN}_{-1} + \lambda[\text{INAS} + \text{ASSALE} - \text{SALE}] + \epsilon_2 \quad (5.3)$$

The first equation involves four regression coefficients that can be unscrambled to obtain estimates of four parameters; the second equation involves five regression coefficients that can be unscrambled to obtain estimates of the five parameters appearing in that equation. But in all there are only six parameters to estimate, and it is clear that the observations now available on INAS create the possibility of conflicting estimates. Indeed, the estimates reported from the pooled firm regressions earlier in this chapter are subject to precisely this same problem.[41] More efficient parameter estimates may be obtained by taking advantage of the *a priori* restrictions rather than estimating equations 5.2 and 5.3 separately. In effect, the procedure practically serves to double the number of degrees of freedom and is obviously superior to the ambiguous parameter estimates provided by the customary realization function approach.[42]

[39] Insignificant coefficients for orders were obtained by Lovell [1967] in realization functions explaining aggregate inventory investment.

[40] Note that without observations on output, we cannot work with the simple sum of the finished goods models of section 6.3 plus the purchased materials and goods in process models of 6.4.

[41] Note that the overidentification problem can be only partially circumvented by exploiting the distinction between λ and λ', discussed in Section 6.3, which has to do with a possible difference between the extent to which firms work to restore inventory to the planned level when surprised and the extent to which they work to revise planned inventories.

[42] The realization function procedure was described briefly in Section 6.3.

Table 6.5.1 reports maximum likelihood estimates of the parameters of equations 5.2 and 5.3.[43] The likelihood function was maximized subject to the restrictions that the β_i be nonnegative and that λ and δ be nonnegative and less than unity. Although asymptotically unbiased and consistent, the estimates are subject to small sample bias because of the sign constraints and the presence of the lagged inventory stock in 5.2.[44] The estimates for the 14 component industries and the durable and nondurable aggregates are based on 35 observations; those obtained by pooling the data over industries are based on 245 observations. We have not undertaken the task of applying the likelihood ratio test procedure appropriate for testing hypotheses; the single and double asterisks over the various parameter estimates indicate, respectively, that the regression procedure yielded coefficients that were at least two or three times their approximate standard errors in magnitude, but these should be interpreted with extreme caution.

Examination of the table reveals that the λ coefficient is exceedingly small in most instances, suggesting that plans are subject to extremely rapid revision. Indeed, the parameter is estimated to have a zero value in three durable industries and one nondurable, implying that INAS is irrelevant as far as the determination of end-of-quarter inventory position is concerned. The aggregate regression suggests that schedules for the delivery of raw materials are, for the most part, subject to extremely sharp revision during the quarterly observation period when actual sales deviate from their anticipated level. The only notable exception is durable industry six, electrical machinery, for which $\lambda - 0.68$. Thus, the aggregate regressions generally tend to suggest a much greater degree of plan revision than our analysis of the pooled regressions revealed. Of course, our low values of λ reported on Table 6.5.1 were obtained with data aggregated by stage-of-fabrication as well as over firms, and this may help to explain the discrepancy.[45] Furthermore, the estimates of λ obtained with the pooled firm data on purchased materials and goods in process were subject to considerable sampling error.

It will be noted that a number of the β_2 coefficients are zero, particularly in nondurables. As may be seen from inspection of equation 4.1, this implies that desired end-of-period inventories are not affected by current sales volume, a not unreasonable result. The zero values of β_3, on the other hand, do not

[43] The estimation procedure is explained in Appendix C of this chapter.

[44] Even if we ignored the sign constraints, we would obtain consistent estimates of the parameters of the model, but the constraints serve to increase the asymptotic efficiency of the estimates when the parameter is actually zero and when either λ or δ is unity; when the parameters are not on these boundary points the asymptotic distributions of the constrained and unconstrained estimators are identical.

[45] Even without any physical increase in the flow of raw materials to the firm, a step-up in production will partially offset the effect of forecast error, for the rise in value added will augment the value of stocks as they are converted from inputs to finished goods inventory.

TABLE 6.5.1. MAXIMUM LIKELIHOOD PARAMETER ESTIMATES

	λ	$\delta\beta_1$	$\delta\beta_2$	$\delta\beta_3$	δ	β_1	β_2	β_3	$\bar{S}_{est}$
DURABLES									
1	0.10	371.9	0	0.043	0.2054	1810	0	0.2093	116.2
2	0.08	2.462	0.0859*	0	0.1061	23.20	0.8096	0	24.5
3	0.68	171.1	0.1581*	0.1427*	0.5070	337.5	0.3118	0.2815	102.4
4	0	1709**	0.0535	0.1514**	0.5536	3087	0.0966	0.2735	131.1
5	0	600.9*	0.0200	0.0892**	0.4117	1460	0.0486	0.2167	140.0
6	0.08	66.15	0.0090	0.0584	0.0946	699.3	0.0951	0.6173	99.8
7	0	309.6	0	0.0520	0.1749	1770	0	0.2973	97.4
Aggregate	0	2374*	0.0975**	0.0721**	0.3411	6960	0.2858	0.2114	363.9
Combined	0.11	12.37	0	0.0262**	0.0421	293.8	0	0.6223	120.6
Sepincep	0.06	419.1**	0	0.0760**	0.2464	1701	0	0.3084	111.1
NONDURABLES									
1	0.10	409.8	0.2004**	0	0.6644	616.8	0.3016	0	204.0
2	0	803.8	0	0	0.2978	2699	0	0	110.3
3	0.05	187.9**	0	0.1613**	0.4505	417.1	0	0.3580	30.9
4	0.15	1926**	0	0.2428**	0.8997	2141	0	0.2699	91.3
5	0.14	1472**	0	0.1251	0.8004	1839	0	0.1563	80.2
6	0.22	229.8**	0	0.2237**	0.5146	446.6	0	0.4347	37.2
7	0.11	724.5*	0	0.2699**	0.8812	822.2	0	0.3063	151.0
Aggregate	0	1597	0.0666	0	0.2257	7076	0.2951	0	258.7
Combined	0.29	42.0	0	0.0043	0.0248	1694	0	0.1734	138.8
Sepincep	0.20	865.1**	0.0323	0.0765**	0.5361	1617	0.0602	0.1427	127.5

appear as reasonable, for they imply that firms do not look to the future in considering what level of inventories is appropriate.

6.6 SUMMARY AND CONCLUSIONS

In this chapter we have tested several variants of the flexible-accelerator buffer-stock inventory model at a variety of levels of aggregation with *ex ante* observations on anticipated sales and planned inventory behavior. Our comparison of the reduced form equations of Section 3.2 with the structural estimates revealed that considerable assistance in explaining realized inventory investment is provided by observations on planned inventory behavior (FINAS), even when this *ex ante* variable is employed in conjunction with a number of other explanatory variables. We also confirmed, in Section 3.3, that precision in explaining inventory investment is sacrificed when use is made of a proxy procedure as a substitute for data on anticipated sales volume. Let us now summarize the more interesting implications and the major limitations of our analysis.

One rather surprising result concerned the behavioral implications of production smoothing. What complications are created for the firm by the difficulties involved in abruptly *changing* the level of output? When we studied the determinants of planned inventory and output, we did not uncover any evidence that plans were influenced by a desire to reduce costs of changing output levels. In contrast, when we looked at realized inventory investment and sales, production smoothing considerations influenced actual behavior in every industry except nonelectrical machinery. This discrepancy, we argued in Section 3.1, may result from a neglect by management of the importance of production smoothing considerations in scheduling output; to the extent that the realities of production smoothing complications influence plant operations, actual production will depart from plan. As a result, finished goods inventory anticipations will not be realized even when sales expectations are correct.

While this proposition concerning production smoothing is a rather interesting result, it must be regarded as quite tentative. The major issue is that of choosing the most appropriate procedure for introducing production smoothing considerations. We used two quite different approaches, and our conclusions are quite insensitive to the particular strategy employed. The simplest approach, utilized by such writers as Johnston [1961], is to interpret seasonal dummy variables as measuring the effects of production smoothing. Insignificant seasonal dummies imply that the seasonal movement in planned output is explicable in terms of the seasonal sales, and that production smoothing factors are neglected.[46] The second and more flexible procedure involves the introduction of lagged production as an additional explanatory variable. Since production is not directly observable, it was necessary for us to add a markup parameter, m, in approximating production with our observations on inventory investment and sales, as indicated by equation 2.6. Unfortunately, the estimates we obtained of the markup coefficient were quite wild, and it is conceivable that we would have obtained a better measure of output by setting $m = 0$ in accordance with the practice followed in many earlier investigations.

Do small firms have an advantage in that they succeed in making more rapid adjustments to changing economic conditions? Our industry-by-industry comparison of small and large firm regressions revealed this tendency in two places. First, consider the parameter δ measuring the extent to which the firm attempts to correct the gap between the current value of equilibrium inventory and the actual stock inherited from the preceding period. Several alternative estimates of δ were provided in the finished goods inventory regressions; specifically, in Tables 6.2.1, 6.3.1, and 6.3.2, we have estimates obtained from the planned inventory regressions, the finished goods inventory structural equation, and the reduced form estimate. With the possible exception of electrical machinery, the pooled small firm regressions generally gave a larger δ, signifying that these firms attempt a more rapid correction of the inventory gap.[47]

Small firms also appear to be more flexible in revising their production schedules in response to surprise. This tendency was revealed by the estimates of the parameter λ reported in Table 6.3.1. We saw that large firm pooled regressions generally yield a quite high value of λ, suggesting that the end-of-quarter outcome for these firms is largely governed by their initial evaluation of economic conditions. In contrast, the small λ obtained with the small firm pooled regressions suggests considerable flexibility in revising production schedules in response to changing economic conditions.

Purchased materials and goods in process stocks are another matter. We still find from Tables 6.4.1 and 6.4.2 that small firms generally have a larger δ, indicating that they plan to correct a greater proportion of imbalances in stocks of purchased materials and goods in process when changing economic conditions have generated a discrepancy between desired and equilibrium stocks. But Table 6.4.2 reveals that in nonferrous metals, chemicals, and petroleum the small firms are less adept than the large at revising the level of

[46] In applying this procedure we used additive dummy variables, and we did not follow Modigliani and Sauerlander [1955] by allowing for a multiplicative effect via changes in such parameters as the marginal desired inventory coefficients.

[47] While the electrical machinery δ is larger for small firms for the realization equation of Table 6.3.1, lower small firm estimates of δ are reported for electrical machinery on the other two finished goods inventory tables.

stocks when surprised during the quarter by changing economic conditions.[48] Large firms in these three industries may invoke greater leverage upon suppliers in revising delivery schedules for their raw materials; that is, the large purchaser may be more successful at negotiating for a rapid delivery of needed supplies when caught short as a result of unexpectedly high sales volume.

Suggestive as they may be, these comparisons are based on rather crude estimates of the parameters. Indeed, we note that while most of the λ coefficients for finished goods inventories are large relative to their standard errors, this claim cannot be made for the purchased materials and goods in process estimates of Table 6.4.2; for this category of stocks, the standard errors of the adaptation coefficient are quite large. Indeed, for two industries, nonferrous metals and electrical machinery, λ is less than twice its standard error on Table 6.4.2, suggesting that firms in these two industries may completely revise their initial delivery schedules within the quarter when surprised by changing market conditions.

We have pointed out that a more efficient set of parameter estimates might have been obtained from the pooled firm data if it had proved computationally feasible to apply the nonlinear maximum likelihood estimation procedure mentioned in Section 5 of this chapter. When this approach was applied to the aggregate industry benchmark data, we usually obtained quite small estimates of λ. Indeed, we obtained a zero value of λ for the nonelectrical machinery, motor vehicles, other durable, and textile industries. For only one of these four industries did we have estimates based on pooled firm data. This is nonelectrical machinery, and the results are quite inconsistent. Quite sizable estimates of λ were obtained with both the finished goods and the purchased materials and goods in process pooled firm regressions. We have argued that this discrepancy may arise from problems of aggregation, for the small estimates of λ reported on Table 6.5.1 were obtained with data aggregated to the industry level and without partition by stage-of-fabrication.

The $\bar{R}^2$'s obtained from the pooled firm regressions are also disappointing, for they are small relative to what we had been led to expect on the basis of studies of aggregate data.[49] We do find that the $\bar{R}^2$'s are generally larger on Table 6.3.1, where we are explaining actual realizations, than on Table 6.2.1, where planned finished goods inventory is being studied. This does not

[48] The difference was significant only in the chemical industry.

[49] The $\bar{R}^2$'s for the inventory models are almost uniformly smaller than those obtained in Chapter 5, when we studied alternative models explaining the generation of sales expectations—but, of course, drawing comparisons of $\bar{R}^2$'s between models involving different explanatory variables is not a very meaningful exercise. As explained in Appendix A, the use of production rather than inventory investment as the dependent variable would yield higher $\bar{R}^2$.

mean, however, that *plans* are harder to explain than *realizations*. Rather, a comparison of the standard errors of estimate reveals that they are of roughly identical magnitude on the two tables, and there is no consistent tendency for the planned equation to provide a looser fit in terms of this criterion than actual realizations. The smaller $\bar{R}^2$'s for planned behavior arise because FINAS generally has a smaller variance than FIN.

It is possible that with inventories, as with many other types of economic activity, models that perform quite well on the aggregates yield loose fits and rather wild parameter estimates because of complicated interfirm behavioral variations. That is to say, to the extent that the complex of factors accounting for differences among firms cancel out in the aggregate, models that are grossly unsatisfactory at the firm level may still perform reasonably well on aggregate data. Unfortunately, direct comparison of firm and aggregate regressions has usually not proved possible because of data limitations.[50] But in two instances in which quite similar models were run on both firm and aggregate data—equations 3.8 and 5.1—much more satisfactory results were obtained with the aggregates.

There are a number of obvious ways in which the accelerator bufferstock framework employed for our study might be elaborated upon when appropriate data are available. As mentioned in Chapter 2.2.2, we have been handicapped throughout our study by the unavailability at the firm level of appropriate data on price movements and orders. The role of price adjustments has been stressed by Edwin Mills [1962]; T. C. Liu [1963] explicitly considered, within the context of a macroeconometric model, the possibility that firms may correct inventory inbalances in part by price rather than output adjustment. Furthermore, the unfilled orders variable has proved of critical importance in prior studies of purchased materials and goods in process; more recently, Gerald Childs [1967] has argued that firms producing to order may simultaneously schedule production and plan future shipments (SALES) on the basis of the information on future demand conditions provided by the incoming flow of new orders. To the extent that either price or order complications invalidate our assumption that sales anticipations are predetermined, our least-squares parameter estimates will be subject to simultaneous equation bias. Fortunately, the orders problem cannot be present for two of the five industries for which we have firm data—chemicals and petroleum—for firms in these industries are classified by the OBE as producing solely to stock. Although we had hoped that the inventory condition dummy variable (COND) might partially fill the gap created by our inability to observe orders, the fact that this variable was insignificant in industries

[50] Since FINAS was not observed at the industry level, we were obviously handicapped. Furthermore, the stage-of-fabrication breakdown of realized inventories could be achieved only for the durable and nondurable sector aggregates.

producing goods to order as well as stock suggests that any effect of the orders complication was fully captured by the sales anticipations term.[51] Further evidence concerning the indirect nature of the influence of the orders variable was obtained from the durable and nondurable sector aggregates, for here we were able to use the orders variable along with sales anticipations in explaining planned inventory accumulation: but in regression 5.1 we saw that the orders coefficient is of incorrect negative sign and small relative to its standard error. Obviously, much more work is required on this issue, but the fragmentary evidence points to the possibility that the influence of orders is primarily felt as a determinant of anticipated sales volume.

[51] Since the regression coefficients and other statistics were virtually unaffected when this variable was introduced, we reported only the regressons with this variable excluded.

Appendix on Estimation Procedures

In this appendix certain statistical problems encountered in the analysis of inventory investment are discussed.

A. INVENTORIES VERSUS PRODUCTION, AND THE CHOICE OF THE DEPENDENT VARIABLE

Equations 2.4′, 2.4, and 2.7 explained the planned levels of finished goods inventory stocks, *ex ante* investment in finished goods, and planned production. We shall see that the same parameter estimates will be obtained regardless of the choice of the dependent variable. To verify this proposition, note that for any given set of estimates of the β_i's and δ, precisely the same residuals will be calculated regardless of whether 2.4′, 2.4, or 2.7 is used for the purpose; consequently, the set of parameter estimates that serves to minimize the sum of squared residuals for any one of these three equations must also minimize it for the other two.

How does the choice between the three alternative regression forms affect the magnitude of $\bar{R}^2$? Since they have the same residuals, they must obviously all yield the same standard error of estimate (and Durbin-Watson coefficient); but the correlation coefficients will not be identical because the variances of the dependent variables are not all the same. In part, as a result of the existence of trend and cyclical movements, the variances of FINAS and QAS are generally larger than the variance of FINAS − FIN_{-1}, or of FIN − FIN_{-1} for that matter. As a consequence, the ratio of the variance of the residuals to the variance of the dependent variable will be larger for regressions 2.4′ and 2.7 than for 2.4. Thus, using FINAS − FIN_{-1} as the dependent variable does not affect the parameter estimates, but it does yield a smaller $\bar{R}^2$ than either planned production or planned inventory.

B. NONLINEAR ESTIMATION OF THE REDUCED FORM EQUATION

The reduced form expression for finished goods inventories, equation 3.7, cannot be estimated directly by linear regression, for λ is not known. It would be possible to split the terms in brackets into separate variables, but this would result in six regression coefficients from which only five parameters are to be determined. That there is no unique way of obtaining estimates of the parameters of the model from the six regression coefficients may be seen as follows. First, adding the coefficient of ASSALE and SALE yields an estimate of $\delta\beta_2$. Dividing the coefficient of ASSALE by this estimate plus unity yields an estimate of λ. But a second estimate of λ may be obtained from the coefficients of ALSALE_{+1} and ASSALE_{+1}.

Our approach is to apply the method of maximum likelihood to this nonlinear estimation problem under the assumption that the error terms are normally distributed. The theorem of Mann and Wald [1943], summarized by Johnston [1963], for obtaining maximum likelihood estimates from equations involving lagged dependent variables requires a slight modification because of the restrictions upon the parameters. The problem is to find, given our sample observations, the values of the unknown parameters λ, β_1, β_2, β_3, and δ that maximize the likelihood function

$$L = (2\sigma^2\pi)^{-n/2} \exp\left(-\frac{\sigma^2}{2}\sum_{t=1}^{T} \epsilon_t^{\,2}\right)$$

where T is the number of observations and ϵ is defined by 3.7; FIN_0 is regarded as nonstochastic. Taking logarithms reveals that maximizing L with respect to the parameters of interest is equivalent to minimizing

$$\begin{aligned}\hat{\sigma}^2 = \frac{1}{n}\sum_{t=1}^{T}\{&\text{FIN} - \delta\beta_1 - \lambda(1 + \delta\beta_2)\text{ASSALE} - \lambda\delta\beta_3\text{ALSALE}_{+1} \\ &- (1 - \lambda)\text{ASSALE}_{+1}[\delta\beta_2 - \lambda(\delta\beta_2 + 1)]\text{SALE} - (1 - \delta)\text{FIN}_{-1}\}^2\end{aligned}$$

The maximum likelihood estimates of the parameters thus involve the method of least squares.

The computations cannot be performed directly by standard regression procedures unless the value of λ is specified. Rather than search simultaneously over the five-dimensional parameter space, we observe that since $\min_{\lambda,\delta,\beta_i} \hat{\sigma} = \min_{\lambda}\left[\min_{\delta,\beta_i} \hat{\sigma}\right]$, a computationally simpler approach is to search over λ for the value minimizing the standard error of the estimate. At each point in the search procedure, a regression run for the given value of λ yields the bracketed expression.

C. SIMULTANEOUS ESTIMATION OF PLANNED AND REALIZED INVENTORY INVESTMENT

Our strategy for obtaining maximum likelihood estimates of the six parameters of the recursive model, equations 5.2 and 5.3, is most easily understood if we first rewrite equation 5.3 as

$$\begin{aligned}[\text{IN} - \lambda(\text{INAS} + \text{ASSALE} - \text{SALE})] \\ = \delta\beta_1[1 - \lambda] + \delta\beta_2[(1 - \lambda)\text{SALE}] + \delta\beta_3[(1 - \lambda)\text{ASSALE}_{+1}] \\ + (1 - \delta)[(1 - \lambda)\text{IN}_{-1}] + \epsilon\end{aligned}$$

Now if the value of λ were known, the problem of estimating the other five parameters would be quite straightforward, for we note that knowledge of the magnitude of λ would enable us to calculate all the expressions in brackets in the above equation; furthermore, it would be possible, knowing λ, to pool in a single regression the observations of this equation with those of equation 5.2.[52] This pooling procedure has an obvious advantage for there are only 17 observations for the above equation and 18 for equation 5.2, while with the pooled regression we would have a total of 35 observations on which to base our estimates; thus, the pooling procedure would yield a substantial gain in efficiency if we were correct in hypothesizing in Section 6.3.1 that the disturbances of the two equations are independently distributed. When λ is not known, it appears intuitively appropriate to search over alternative values of λ, running a regression for each trial value, selecting as the final estimate of λ that value which yields the smallest standard error of estimate, and using as the estimate of the other parameters the coefficient of the tightest regression. As a first step in evaluating this procedure, note that under the assumption that the disturbances of equation 5.2 are normally and independently distributed, the likelihood of obtaining the n observed values of INAS is

$$L_1 = \left(\frac{1}{\sigma_{\epsilon_1}\sqrt{2\pi}}\right)^n \exp\left(-\frac{1}{2\sigma_{\epsilon_1}^2}\sum \epsilon_1^2\right)$$

where the disturbance ϵ_1 is a function of observed variables and the unknown parameters as given by equation 5.2. Similarly, the likelihood of obtaining the n' observed values of IN is

$$L_2 = \left(\frac{1}{\sigma_{\epsilon_2}\sqrt{2\pi}}\right)^{n'} \exp\left(-\frac{1}{2\sigma_{\epsilon_2}^2}\sum \epsilon_2^2\right)$$

[52] Care was required in estimating the intercept; the first explanatory variable consists of unity for each of the observations on equation 5.2 and $(1 - \lambda)$ for the observations from the other equation.

where the disturbance ϵ_2 is a function of observed variables and the unknown parameters as given by equation 5.3. The likelihood of obtaining the combined set of observations, given the assumption that ϵ_1 and ϵ_2 are independently distributed, is simply $L = L_1 L_2$. Taking logarithms, we have

$$\log L = \text{constant} - \frac{1}{2\sigma_{\epsilon_1}^2} \sum \epsilon_1^2 - \frac{1}{2\sigma_{\epsilon_2}^2} \sum \epsilon_2^2$$

Consequently, the values of δ, β_1, β_2, β_3, and λ that maximize L also minimize

$$\sigma^2 = \frac{\sum \epsilon_1^2 + \rho \sum \epsilon_2^2}{n + n'}$$

where $\rho = \sigma_{\epsilon_1}^2 / \sigma_{\epsilon_2}^2$. Our procedure was to maximize the likelihood function subject to the homogeneity assumption that $\rho = 1$.[53] Rather than search simultaneously over the five-dimensional parameter space, we saved computational effort by iterating over λ, minimizing the sum of squared residuals for the specified value of λ; that is, for each specified value of λ we ran a least-squares pooled regression. Because of the restriction $0 \leq \lambda \leq 1$, it was possible to economize further on the computations by employing a Fibonacci search procedure.[54]

[53] Inspection of the residuals for the individual industries suggested that this homogeneity assumption was not grossly violated. If it had been, the estimates of ρ obtained from the residuals would have been employed in an application of the theory of weighted regression in order to obtain maximum-likelihood estimates. It is interesting to observe that *if* the variance of the disturbance term of equation 5.2 is exceedingly small, relative to that of equation 5.3, so that ρ is close to zero, the appropriate weighted regression procedure is equivalent to the use of equation 5.2 to estimate all of the parameters except λ; an estimate of λ is then obtained with a regression based on equation 5.3, after simplification with the aid of the estimates, already obtained, of the other parameters from 5.2.

[54] For a description of this search procedure, see Wilde [1964]. The Fibonacci search procedure presumes that the minimization problem is unimodal. We have not verified analytically that this condition is satisfied; on the other hand, examination of the results of the iterations suggested that the conditional variance is a convex function of λ.

Epilogue

In this study we have had the good fortune to be able to replicate a variety of investigations that had, for the most part, been initially executed on much less adequate data. Many of the variables we used were not available to earlier investigators. Furthermore, we have had a unique opportunity to observe dynamic behavior at the level of the individual firm as well as with industry aggregates. Although, in many respects, earlier hypotheses have been confirmed, our study has not been free of surprises and we found at a number of points that hypotheses that had appeared to be at least tentatively established in earlier work are now open to serious question. Our results were summarized in detail at the end of each chapter, and there is no need to review them here. But it is necessary for us to reflect on the implications of our empirical research for the theory of the inventory cycle.

Is it reasonable to attempt to advance tentative propositions concerning the nature of the inventory cycle on the basis of data covering a relatively short span of years? With the exception of the 1960 recession, the period covered by our study was characterized by reasonably steady growth; obviously, it is dangerous to generalize from a single historical experience. Fortunately, the sales of the individual firms we observed were subject to considerable fluctuation; the industry aggregates displayed much greater variation than the overall level of economic activity. Pending the accumulation of additional observations, the evidence of the OBE survey provides tentative evidence concerning the role of inventories and sales expectations in the business cycle.

That sales anticipations are much more accurate than earlier studies had suggested was a major surprise of Chapter 3. We found that business firms are able to predict sales developments three months ahead with about the same degree of precision as is currently achieved with econometric models in annual forecasting of aggregate economic activity. This was true for industries in which production is only for stock as well as in sectors which produce to order; indeed, there is no systematic tendency for firms producing to order and to stock to forecast shipments more precisely than do firms producing only to order. We conclude that firms predict sales developments with much greater precision than has been customarily assumed in theoretical models of the inventory cycle. In contrast, the pioneering empirical study of Ferber [1953] had suggested that firms guess the direction of actual change incorrectly approximately half the time. The earlier evidence had suggested that it was not unreasonable to use the static no-change hypothesis of expectations formation in building theoretical models of the inventory cycle, and we invoked this assumption in order to simplify the task of reviewing the elementary theory of the inventory cycle in Chapter 1. Our new data confirm the suggestion of Edwin Mills that it is more appropriate to assume that firms correctly estimate the change than to suppose that they anticipate no change in sales volume.

It may be tempting to conjecture that the contrast between the picture of accurate firm forecasting provided by our study and the gross inaccuracies suggested by investigations of data for earlier periods might be indicative of an actual improvement in the art of forecasting. A partial test of this proposition was provided by our examination of the performance of the railroad shippers' forecasts in recent years; we found that while there was probably some improvement in the precision of the forecasts, there appears to be a systematic tendency for the type of evidence provided by the shippers' forecast data analyzed by Ferber to exaggerate the errors that firms make in forecasting. Furthermore, it would be a mistake to conclude that whatever improvement did occur in the art of forecasting must have contributed to greater economic stability; a theoretical study of the inventory cycle by Lovell [1962] shows that more accurate prediction by business firms will not necessarily serve to dampen the inventory cycle.

The elementary theory of the inventory cycle suggests that firms should be able to forecast finished goods inventory investment and sales volume with approximately equal precision, for stocks are drawn down below planned levels by an amount equal in magnitude to the forecast error. In fact, we found that firms do not forecast quarterly inventory investment as accurately as they predict sales movements; we conjectured that the lower precision in predicting inventories arises in part because the occurrence of machinery breakdowns and other interruptions in the production process contribute, along with the errors in forecasting sales, to inaccurate forecasting of finished goods inventory.

We did not find evidence supporting the Pigouvian notion that the business cycle is caused by waves of optimistic and pessimistic error. In the first place, the errors made by firms in forecasting sales do not appear to be of sufficient magnitude to account for observed cyclical phenomena. Furthermore, we found in Chapter 4 that the relationship among the errors of forecasting, both among firms in the same industry and among aggregates of different industries, was no closer than one would expect to occur if anticipations were formed by a simple projection of recent sales experience. Admittedly, this is a weak test of Pigou's proposition, but we have no evidence suggesting that we should reject the alternative hypothesis that at least a portion of the observed correlation among errors in sales forecasts is caused by the correlation in the movements of actual sales, rather than the reverse. Certainly, we are compelled to conclude that if firms relied upon no-change predictions, the resulting forecast errors would be of much greater magnitude and more closely correlated than are the actual mistakes that firms make in predicting future demand conditions.

Inventory cycle models can be classified according to the type of assumption that is invoked about the formation of sales expectations, and a variety of competing hypotheses concerning the way in which expectations are generated were evaluated in Chapter 5. Both the adaptive expectations model of Nerlove and simplified versions of Ferber's law have been employed in inventory cycle models; both models performed quite well on our data, with Ferber's performing better on the industry aggregates and the adaptive expectations model dominating in explaining individual firm behavior. But we also found that sales expectations are sufficiently accurate to make the use of the actual realization as a proxy for the anticipation a particularly attractive alternative. Nonetheless, expectations do not appear to fully satisfy Muth's "rationality" postulate, and we argued that it is better to assume that the forecast error is a function of the realized change rather than a purely random variable.

Our study revealed three rather surprising facets of production behavior that are of obvious relevance to the problem of explaining how inventories behave over the course of the business cycle. One striking result is the substantial evidence provided by our study that both large and small firms are much more flexible at adjusting production schedules to unexpected changes in market conditions than is customarily assumed in theoretical models of the inventory cycle. If firms actually made the substantial errors in forecasting sales volume that the earlier empirical studies had suggested, it would be extremely difficult for them to move far in the direction of error correction within our three-month observation period. But since forecast errors are small in magnitude, error correction is feasible, and the evidence suggests that production plans and schedules for the delivery of inputs are sufficiently flexible to permit considerable adjustment within the quarter to whatever errors are made in forecasting sales volume.[1] This provides further evidence that the role of forecast errors as a determinant of cyclical fluctuations is exaggerated in the Metzler model of the inventory cycle.

A comparison of the behavior of large and small firms did not reveal a noticeable difference in the degree of forecasting precision achieved, but we did find empirical evidence suggesting that an advantage of being small is that it permits a more rapid realignment of production schedules when unexpected market developments cause errors in forecasting sales. On the other hand, there is at least some evidence that large firms are able to obtain from their suppliers prompt correction in the timing of raw material deliveries when stocks of purchased materials are out of adjustment. These distinctions suggest that the problem of aggregation, in both empirical and theoretical investigations, may deserve more attention than it customarily receives.[2] It is also conceivable that the optimal size of the firm may be determined by the relative flexibility and ease with which small and large firms are able to adjust to the constantly changing environment characterizing stochastic equilibrium.[3]

Finally, we should note that there are three types of systematic error that appear to be involved in the typical firm's short-run response to its changing environment. One aspect, encountered when we investigated Muth's "rational expectations" concept in Chapter 5, is the apparent failure of firms to fully exploit the information provided from past experience in formulating their expectations about the future. Second, there is at least some evidence in Chapter 6 that firms do not adequately consider production smoothing considerations in initially formulating their production schedules; as a result, actual production may systematically deviate from plan when the costs involved in changing production become manifest during the production

[1] Metzler [1947, pp. 2, 12] defined the "production planning period" as having the property that "the rate of production for all commodities is fixed at the beginning of each period and remains unchanged throughout the period" and estimated that "the average planning period has a duration of approximately five months." While the possibility of production plan revision has been ignored in many empirical studies of inventory investment, the problem received careful consideration in the pioneering study of Modigliani and Sauerlander [1955]; on the basis of their fragmentary evidence consisting of eleven observations from the Dun and Bradstreet survey, they estimated the "feed-in" coefficient for manufacturing to be about 0.8.

[2] The aggregation problem posed for the econometrician concerned with estimation and hypothesis testing is quite different from that involved in the construction of dynamic models of the business cycle. The strong uniformity assumption invoked by Lovell [1962] and Foster [1963] in multisector models of the inventory cycle presupposes that the distinctions between large and small firms in the same industry may be ignored.

[3] It is unfortunate that such dynamic costs as those related to changing output are neglected in most empirical studies attempting to determine whether cost functions display increasing or decreasing returns to scale.

period. Third, we found in conformity with the "controller effect" of Murray Foss [1961] that firms in our sample have a systematic tendency to underestimate the magnitude of future inventory stocks; as a result of this unwarranted optimism, the average firm generally finds itself with more capital than planned tied up in inventory.

Bibliography

Abramovitz, Moses [1950], *Inventories and Business Cycles*, New York: National Bureau of Economic Research.

Anderson, T. W. [1958], *An Introduction to Multivariate Statistical Analysis*, New York: John Wiley & Sons.

Ando, Albert, E. Cary Brown, John Kareken, and Robert M. Solow [1963], "Lags in Fiscal and Monetary Policy," in *Stabilization Policies*, Research Studies prepared for the Commission on Money and Credit, Englewood Cliffs, N.J.: Prentice-Hall.

Ando, Albert, and Franco Modigliani [1963], "The 'Life Cycle' Hypothesis of Saving," *American Economic Review*, **53** (March, 1963), 55–84.

Arrow, Kenneth J. and M. Nerlove [1958], "A Note on Expectations and Stability," *Econometrica*, **26** (April, 1958), 297–305.

Ball, Robert J. and P. S. Drake [1963], "Stock Adjustment Inventory Models of the United Kingdom Economy," *Manchester School of Economics and Social Studies*, **31** (May, 1963), 87–102.

Beckmann, Martin [1961], "Production Smoothing and Inventory Control," *Operations Research*, **9** (July–August, 1961), 456–467.

Belsley, David A. [1965], *Industry Production Behavior: An Econometric Analysis*, unpublished Doctoral Dissertation, Massachusetts Institute of Technology.

Bossons, John and Franco Modigliani [1960], "The Source of Regressiveness in Surveys of Businessmen's Short-Run Expectations," in *The Quality and Economic Significance of Anticipations Data, A Conference of the Universities-National Bureau Committee for Economic Research* (edited by Hart, Modigliani, and Orcutt), Princeton: Princeton University Press.

Bossons, John and Franco Modigliani [1966], "Statistical vs. Structural Explanations of Understatement and Regressivity in 'Rational' Expectations," *Econometrica*, **34** (April, 1966), 347–353.

Brown, Murray [1961], "*Ex Ante* and *Ex Post* Data in Inventory Investment," *Journal of the American Statistical Association*, **56** (September, 1961), 518–534.

Brown, R. G. [1959], *Statistical Forecasting for Inventory Control*, New York: McGraw-Hill.

Butler, William F. and Robert A. Kavesh [1966], *How Business Economists Forecast*, Englewood Cliffs, N.J.: Prentice-Hall.

Cagan, Phillip D. [1956], "The Monetary Dynamics of Hyperinflation," *Studies in the Quantity Theory of Money* (edited by Milton Friedman), 25–117, Chicago: University of Chicago Press.

Carlson, J. A. [1967a], "Forecasting Errors and Business Cycles," *American Economic Review*, **57** (June, 1967), 462–481.

——— [1967b], "The Stability of an Experimental Market with a Supply-Response Lag," *Southern Economic Journal*, **33** (January, 1967), 305–321.

Childs, Gerald L. [1967], *Unfilled Orders and Inventories, A Structural Analysis*, Amsterdam: North-Holland Publishing Co.

Corley, T. A. B. [1962], "How Do Businessmen Plan Production? A Case Study of the Radio and Television Industry, 1951–60," *Journal of Industrial Economics*, **10** (March, 1962), 139–154.

Courchene, T. J. [1967], "Inventory Behavior and the Stock Order Distinction: An Analysis by Industry and Stage Fabrication with Empirical Application to the Canadian Manufacturing Sector," *The Canadian Journal of Economics and Political Science*, **33** (August 1967), 325–357.

Crawford, C. M. [1955], "Sales Forecasting Methods of Selected Firms," *University of Illinois Bulletin*, vol. 52.

Darling, Paul G. [1959], "Manufacturers' Inventory Investment, 1947–1958: An Application of Accelerator Analysis," *American Economic Review*, **49** (December, 1959), pp. 950–962.

Eisner, Robert [1958], "Expectations, Planned Capital Expenditures: A Synthesis of *Ex Post* and *Ex Ante* Data," in *Expectations, Uncertainty and Business Behavior*, (edited by Mary Jean Bowman), Social Science Research Council.

——— and Robert H. Strotz [1963], "Determinants of Business Investment," in *Impacts of Monetary Policy*, a volume prepared for the Commission on Money and Credit. Englewood Cliffs, N.J.: Prentice-Hall.

Enthoven, Alain C. [1956], *Studies in the Theory of Inflation*, unpublished Doctoral Dissertation, Massachusetts Institute of Technology.

——— and Kenneth J. Arrow [1956], "A Theorem on Expectations and the Stability of Equilibrium," *Econometrica*, **24** (July, 1956), 288–293.

Ferber, Robert [1953], *The Railroad Shippers' Forecasts*, Urbana: Bureau of Economic and Business Research, University of Illinois.

——— [1958], "The Accuracy and Structure of Industry Expectations in Relation to those of Individual Firms," *Journal of the American Statistical Association*, **53** (June, 1958), 317–335.

——— [1960], "The Railroad Shippers' Forecasts and the Illinois Employers' Labor Force Anticipations: A Study in Comparative Expectations," in *The Quality and Economic Significance of Anticipations Data, A Conference of the Universities-National Bureau Committee for Economic Research*, (edited by Hart, Modigliani and Orcutt), Princeton: Princeton University Press.

Foss, Murray F. [1961], "Manufacturers' Inventory and Sales Anticipations: A New Survey," *Proceedings, Business and Economics Statistics Section*, American Statistical Association, 234–251.

Foster, Edward [1963], "Sales Forecasts and the Inventory Cycle," *Econometrica*, **31** (July, 1963), 406–421.

Fromm, Gary [1962], "Inventories, Business Cycles and Economic Stabilization," in *Inventory Fluctuations and Economic Stabilization*, Part IV, Joint Economic Committee, Congress of the United States, 37–133, Washington: U.S. Government Printing Office.

Hammer, Frederick S. [1964], *The Demand for Physical Capital; Application of a Wealth Model*, Englewood Cliffs, N.J.: Prentice-Hall.

Hart, Albert G. [1960], "Quantitative Evidence for the Interwar Period on the Course of Business Expectations: A Revaluation of the Railroad Shippers' Forecast," in *The Quality and Economic Significance of Anticipations Data, A Conference of the Universities-National Bureau Committee for Economic Research* (edited by Hart, Modigliani and Orcutt), Princeton: Princeton University Press.

Hastay, Millard [1960], "The Formation of Business Expectations about Operating Variables," in *The Quality and Economic Significance of Anticipations Data, A Conference of the Universities-National Bureau Committee for Economic Research* (edited by Hart, Modigliani, and Orcutt), Princeton: Princeton University Press.

Hawtrey, R. G. [1928], *Trade and Credit*, London: Longmans, Green & Co.

——— [1937], *Capital and Employment*, London: Longmans, Green & Co.

Hicks, J. R. [1939], *Value and Capital*, Oxford: The Clarendon Press.

Holt, Charles C., Franco Modigliani, John F. Muth, and Herbert A. Simon [1960], *Planning Production, Inventories, and Work Force*, Englewood Cliffs, N.J.: Prentice-Hall.

——— and Franco Modigliani [1961], "Firm Cost Structures and the Dynamic Responses of Inventories, Production, Work Force, and Orders to Sales Fluctuations," in *Inventory Fluctuations and Economic Stabilization*, Part II, Joint Economic Committee, 87th Congress, 1st session.

Hurwicz, L. [1950], "Least-Squares Bias in Time Series," in *Statistical Inference in Dynamic Economic Models* (edited by T. Koopmans), New York: John Wiley & Sons.

Johnston, John [1961], "An Econometric Study of the Production Decision," *Quarterly Journal of Economics*, **75** (May, 1961), 234–261.

Jorgenson, Dale W. [1963], "Capital Theory and Investment Behavior," *American Economic Review*, **53** (May, 1963), 247–259.

Katona, George [1951], *Psychological Analysis of Economic Behavior*, New York: McGraw-Hill.

Keynes, John Maynard [1936], *General Theory of Employment, Interest and Money*, London: Macmillan and Co., Ltd.

Klein, Lawrence, R. [1950], *Economic Fluctuations in the United States*, 1921–1941, New York: John Wiley & Sons.

——— and Joel Popkin [1961], "An Economic Analysis of the Postwar Relationship Between Inventory Fluctuations and Changes in Aggregate Economic Activity," in *Inventory Fluctuations and Economic Stabilization*, Part III, Joint Economic Committee, Congress of the United States, 71–89, Washington: U.S. Government Printing Office.

Kloek, T. and R. Bannink [1961], "Principal-Component Analysis Applied to Business Test Data," *Econometric Institute Report* 6112.

Krishnamurty, K. and D. U. Sastry [1966], *Inventories in the Organized Manufacturing Sector of the Indian Economy: A Disaggregative Study*, Delhi: Institute of Economic Growth, University Enlave.

Kuh, Edwin [1963], *Capital Stock Growth, A Micro-econometric Interpretation*, Amsterdam: North-Holland Publishing Co.

Kuznets, Paul W. [1964], "Financial Determinants of Manufacturing Inventory Behavior: A Quarterly Study Based on United States Estimates, 1947–1961," *Yale Economic Essays*, **4** (Fall, 1964), 331–370.

Ladd, George W. [1963], "Distributed Lag Inventory Analyses," *Research Bulletin 515*, Agricultural and Home Economics Experiment Station, Iowa State University, (April, 1963).

Liu, T. C. [1963], "An Exploratory Quarterly Model of Effective Demand in the Postwar U.S. Economy," *Econometrica*, **31** (July, 1963), 301–48.

Longley, James W. [1967], "An Appraisal of Least Squares Programs for the Electronic Computer from the Point of View of the User," *Journal of the American Statistical Association*, **62** (September, 1967), 819–841.

Lovell, Michael C. [1961], "Manufacturers' Inventories, Sales Expectations, and the Acceleration Principle," *Econometrica*, **29** (July, 1961), 293–314.

——— [1962a], "The Contribution of Inventory Investment to Cyclical Reversals in Economic Activity," in *Inventory Fluctuations and Economic Stabilization Hearings*, Joint Economic Committee, Congress of the United States, July 1962, 245–263, Washington: U.S. Government Printing Office.

——— [1962b], "Buffer Stocks, Sales Expectations, and Stability: A Multi-sector Analysis of the Inventory Cycle," *Econometrica*, **30** (April, 1962), 267–296.

——— [1963], "Seasonal Adjustment of Economic Time Series and Multiple Regression Analysis," *Journal of the American Statistical Association*, **58** (December, 1963), 993–1010.

——— [1964], "Determinants of Inventory Investment," in *Models of Income Determination* (edited by Irwin Friend), Princeton: Princeton University Press.

——— [1967] "Sales Anticipations, Planned Inventory Investment, and Realizations" in *Determinants of Investment Behavior* (edited by Robert Ferber), New York: Columbia University Press.

——— [1968], "Department Store Inventory, Sales, Order Relationships," in *The Brookings Model: Some Further Results* (edited by Duesenberry, Fromm, Klein, and Kuh), Amsterdam: North-Holland Publishing Company.

Lundberg, Eric [1937], *Studies in the Theory of Economic Expansion*, London: P. S. King and Son; as reprinted in New York: Kelley and Millman, 1955.

Mack, Ruth P. [1967], *Information, Expectations, and Inventory Fluctuations*, New York: Columbia University Press.

Mann, H. B. and Abraham Wald [1943], "On the Statistical Treatment of Linear Stochastic Difference Equations," *Econometrica*, **11** (July–October, 1943), 173–220.

Meiselman, David [1962], *The Term Structure of Interest Rates*, Englewood Cliffs, N.J.: Prentice-Hall.

Metzler, Lloyd [1941], "The Nature and Stability of Inventory Cycles," *Review of Economic Statistics*, **23** (August, 1941), 113–129.

——— [1947], "Factors Governing the Length of Inventory Cycles," *Review of Economic Statistics*, **29** (February 1947), 1–15.

Meyer, John R. and Robert R. Glauber [1964], *Investment Decisions, Economic Forecasting, and Public Policy*, Boston: Division of Research, Graduate School of Business Administration, Harvard University.

Mills, Edwin S. [1957], "The Theory of Inventory Decisions," *Econometrica*, **25** (April, 1957), 222–238.

——— [1959], "Uncertainty and Price Theory," *Quarterly Journal of Economics*, **73** (February, 1959), 116–130.

——— [1961], "The Use of Adaptive Expectations in Stability Analysis, Comment," *Quarterly Journal of Economics*, **75** (May, 1961), 330–335.

——— [1962], *Price, Output, and Inventory Policy*, New York: John Wiley & Sons.

Mincer, Jacob [1966], "The Evaluation of Economic Forecasts," Preliminary Paper, New York: National Bureau of Economic Research.

Modigliani, Franco and Owen H. Sauerlander [1955], "Economic Expectations and Plans in Relation to Short-Term Forecasting," in *Short-Term Economic Forecasting*, New York: Princeton University Press.

——— and H. M. Weingartner [1958], "Forecasting Uses of Anticipatory Data on Investment and Sales," *Quarterly Journal of Economics*, **72** (February, 1958), 23–54.

——— and Kalman J. Cohen [1961], *The Role of Anticipations and Plans in Economic Behavior and Their Use in Economic Analysis and Forecasting*, Urbana: University of Illinois.

Mood, Alexander McFarlane [1950], *Introduction to the Theory of Statistics*, London: McGraw-Hill.

Moriguchi, Chikashi [1967], *Business Cycles and Manufacturers' Short-Term Production Decisions*, Amsterdam: North-Holland Publishing Co.

Muth, J. F. [1960], "Optimal Properties of Exponentially Weighted Forecasts of Time Series with Permanent and Transitory Components," *Journal of the American Statistical Association*, **55** (June, 1960), 299–306.

——— [1961], "Rational Expectations and the Theory of Price Movements," *Econometrica*, **29** (July, 1961), 315–335.

Nagar, A. L. [1962], "Statistical Testing of the Accuracy of Forecasts," *Statistica Neerlandica*, **16**, 237–247.

National Industrial Conference Board [1963], *Forecasting Sales*, Studies in Business Policy No. 106, New York.

Nerlove, Marc [1958a], "Adaptive Expectations and Cobweb Phenomena," *Quarterly Journal of Economics*, **72** (May, 1958), 227–240.

——— [1958b], *The Dynamics of Supply: Estimation of Farmers' Response to Price*, Baltimore: The Johns Hopkins Press.

——— and S. Wage [1964], "On the Optimality of Adaptive Forecasting," *Management Science*, **10** (January, 1964), 207–224.

Orr, Daniel [1963], "A Stochastic Income Model Using Optimal Inventory Rules," *Review of Economic Studies*, **30** (June, 1963), 84–92.

Orr, Lloyd D. [1966], "Expected Sales, Actual Sales, and Inventory-Investment Realization," *The Journal of Political Economy*, **74** (February, 1966), 46–54.

——— [1967], "A Comment on Sales Anticipations and Inventory Investment," *International Economic Review*, **8** (October, 1967), 368–373.

Pashigian, B. Peter [1964], "The Accuracy of the Commerce-S.E.C. Sales Anticipations," *Review of Economics and Statistics*, **46** (November, 1964), 398–405.

——— [1965], "The Relevance of Sales Anticipatory Data in Explaining Inventory Investment," *International Economic Review*, **6** (January, 1965), 65–91.

Pigou, A. C. [1929], *Industrial Fluctuations*, London: Macmillan and Co.

Popkin, Joel [1965], "The Relationship Between New Orders and Shipments: Analysis of the Machinery and Equipment Industries," *Survey of Current Business* (March, 1965), pp. 24–32.

Raiffa, Howard and Robert Schlaifer [1961], *Applied Statistical Decision Theory*, Boston: Division of Research, Graduate School of Business Administration, Harvard University.

Schramm, Richard [1967], *Optimal Adjustment of Factors of Production and the Study of Investment Behavior*, unpublished Doctoral Dissertation, Carnegie-Mellon University.

Simon, H. A. [1956], "Dynamic Programming under Uncertainty with a Quadratic Criterion Function," *Econometrica*, **24** (January, 1956), 74–81.

Smyth, D. J. [1966], "How Well Do Australian Economists Forecast?" *Economic Record*, **42** (June, 1966), 293–311.

Stanback, Thomas J., Jr. [1962], *Postwar Cycles in Manufacturers' Inventories*, New York: National Bureau of Economic Research.

Stekler, H. O. [1967], "Data Revisions and Economic Forecasting," *Journal of the American Statistical Association*, **62** (June, 1967), 470–483.

Theil, Henri [1957], "A Note on Certainty Equivalence in Dynamic Planning," *Econometrica*, **25** (April, 1957), 346–349.

——— [1961], *Economic Forecasts and Policy*, 2nd edition, Amsterdam: North-Holland Publishing Co.

——— [1966], *Applied Economic Forecasting*, Chicago: Rand McNally & Co.

——— and Myron Scholes [1967], "Forecast Evaluation Based on a Multiplicative Decomposition of Mean Square Errors," *Econometrica*, **35** (January, 1967), 70–88.

——— and S. Wage [1964], "Some Observations on Adaptive Forecasting," *Management Science*, **10** (January, 1964), 198–206.

Thonstad, T. and D. B. Jochems [1961], "The Influence of Entrepreneurial Expectations and Appraisals on Production Planning," *International Economic Review*, **2** (May, 1961), 135–153.

Thornber, Hodson [1966], *Applications of Decision Theory to Econometrics*, unpublished Doctoral Dissertation, University of Chicago.

Tintner, Gerhard [1952], *Econometrics*, New York: John Wiley & Sons.

Wallis, Kenneth F. [1966], "Some Econometric Problems in the Analysis of Inventory Cycles," Cowles Foundation Discussion Paper No. 209.

Watts, Harold W. [1958], "Long-Run Income Expectations and Consumer Saving," in *Studies in Household Economic Behavior*, by Dernburg, Rosett, and Watts, New Haven: Yale University Press.

Whitaker, Gilbert R., Jr. [1966], *A Decision Unit Model of Short-Run Production and Inventory Decisions of Manufacturing Firms*, Madison: University of Wisconsin, Bureau of Business Research and Service.

Wilde, Douglass J. [1964], *Optimum Seeking Methods*, Englewood Cliffs, N.J.: Prentice-Hall.

Winters, P. R. [1960], "Forecasting Sales by Exponentially Weighted Moving Averages," *Management Science*, **6** (April, 1960), 324–342.

Zarnowitz, Victor [1962], "Unfilled Orders, Price Changes and Business Fluctuations," *Review of Economics and Statistics*, **44** (November, 1962), 367–394.

——— [1967], *An Appraisal of Short-Term Economic Forecasts*, New York: National Bureau of Economic Research.

Zellner, A., D. S. Huang, and L. C. Chau [1965], "Further Analysis of the Short-Run Consumption Function with Emphasis on the Role of Liquid Assets," *Econometrica*, **33** (July, 1965), 571–581.

Author Index

Abramovitz, Moses, 4
Anderson, T. W., 110
Ando, Albert, 113
Arrow, Kenneth J., 112

Ball, Robert J., 113, 142, 171, 217
Bannink, R., 101
Beckmann, Martin, 245
Belsley, David A., 20
Bossons, John, 129
Brown, E. Cary, 217
Brown, Murray, 25
Brown, R. G., 142
Butler, William F., 112

Cagan, Phillip D., 142–143
Carlson, J. A., 204–205
Chau, L. C., 113, 142
Childs, Gerald L., 20, 199, 220, 232
Cohen, Kalman J., 161
Corley, T. A. B., 246
Courchene, T. J., 20, 220
Crawford, G. M., 246

Darling, Paul G., 246
Drake, P. S., 113, 142, 171, 217

Eisner, Robert, 12, 114, 191, 207, 220
Enthoven, Alain C., 112, 113

Ferber, Robert, 27, 41–42, 45, 49–50, 79, 113, 115–141, 144, 149, 157–161, 189–192, 240–241
Foss, Murray F., 16–19, 73, 107, 243
Foster, Edward, 112, 115, 242
Fromm, Gary, 4

Glauber, Robert R., 38

Hammer, Frederick S., 142
Hart, Albert G., 24, 45, 51, 79, 116
Hastay, Millard, 25
Hawtrey, R. G., 3
Hicks, J. R., 141
Holt, Charles C., 37, 73, 142, 145, 197–199
Huang, D. S., 113, 142
Hurwicz, L., 32

Jochems, D. B., 25
Johnston, John, 113, 116–117, 177, 194, 199, 203, 229, 235
Jorgenson, Dale W., 113

Kareken, John, 217
Katona, George, 22
Kavesh, Robert A., 112
Keynes, John Maynard, 2, 171
Klein, Lawrence R., 4, 177
Kloek, T., 101
Krishnamurty, K., 247
Kuh, Edwin, 31
Kuznets, Paul W., 19

Ladd, George W., 113
Liu, T. C., 232
Longley, James W., 34
Lundberg, Erik, 3, 6–11

Mack, Ruth P., 248
Mann, H. B., 143, 235
Meiselman, David, 114, 144, 161, 169, 191
Metzler, Lloyd, 4, 6–11, 21, 195, 205, 242
Meyer, John R., 38
Mills, Edwin S., 24, 98, 100, 112, 114, 177, 189, 194, 197, 199–200, 232
Mincer, Jacob, 79, 161
Modigliani, Franco, 24–25, 37, 41, 49–50, 59, 62, 73, 79, 80, 113, 129, 142, 145, 161, 197–199, 206–207, 230, 242
Mood, Alexander, 31

Moriguchi, Chikashi, 177
Muth, J. F., 37, 73, 76, 98, 100, 112, 114, 142, 145, 153, 169, 198–199, 242

Nagar, A. L., 39
National Industrial Conference Board, 112
Nerlove, Marc, 112, 141–142, 149, 161, 185, 189

Orr, Daniel, 249
Orr, Lloyd D., 205, 208

Pashigian, B. Peter, 25, 77, 206, 208
Pigou, A. C., 2–3, 62, 100, 241
Popkin, Joel, 4

Raiffa, Howard, 73

Sastry, D. U., 247
Sauerlander, Owen H., 24, 25, 41, 49–50, 59, 62, 79, 80, 199, 206, 230, 242
Schlaifer, Robert, 73
Schramm, Richard, 142
Simon, H. A., 37, 73, 142, 145, 198–199
Smyth, D. J., 250
Solow, Robert M., 217
Stanback, Thomas, Jr., 4
Stekler, H. O., 59
Strotz, Robert H., 12, 207, 220

Theil, Henri, 25, 28–29, 37, 60, 62, 74, 77, 79, 81, 93, 108, 142, 171
Thonstad, T., 25
Thornber, Hodson, 28
Tintner, Gerhard, 110

Wage, S., 142
Wald, Abraham, 143, 235
Wallis, Kenneth F., 250
Watts, Harold W., 113
Weingartner, H. M., 25, 207
Whitaker, Gilbert R., Jr., 25
Wilde, Douglass J., 237
Winters, P. R., 142

Zarnowitz, Victor, 79, 81
Zellner, A., 113, 142

Subject Index

Advertising expenditure, 20–21
AGGREGATE regression, 33
Aggregation, effects on forecast accuracy, 52–53, 55–56
  perfect, 30
  problems of, 242
ALSALE, 14
ASSALE, 14

Behrens-Fisher problem, 204
Benchmark alignment, 17–18
Bias correction, compiler, 19
  optimal linear, 75–76
Business cycle, error theory, 2
  and inventory investment, 4–5
  and monetary factor, 2–3
  and psychological factors, 2, 109

Certainty equivalents, 73, 170
Cobweb cycle, 112
COND, 14, 195, 232
Controller effect, 73, 107, 212, 243
Covariance analysis, 31
Cross-section versus time-series estimates, 54, 111
Cyclical fluctuations and magnitude of forecast errors, 40

Data mining, 29
Data pooling, 30–31
Data processing, blind, 26, 34
  computer editing, 18
Delayed adjustment behavior, 195
Demand functions, *ex ante,* 21–22
Dependent variable, choice of, 234
Diffusion indices, 101
Dun and Bradstreet survey, 25, 49–50, 242
Durbin-Watson statistic, 32
  pseudo-pooled, 33

Economies of scale, 204, 212, 230
Expectations, adaptive, 113, 141–169, 189
  myopic, 198
  no-change hypothesis, 240–241
  normal, 141
  optimal, 153
  point versus interval, 16
  rational or implicit, 76, 169–192
  regressive, 24, 129–141, 192
  revision, 161–169
  sufficiency, 171–192
Exponential smoothing, *see* Expectations, adaptive

Ferber's law, 18, 115–141, 157, 161, 181, 189, 240–241
Fibonacci search, 237
FIN, 14
FINAL, 14
FINAS, 14
Forecast horizon, 15–16
Forecasting procedures, customer survey, 170
  end-use, 114
  same-as-last-quarter, 115
  technical, 114
Fortune's Business Roundup Survey, 25, 49–50
F statistic, 31

Homoscedasticity assumption, 31, 121
Hurwicz bias, 32, 143
Hypothesis testing, and binomial theorem, 28
  choosing among alternatives, 27–29

IFO-institut fur Wirtschaftsforschung, 25
"Implicit" forecasts, 24, 177
IN, 14
INAL, 14
INAS, 14
Industry identification codes, 15
Inequality coefficient, 38
Input-output tables, 114

Interest rate term structure, 161
Inventory, anticipated equilibrium,
cycle, hypothetical data, 10
equilibrium, 7
planned inventory, 7, 201–204
stage of fabrication, 20
Inventory cycle, 240

Klein-Goldberger econometric model of the United States, 4

Law of Large Numbers, 56
LIFO accounting procedures, 18
Liquid assets, 207

McGraw Hill Survey, 25
Market share decomposition, 95–100
forecasting, 96
Markup coefficient, 196
Merged firms, 27
MSE, 37
Munich Business Test, 19

Nature, perverse, 75
Nature's urn, 80
Netherlands Central Planning Bureau, 60, 79
No-change prediction, 96, 108

OBE-SEC Plant and Equipment Expenditure Survey, 55
Optimal size of firm, 242
Optimist, naive, 45
perennial, 71
Orders, new and unfilled, 20, 195, 199, 220, 225–226, 232

Partial $\bar{R}^2$, 34
PF, 14
PM, 14
PMAL, 14
PO, 14
POOLED and POOLED WITH SEPARATE INTERCEPT regressions, 33
Price, adjustments, 21–22, 232
data, 22
deflation, 21–23
hedging, 20
Principal components, 104–107
Production, *def,* 194, 196
as dependent variable, 234–235
to order, 21, 115, 199, 220, 225, 240
period, 204, 242
plan revision, 200, 204–205
smoothing, 197, 203, 208, 211, 215, 229
Proxies for anticipations, 177, 181
naive, 185
Psychological factors in business cycle, 2, 109
PT, 14

Quadratic cost functions, 198

r_1^2, 39
r_2^2, 39
r_3^2, 40
Railroad shippers forecasts, 24, 41, 51, 59, 79, 108, 116, 240
transformed, 189
Realization function, 193, 207, 226
Recursive model, 193, 206, 215, 236–237
Reduced form equation, 8, 212–217, 235
Regional Shippers Advisory Boards, *see* Railroad shippers forecasts
Regression table format, 33–34
Response date, average, 15
Reversal coefficient, 129, 133, 137
RMSE, 37
Roundoff error, 34

SALE, 14
Sales proxies, 217
Sample design, 26
Seasonal adjustment, 18
dummy variables, 18
movements, 115
Security restrictions, 26
Socialism, 2
Survey, customer, 74
nonresponse, 18

"Technical" forecasts, 114
Turning-point errors, 42–46
and seasonal adjustment, 42

U, 38
U_1, 37
Underestimation of change, probability of, 79–91
regression analysis of, 91–95
and seasonal adjustment, 91
UOR, 225

Waves of optimism and pessimism, 3, 100–107, 240–241
Weighted regression, 31

OHIO UNIVERS[illegible] LIBRARY

Please return this [illegible] as y[illegible] have finished with it. [illegible] fin[illegible] [illegible] returned by [illegible]

SLC 12-11-69